SEXUALITIES LOST AND FOUND

Lesbians, Psychoanalysis, and Culture

SEXUALITIES LOST AND FOUND

Lesbians, Psychoanalysis, and Culture

Edited by

Edith Gould
Sandra Kiersky

International Universities Press, Inc.
Madison   Connecticut

Manufactured in the United States of America

Library of Congress Cataloging-in-Publication Data

Sexualities lost and found / edited by Edith Gould, Sandra Kiersky.
    p. cm.
  Includes bibliographical references and index.
  ISBN 0-8236-6062-1 (paperback : alk. paper)
    1. Lesbianism—Psychological aspects. 2. Lesbians—Counseling of
  3. Psychoanalysis and homosexuality. I Gould, Edith. II. Kiersky, Sandra.

RC558.5 .S49 2001
616.89′17′086643—dc21

2001016859

Contents

Part IV. Twenty-Five Years of Psychoanalysis in the Lesbian Community

Contributors

Donna Bassin, Ph.D., Member and Faculty, Institute for Psychoanalytic Training and Research (IPTAR), New York City; Assistant Professor, Pratt Institute, psychoanalyst in private practice, New York City.

Virginia Blum, Ph.D., Associate Professor, Department of English, University of Kentucky.

Lee Crespi, C.S.W., Executive board member, teacher, and supervisor, Psychoanalytic Psychotherapy Study Center; private practice, New York City.

Ann D'Ercole, Ph.D., Clinical Associate Professor of Psychology, Postdoctoral Program in Psychotherapy and Psychoanalysis, Graduate School of Arts and Sciences, New York University.

Jack Drescher, M.D., Supervising analyst and faculty member, William Alanson White Institute, New York City; private practice, New York City.

Deborah F. Glazer, Ph.D., Supervisor and faculty member, Psychoanalytic Institute, Postgraduate Center for Mental Health; private practice, New York City.

Edith Gould, B.C.D., Senior supervisor and training analyst, Psychoanalytic Institute of the Postgraduate Center for Mental Health, New York City; private practice.

Suzanne Iasenza, Ph.D., Associate Professor of Counseling, John Jay College, City University of New York; psychologist and sex therapist in private practice, New York City.

Sandra Kiersky, Ph.D., Faculty member and supervisor, Institute for Psychoanalytic Study of Subjectivity, the National Institute for the Psychotherapies, and the Parent-Infant Program, Columbia University Center for Training and Research, New York City.

Ronnie C. Lesser, Ph.D., Private practice, New York City.

Joyce McDougall, Supervisor and training analyst, Paris Psychoanalytic Society and Institute of Psychoanalysis.

Donna M. Orange, Ph.D., Psy.D., Faculty and supervising analyst, Institute for the Psychoanalytic Study of Subjectivity, New York City; member, Wiener Kreis fur Psychoanalyse und Selbstpsychologie, Vienna; faculty and supervising analyst, Instituto di Specializzizione in Psicologia psicoanalotica del se e psicoanalisi relazionale, Rome.

Arlene Kramer Richards, Ed.D., Training and supervising analyst, New York Freudian Society; fellow, Institute for Psychoanalytic Training and Research; member, American Psychoanalytic Association, International Psychoanalytic Association.

Shara Sand, Psy.D., Psychologist, Barnard College Mental Health Service; Adjunct Assistant Professor of Psychology, Ferkauf Graduate School of Psychology, Yeshiva University; lecturer, Barnard Pre-College Program; private practice, New York City.

Erica Schoenberg, Ph.D., Supervisor, Institute for Human Identity; private practice, New York City and Westchester.

Adria E. Schwartz, Ph.D., Clinical supervisor and training analyst, Postdoctoral Program in Psychoanalysis and Psychotherapy, New York University.

Ellen Shumsky, C.S.W., Faculty member, supervisor, Institute for Contemporary Psychotherapy, Psychoanalytic Psychotherapy Study Center, and Research Institute for Self Psychology; private practice, New York City.

Sheldon Waxenberg, Ph.D., Professor Emeritus of Counseling and Psychology, John Jay College of Criminal Justice, City University of New York.

Introduction

Edith Gould and Sandra Kiersky

The collective resistance in psychoanalysis to recognizing and addressing the lesbian was recently reflected in a symposium entitled "Love and Desire in the Analytic Situation." A panel consisting of a group of the most prominent theory crafters in the field, completely avoided any reference to love and desire in the same-sex analytic pair. The male psychoanalysts on the panel presented cases where the traditional dyad of psychoanalysis, the Ur dyad of psychoanalysis, that of the older male physician with the younger female patient, was once again trotted out (Geller and Gould, 1998). (Hill [1994] refers to the " 'ur-like' place of the erotic transference in the development of psychoanalytic ideas . . . as the original transference of Anna O to Freud" [p. 488].) Despite the fact that a feminist revolution in psychotherapy has taken place, where the majority of both clinicians and patients are women, when it comes to women and same-sex desire, there continues to be an appalling blindspot in the literature. Castle's (1993) "apparitional lesbian" lives on in conference halls, classrooms, and consulting rooms. This collection of papers is a way to remedy the traditional exiling of the lesbian and same-sex love to the margins of human experience.

The first parts of this book originated in a special issue of *Psychoanalysis and Psychotherapy: The Journal of the Psychoanalytic Institute of the Postgraduate Center for Mental Health*, edited by Sandra Kiersky, entitled "Sexualities Lost and Found: Psychoanalytic Perspectives on Lesbian Experience," which was published in 1996.

The issue was dedicated to Ted Riess, who was one of the first psychoanalysts to oppose the traditional psychoanalytic pathologizing of homosexuality. In his research and papers (Gundlach and Riess, 1968; Riess, 1987) Ted argued for a therapeutic stance in which "homoeroticism is seen as non-pathological, but requiring analysis to evaluate the positive potentials and the conflicts arising from it." He strongly believed that "analysis should provide a positive, corrective experience against homophobia" (p. 128). Rejecting the Freudian notion of procreation and genital difference as the hallmark of natural and normal sexuality, Ted focused on the interplay between the sociocultural and the psychological in lesbian experience. Believing that psychoanalysis had to reorganize itself, generally, in the areas of gender and the psychology of women, Ted and his research collaborator, Ralph Gundlach, conducted a large-scale project designed to highlight the multiplicity and diversity of female sexual identities. One phase of this was a study of lesbians, the largest population of lesbian women studied to date anywhere in the world. Prefiguring the current reconceptualizations of gender and sexuality, the issues defined by Ted's work remain a focal point of psychoanalytic concern today. As Ted hoped, sexuality has undergone a transformation in our culture. Despite this, many psychoanalysts continue to see anatomy as destiny and have moved very little from the early psychoanalytic vision of lesbians as masculine and arrested at infantile stages of development. Though the contributors to this volume come from very different perspectives, none shares Freud's early view of homosexuality as abnormal, nor the current pathologizing views of analysts like Socarides and Siegel in the United States.

This book evolved as we added ten more papers to the original collection published in *Psychoanalysis and Psychotherapy*. We have called it *Sexualities Lost and Found,* because it is a set of papers about the subversion and reemergence of lesbian experience as it is actually lived.

Recently, these theories seem to be moving in a more positive direction. This collection of essays reflects the changing and diverse views of women and of psychoanalysts. The papers present multiple representations of women, in a variety of contexts and cultural identities. They describe and bear witness to lesbians as mothers, daughters, lovers, friends, couples, poets, analysts, patients, and rock stars. In this spirit of inclusiveness, we have offered a wide range of voices from different theoretical perspectives and technical approaches. The contemporary Freudian, interpersonal, intersubjective, relational, and postmodern frameworks are all represented, as well as queer theory, and sociocultural, philosophical, and performative points of view. Although theory and practice are inextricably linked, the papers lean naturally toward one or the other, in that some focus on theory while others weigh in more heavily on the side of the clinical moment.

A number of exciting books (Butler, 1990; O'Connor and Ryan, 1993; Domenici and Lesser, 1995) have offered postmodern deconstructions of theories about lesbians, but the literature in general is sparse in regard to the lesbian patient in the clinical situation. Therefore the papers in this volume by McDougall, Kiersky, Gould, Shumsky, Bassin, and Drescher move into relatively uncharted clinical territories that include lesbian infertility and the previously unacknowledged dyad of the gay male analyst and the lesbian analysand. McDougall's paper on gender identity and creativity represents a critical shift in her conceptualization of lesbian identity. Her paper illustrates the ways in which theories evolve over time, as they are shaped and transformed by culture and the crucible of clinical experience. These papers create a bridge "between the densely academic, yet inspiring postmodern theorizing about sex, gender and sexuality and the intense thoughts and feelings involved in [the] lived experience" (D'Ercole, 1998) of female desire.

The more theoretical papers of Orange, Lesser, Schoenberg, and Blum address the difficulty of defining who is a lesbian and what this category actually means. Theories of lesbian desire, from various points of view, are deconstructed and revisioned, as is the absence of a theory of desire in Kohut's body of work.

The impact of culture is taken up as D'Ercole unpacks the relationship between gender, sexuality, and performativity; Richards analyzes a lesbian poet and her work; Schwartz thinks about queer theory and its contributions to clinical process; Sand theorizes lesbian sexuality through the music of two popular lesbian singers; and Glazer addresses the psychological complexities of being a lesbian mother.

As a group, these authors underscore the multiplicity, complexity, and contextual nature of love between women and envision psychoanalytic theories that include these qualities. With these voices, the "apparitional lesbian" is brought into focus and given substance.

Finally, our tribute to Ted Riess comes full circle with papers by Crespi and Iasenza and Waxenberg. Crespi traces the transformations that have occurred during twenty-five years of psychoanalysis in the lesbian community. Iasenza and Waxenberg offer a postmodern reinterpretation of the original figure-drawing data Gundlach and Riess collected during their groundbreaking study.

The times, of course, have changed and nowhere is this clearer than in the present volume as contributors delineate major shifts in our understanding, as psychoanalysts, of the body, of relatedness, subjectivity, desire, and the role of culture and apply these to the question of same-sex desire in women.

References

Butler, J. (1990), *Gender Trouble: Feminism and the Subversion of Identity.* New York: Routledge.

Castle, T. (1993), *The Apparitional Lesbian: Female Homosexuality and Modern Culture.* New York: Columbia University Press.

D'Ercole, A. (1998), Discussion of E. Gould, The body politic, and D. Glazer, Same sex desire and the trauma of sexual difference. International Federation for Psychoanalytic Education, Ninth Annual Interdisciplinary Conference, "How Will the Body Speak in the 21st Century?" New York.

Domenici, T., & Lesser, R., eds. (1995), *Disorienting Sexuality: Psychoanalytic Reappraisals of Sexual Identities.* New York: Routledge.

Geller, J., & Gould, E. (1998), A contemporary psychoanalytic perspective: Rogers' brief psychotherapy with Mary Jane Tilden. In: *The Psychotherapy of Carl Rogers: Cases and Commentary,* ed. B. Farber, D. Brink, & P. Raskin. New York: Guilford Press, pp. 211–230.

Gundlach, R., & Riess, B. F. (1968), Self and sexual identity in the female: A study of female homosexuality. In: *New Directions in Mental Health,* Vol. 2, ed. B. F. Riess. New York: Grune & Stratton.

Hill, D. (1994), The special place of the erotic transference in psychoanalysis. *Psychoanal. Inq.* (Spec. Issue), 14:483–498.

O'Connor, N., & Ryan, J. (1993), *Wild Desires and Mistaken Identities: Lesbianism and Psychoanalysis.* New York: Columbia University Press.

Riess, N. F. (1987), Transference and countertransference in therapy with homosexuals. *Dynam. Psychother.,* 5:117–129.

Part I

Introduction:
From Theory Construction to the Lived Experience

1

Gender Identity and Creativity: From Inhibition to Inspiration

Joyce McDougall

This paper offers a modest contribution to the understanding of sexual role identity, including its role in creativity. Whether we are considering homosexual or heterosexual object orientation, there is no evidence that a psychic representation of core gender identity is *inborn*. Core gender and sexual role identity are shaped in large part by the experiences of early childhood and the parental discourse on sexuality and sexual role. Freud himself emphasized that the objects of sexual desire are not innate, they have to be "found."

Over thirty years ago I wrote a paper on Homosexuality in Women based on a very small number of analysands, and drew conclusions that, at that time, as a young and relatively inexperienced analyst, I believed could apply to female homosexuality in general. But as the years went by, my increasing experience, both with my ongoing self-analysis and with many lesbian analysands, led me to conclude that the generalizations

This paper will be published in the *Journal of Gay and Lesbian Psychotherapy*, Volume 5, Number 1, pp. 5–28, 2001, Haworth Press. Published by permission of the publisher.

I had made in my 1980 paper were inappropriate and applied only to the analysands quoted in that paper.

I have chosen the case of a female patient in order to explore to what extent family circumstances and the unconscious wishes of parents may have contributed to her adult sexual orientation. Before discussing an important session that took place in the sixth year of our work together, I shall give a brief account of her family background.

Initial Interview

Mia came to see me some eight years ago. I opened the door of my waiting room to a woman in her early forties, modishly dressed in a gray pantsuit in professional businesswoman style. She began by saying she had an important post in the Ministry of Cultural Affairs and that she was charged, among other duties, with writing cultural surveys of litera- ture and art, but that the quality of her work was falling off. She then went on to say that she was a lesbian and was desperately unhappy following the breakdown of a fifteen-year love relationship with Claire, a French actress, and that this was the main reason she was having difficulty in working. The break in the relationship was precipitated by Mia's discovery a year earlier, that Claire had begun a secret love affair with a young Englishwoman, Nathalie.

Mia said:

> I'm so unhappy—as if my life is no longer worth living. Claire and I have been lovers for so many years and I trusted her completely. She seemed to need me as much as I needed her. She was the total background to my life. Nothing has any meaning without her. She says she can't give up her affair with Nathalie but that it changes *nothing* so far as our relationship is concerned. It's just an adventure.

She added that Claire is approaching 60 and had stressed her age to support her right to have this "extramarital" affair. The culminating insult, as Mia put it, was Claire's suggestion that she might enjoy meeting Nathalie and thought that the three of them could establish some kind of menage a trois. This released a flood of violent quarreling during which time Mia had thoughts of committing suicide. Finally, she had taken her courage in both hands and precipitously left the apartment for which they had shared all costs over the past fifteen years. Much of Mia's furniture was still there and Claire did everything to prevent her from taking her stuff away.

Mia continued:

> That's more than a year ago yet I still cry every night and still feel totally lost. I try to work on the book I'm doing for the Ministry, but I can't concentrate; I try to play my piano and I start crying. Nothing helps. Claire keeps begging me to come back, saying she doesn't want to live without me; that I'm childish and moralistic to have created this rupture for such a minor matter. It's like an unbreachable gap in understanding between us. I've been living an illusion all these years. I can't go back—and I can't go forward either. I can't bear the pain of knowing she loves another woman—why is it so unbearable? I wonder if I shall ever love again. Why is it such a life-and-death matter? Can I be helped?

I felt very moved by Mia's pain and her questions. I also found myself thinking back over former patients who had faced similar catastrophic ruptures, in both heterosexual and homosexual love relations, and how the hurt partner often rushed into a new relationship with the hope of avoiding the pain. Mia, on the other hand, was eager to understand *why* the loss of Claire was so intolerable to her and why she could not even imagine ever meeting a new lover.

Toward the end of our initial interview, I reviewed what she had told me and said it seemed as though she had left some very important parts of herself with Claire: her capacity to love, her joy in her work, the pleasure she took in writing and in playing music. I then explained briefly what a psychoanalytic engagement involved, and said it might help her understand the painful process of mourning, and why she was not yet able to take back many precious parts of herself that bound her to Clare.

She looked quite surprised and said that this would give her food for thought, and then asked if she might see me once more. At our second interview she said, "When I left your office the other day I felt that a new world might open up inside me." She also told me on this occasion that her mother, who was in her seventies, was dying of AIDS. My shock was visible, and she explained that she and her sisters had only just received the verdict: the HIV virus was traced back to some years earlier when her mother had received a blood transfusion during a minor surgical intervention—it was contaminated blood. Mia would now have to arrange, somehow, to find time to see her mother regularly, and give her support to face the treatment and the fear of death. Within the next few weeks we had a few scattered sessions in which Mia referred continually to the gravity of her mother's condition as well as to her recurring pain over the loss of Claire. (I began to sense that the two losses might have something in common and wondered if Claire had been invested as a maternal figure for Mia.) She also brought a couple of dreams in which she played the role of a child who had lost her way.

At the end of our first year of intermittent sessions, Mia asked whether I could manage to see her on a regular basis in spite of her frequent absences due to her professional occupation. We are now in the eighth year of our analytic voyage, and my interest and fondness for this patient are such that I have usually managed to replace the innumerable sessions she has had to miss because of her work, and she has made the same effort, agreeing to come very early in the morning, late in the day, and so on.

I shall briefly review certain elements of Mia's childhood background insofar as they may shed some light on her adult sexual orientation. Most of these details came to light in the first few weeks of our therapeutic voyage, but other important events that had been totally forgotten only came on the analytic scene as the years went by.

Mia's Family Background

Mia's mother was a high-school teacher and her father was a government administrator. She has a sister ten years older than herself (whose name also happens to be Claire!). Nine years after Claire was born, the mother gave birth to a stillborn child—a boy. The following year mother became pregnant again—and Mia arrived. When Mia was 5 years old another sister (Florence) was born. The two sisters are married with children and Mia is very attached to her nieces and nephews.

Mia recalled that, when she was 9, her father received a post some distance from the town where they lived and only returned home on weekends. This work continued until Mia was 16. She felt his absence keenly during those seven years and her belief that her mother needed special support from her became acute during this long period. Mia always suspected that her father had a lover in the town where he was living and working, but she has no evidence of this. Her sisters are skeptical about this belief, and in addition, unlike Mia, neither of them has the feeling of having been abandoned by their father, or that the mother was depressed throughout those years.

Later, Mia left France to take up a teaching post in Los Angeles and remained there for several years. During a return visit to France in her late twenties, her father died suddenly of a lightning cancer. She recalled vividly the scene in which her sisters and her mother were talking with the hospital doctors about the measures to be adopted in an attempt to save him, and that she was alone with him at the instant of his death. She sobbed uncontrollably for hours, to the concern of the other members of the bereaved family.

Mia then explained:

> It was in Los Angeles that I had my first serious love affair with a woman. Up until then I'd been involved in various sexual adventures with different boys but those encounters never meant anything to me—just the feeling that I was doing the right thing; it took some time, and courage, to admit to myself and to my mother that I could only love a woman. Mother was most understanding and said I should follow my heart. [She then added] Of course I could never have told my father about it! [Then a long pause before she continued] After my father's death I decided to return permanently to France—and that's when I changed professions.

Mia seemed to indicate that in some tragic way her acceptance of her lesbian identity had become associated with her father's death, but it took several years before the implications of this link could be analyzed, thereby enabling Mia not only to freely assume her sexual orientation but also to write her first novel—but I shall come back to these aspects later.

During the early years of regular work together, we had many occasions for exploring Mia's hitherto unacknowledged feelings of dependency and separation anxiety. The first noticeable reactions to abandonment came through transference manifestations. Mia knew in advance, as all my analysands do, that I am always absent at the time of the Paris school vacations, but it was necessary to remind her of this on every occasion. Each impending absence released a number of anxiety dreams whose themes tended to reveal an alarming disinvestment of her value as an individual. Moreover, she frequently had unusual somatic manifestations during my absence. She would catch colds or flu whenever

I was away and on two occasions suffered from alarming cardiac symptoms. At my insistence, she consulted a leading cardiologist who declared that there was no cardiac pathology. I then learned that Mia's cardiac troubles were not new, they had begun shortly *after her father's death.* As Mia slowly became convinced that her somatizations were a reaction to separation and loss she came to question seriously, for the first time, the emotional events that may have surrounded her birth and her place in the family.

The Dead Boy

On a couple of occasions when Mia brought a dream, and later a fantasy, concerning a dead child, I asked what she thought may have been the attitude of her parents toward her birth following so closely that of the little dead son. She treated the notion that this fact could have had any importance with total denial. "I was sure I was my mother's favorite. I did more to help her than anyone else—and also in a way I was my father's special child too because I was the only one who was keenly interested in intellectual pursuits—he was proud of my academic success."

Then came a dream in which a child was killed and Mia was to be charged with the murder. My immediate reaction was to ask whether it was a little boy or a little girl who died in this dream, but I did not say this and I was pleased when Mia herself said, "Now this time I have to find out what effect that baby's death may have had on my life."

As a result, she then decided to ask Claire her sister who was 10 years old when Mia was born, if she recalled anything about her birth. Claire replied, "My goodness how could I forget it! But I was always careful not to talk to you about it. Well, Mom and Dad were both convinced it would be a boy, then on the day you were born Dad called me into his study and said, 'I've some very sad news for you—it's a girl.' And he burst into tears."

This led to much construction and reconstruction concerning Mia's vision of her role in the family. Among the different fantasy constructions, she uncovered a feeling of guilt at not having fulfilled her parents' wish for a son and came to connect this with her determination from a very young age that she must do everything she could to "make mother happy.'' She recalled innumerable efforts to comfort her mother during the seven lonely years when the father was working away from home. She came to feel that she had attempted to take her father's place in caring for her mother—and after acknowledging the importance this had in her inner psychic world she went on to tell me that in her love relationships she thought only of her partner's pleasure, sexually and otherwise. In fact her lover Claire had often complained that Mia was too insistent on their sexual relationship and said she much preferred to sleep. Out of love for Claire, Mia accepted the partial abstinence that had marked the last years of their conjugal relationship and was therefore all the more shocked and hurt when she discovered the existence of Nathalie.

We also came to understand that, under the pressure of the unconscious belief that she should have been a boy and that she was supposed to play her father's role to her abandoned mother, she had fought for her *right to be a girl*. Apart from her identification with the ''father-lover'' who brings sexual gratification to the ''mother-woman,'' Mia was extremely critical of those of her homosexual acquaintances who were notably masculine in their dress, attitudes, and manner. When I asked her the reason for this intolerance she came around to understanding that she had fought all her life *against* the idea that she should have been a boy, and had done everything in her power *to protect her feminine identity*. This was a powerful factor in her giving active support to many political issues, particularly when they involved the ill-treatment of women or the problems of children who were the victims of sexual abuse.

The Little Sister

Mia had repressed all knowledge of her childhood pain and confusion about being born a girl to parents who desired and expected a boy. Similarly, she also had difficulty in recognizing—and reconstructing—what she had experienced at the time of Florence's birth. From time to time she would mention younger quarrelsome relations with her sister, whom she always referred to as ''Flo,'' which puzzled her. When I asked her if she recalled any jealousy at the time of Flo's arrival in the family she said, ''Not at all! I cherished my little sister and was always concerned for her welfare.'' Yet certain dreams and Mia's reports of numerous quarrels and disagreements with Flo tended to reveal the opposite. She slowly recalled how she had become withdrawn around the time of Flo's birth, and how, in her early school years, she closed herself off from the others for hours, reading her picturebooks and listening to music. She also fell in love with another little girl when she was 6, only to discover that the intensity was not shared. It seemed that this first love affair outside the family circle was an attempt to give to another what she desperately desired for herself as well as being an effort to resolve her pain around the birth of Flo. We gradually found further evidence that Flo's birth had been a profoundly traumatic event, particularly since her father had shown considerable interest in the new baby. Mia finally admitted that she thought Flo had been her father's real favorite and came to envision herself as a very lonely little girl with mother and Claire on one side and father and Flo on the other.

A typical incident that had occurred a couple of years back confirmed these reconstructions. Mia had gone to have lunch with Flo and her two children. She came to her session later that day saying that she had tried to talk to Flo about their ambivalent relationship, which had become increasingly evident as the death of their mother approached.

Mia: I got home from Flo's and was preparing to come here when I discovered I'd lost all my papers: my identity card, my car papers, my credit cards. My first thought was that they must have been stolen, then I realized that I'd left them at Flo's place. I phoned her and explained where I thought they would be. She searched everywhere and said they weren't there. Somehow I don't trust her.

JM: As though she's stealing your identity once again?

Mia: Oh, I'm sure you're right! She said she spent thirty minutes searching through every room where I'd been. Why do I still maintain such an infantile attitude toward her? [Mia was so anxious that she couldn't pursue this important question and went on] So where did I lose the papers? I've looked everywhere in my place and they're not there.

At the end of the session she said, "What shall I do without my papers—I'm leaving for China in three days and I've no time to replace them." Then rather unexpectedly, a little like a child—which did not in any way resemble her usual adult manner—she said piteously, "What would *you* do in such a situation?" I said, "Well, if your papers haven't been stolen, then unconsciously *you know* where they are. I'd go back home and let myself wander without reasoning, to any place that comes to mind with the hope that I might find them.'' She said, ''Is that a psychoanalytic theory?'' I replied that I didn't think so but that it often worked.

Later that evening I found a message on my answering machine saying, ''I did what you said and without reasoning I went through the pockets of a raincoat that I had not worn and there I found my papers and identity cards—I must have put them there absent-mindedly when I was wondering whether it might rain. Please accept my grateful thanks. See you in a couple of weeks time.''

Two major events occurred in our third year of working together: the first was Mia's meeting with Florence (the same name as Mia's younger sister) who was to become her new lover.

Mia's New Companion

Mia met Florence at a meeting of professional women concerned with the ill-treatment of women in Bosnia and North Africa—Florence is a lawyer six years younger than Mia. They were attracted to each other intellectually, and each learned that the other had lived through the painful rupture of a long-standing love affair. Mia was, for the first time, able to contemplate forming a new relationship, although with many misgivings, and the two women eventually decided to live together. After a few months of conjugal life there were quarrelsome exchanges between them (largely stimulated, according to Mia, by Florence's extreme jealousy over Mia's constant preoccupation with her dying mother). She encouraged Florence to consult an analyst in order to preserve the relationship. Mia reported that Florence had become much more agreeable to live with since beginning her analysis and they formed a more loving couple.

Mother Dies

A year-and-a-half later came the mother's slow and painful death. Mia went through a normal period of great sadness and much reminiscing, alone and with her sisters. There were disputes among the sisters regarding the handling of the small legacy—in particular the three sisters now owned in common a country house that had been in the family for many years. Flo and Claire both claimed they needed the country house more often than Mia since they had children, whereas Mia had only herself to look after—and so on. During this difficult period, Mia was able to sort out the different projections and settlings of accounts with the past that added to the intensity of these quarrels—and began very sensitively to explore the competitive feelings of the three sisters toward their mother. This also enabled Mia to put together her own narcissistic need for the omnipotent fantasy that she alone could ''repair'' mother, and came to better understand why she had shown more devotion and given more time to visiting the dying woman than her two sisters had done. Her view of the family constellation at this point presented the two sisters as married with special responsibilities, while she was in some sense ''married'' to their mother and therefore had special responsibilities toward her.

After the mother's death, the daughters were advised to sue the doctors responsible for the contaminated blood through which the mother had contracted AIDS. The case was thrown out by the medical legal authorities who said that people of that age were not entitled to compensation. But Florence, in her capacity as a lawyer, fought the legal decision, claiming that it was a scandalous decision, that a woman in excellent health might well have lived on into her eighties, and she won the case. The daughters received compensation, but Mia cried throughout the following session saying that this money did not bring her mother back and she in fact decided she would give the money to AIDS research.

At this point in our analytic voyage, Mia had integrated all that we had explored together concerning her painful mourning process over the loss of Claire. Mia was able to say during one session, ''I now understand that those who commit such treachery are making others suffer the pain to which they have had to submit as though to prove their own power to annihilate another.'' This statement reflected Mia's attempts as time went on to understand the extent to which Claire was *compelled to repeat* some of her own traumatic past.

Incidentally, I would like to make a couple of remarks here concerning those patients whose suffering stems mainly from the traumatic effect of the onslaught of either a primary caretaking or present-day love object. When the analysand is able—and *willing*—to want to understand what may be taking place in the internal world of the hurtful person that might give meaning to their behavior, it frequently follows that the pain of the abandonment, cruelty, absence, or treachery, becomes more bearable.

Thus, when the analysand begins to understand that *her* suffering arises from dramatic situations in her own inner psychic world, this acquisition of meaning is a powerful factor toward promoting psychic change. But so often our analysands do not apply this form of insight to the individuals whom they prefer to believe are the cause of their misery!

I encouraged Mia to try to imagine the blind forces that may have shed light on Claire's behavior. I shall not go into the lover's childhood background and the extent to which it illuminated the totally unexpected "treachery," but our analytic work on this theme proved helpful in enabling Mia to continue with the work of mourning—and was also instrumental in freeing her to meet her new partner long after the rupture with Claire. In all, this had required two years of intensive therapeutic endeavor on Mia's part as well as mine.

The second point I want to emphasize is that clinical experience has led me to discover that when an analysand can make sense out of the other's hurtful behavior (particularly in the case of an internal parental figure experienced by the child within as a consistently traumatizing object) this frequently *releases* creative capacities that have been paralyzed.

Although Mia suffered still from her moments of longing for the lost paradise she had known, she began to analyze the factors in Claire's own life history that could account for her treachery toward Mia. She agreed to see Claire from time to time but resisted all of Claire's attempts to induce her to come back. "Claire says I talk about nothing but her treachery, and that this has no meaning in a love relationship, that true love does not submit to obligations." As she later wrote, "The love we shared, which I believed was evidence of an enduring peace, was nothing but an armistice."

The beneficial effect of Mia's attempts to identify with Claire's hurtful or incomprehensible behavior was noticeable in that it led Mia to take notes on two central themes: one on the internal and contrasting family dramas of the three sisters and their widely different images and ways of relating to the mother, while another notebook series dealt with her fractured love relationship and her growing awareness of this kind of drama among her lesbian friends.

The Novel

As Mia slowly came to terms with the loss of Claire and the place that she had held in her life, she began to write her first novel, which was autobiographical. This was a breakthrough in that her former published works were essays dealing with sociocultural themes, whereas this, she knew, would be different from anything she had written before. I followed this creative endeavor with the greatest of interest. Then, when the novel was finished, Mia suddenly announced, ''Now I must destroy it because I would never dare publish it.''

We spent many a session on this conflict in which she expressed great concern that her colleagues in the Ministry (mostly men) would be shocked by the revelation of her lesbianism. I helped her examine these projections from all angles and as a result she finally decided to send the manuscript to one or two publishing houses, expecting rejection. In fact it was signed up by a well-respected publishing house. There was some argument about the title of the book: Mia wished it to have a title referring to human passion and the pain involved in broken love relationships, but the editor was adamant that it should have a title referring to lesbian love.

When Mia finally received the page proofs, to her shock a subtitle had been added which caused her further irritation. The subtitle read ''marginal lovers,'' which, Mia felt, suggested that the book was focused on lesbian secrets whereas its central focus was on the drama of treachery and of the emotional turmoil that follows fractured love relationships in all human beings.

The book had considerable success: there were laudatory reviews and an interview on Radio France, during which she steered the interview, as she put it, ''toward myself as a female *writer* rather than a female *homosexual*.''

Around this time, Mia asked whether her analysis would be soon coming to an end. It seemed possible that our work was drawing to a close so I proposed the possibility of terminating perhaps in a year's time, which may have precipitated the following dream. The new material that came to light led to my noting the session rather fully.

The Session

THE BROKEN PLATE

Mia: I dreamed about you for the first time in a long while! You were entertaining many guests in your home. Your place was a magnificent manor with exquisite gardens and trees everywhere. Somebody who was supposed to be your husband—a very tall man—was looking after things. I had broken a beautiful plate and I was looking for you so I could give you the broken pieces that I was holding in my hands. I don't remember the end of the dream but I know it was a happy feeling, as though, in spite of my having broken the plate, this would be a peaceful matter between us.

Mia went on to say that she didn't understand the dream at all and could not associate to any of its elements.

JM: [Thinking to myself that the plate might represent something belonging to me that she wished to break—or some broken parts of herself that required mending, perhaps related to the tentative idea of our work terminating someday in the near future I said] and the broken plate?

Mia: I'm not someone who breaks plates. I'm a *very* careful person.

JM: Only my things? And only in a dream? [She laughed, then said]

Mia: Wait a minute—I've just thought of something. Mon Dieu! I haven't thought of this in years! I was—er—about 6 and I was helping my mother set the table because we were expecting guests. I always tried desperately to help—like a grown-up?—so I had taken four or five plates together to put on the table, but they were so heavy I dropped them and *every one was broken.* [Her voice suddenly sounded like that of a terrified 6-year-old. After a relatively long silence, imagining that I myself had broken the plates, I asked]

JM: And what did mother say?

Mia: Oh, she said, "Those who break plates pay for them"—and I paid for months and months out of my pocket money until every plate had been paid for.

JM: You said my husband was in the dream; was your father in the real scene on that occasion?

Mia: Oh yes he was! Tiens! Now I remember he came forward and said, "But she's only trying to help, she didn't *mean* to break the plates!" But my mother was adamant, and of course she was right! I'd done something quite unpardonable. [She makes a gesture toward my chair as though to convince me of the seriousness of her misdeed. Impulsively I wanted to say something like "Why are you so hard on yourself" but I immediately recognized that this was my problem. Then I began to imagine the situation as the 6-year-old Mia may have experienced it and said]:

JM: As though you'd broken your mother into pieces?

Mia: Hmm . . . just the kind of fantasies I never want to admit to having. . . . You know I still worry about her and whether I really looked after her properly all those years. I did everything I could to make her feel cared for. Did I smash her in my childish mind?

JM: [Thinking back to those sessions where Mia had come to feel in a childlike megalomanic way that she was responsible for the baby boy's death] Well, you smashed her tummy when you got rid of that baby boy—and maybe you wanted to do it again when Flo was inside her?

Mia: Yeah . . . I know now that all my fears of dying when I was a kid are connected with such wishes. [Long pause] Those broken plates are still a searing memory. I felt so humiliated.

JM: Perhaps you too were the broken plate—the image of yourself as a helpful little girl was smashed.

Mia: In last night's dream I was bringing *you* the broken pieces in quite a happy frame of mind. And you and your husband seemed quite happy about everything too and I thought that you seemed to be a loving couple.

JM: Could the happy couple also represent your own parents? And perhaps feeling that the broken plate was not catastrophic may express a wish for your parents to be a loving sexual couple?

Mia: It's true! I always thought of them as disunited. Maybe that's what I wanted to believe! [Pause] Since it was *you* and *your husband* does the dream relate to us also?

JM: Maybe you were counting on me to mend the broken pieces of yourself, to give you a better image of yourself as the helpful and caring little girl you tried so hard to be? And it might also suggest that you can envision our separating one day without your feeling broken or abandoned?

Mia: Yes, I'm beginning to think that's possible. The most precious thing I have gained in these years of working with you is to have discovered my identity, not only my identity as a woman but also who I am as a person. I no longer feel broken—and I want to thank you for that.

I communicated my feeling that themes of separation and loss had been predominant throughout our psychoanalytic relationship and that we might look more closely at losses that had been traumatic for her, before the break with Claire.

Mia: [After a long pause]: I'm thinking once again of how bad I felt every weekend when my father left town, leaving mother alone. [Pause] And also how important it has been for me to discover that I was not the boy my parents wanted. I had to lose some illusions there too. [Long pause] But you showed me how I always fought to protect my feminine identity—and thanks to our work here I now feel I have a perfect right to my lesbian identity. I still remember your saying, "That little girl of the past made a creative choice in a very painful situation." [Another long pause before she continued]: For some strange reason I've never told you something my mother confided to me when I was an adolescent and which she never told my sisters: that she had been *sexually abused by her own father*. [I was taken aback by this revelation and also thought to myself that this gave a glimpse into special projections that the mother may have made onto this particular daughter. Mia continued]: Mom always used to say to me, "Don't ever depend on a man for support. Be sure to have your own career and keep your independence." [Another pause]

Mia: All those adventures I had with different men up to my twenties were just a cover-up. I was trying to do what my mother proclaimed the world expected of me. [For a moment I felt somewhat confused—just as Mia might have felt in listening to her mother's implicit messages.]

JM: Were you trying to do what your mother said was expected—get yourself a man—while at the same time receiving another message: "trust no man"?

Mia: [She laughed and said]: Oh yes! That was the *main* message! And I now understand in a new way, why, when I'm making love, in my mind I always imagine I am bringing my woman lover what a man could have brought her if that had been her sexual choice. To give my lover pleasure has always been my greatest pleasure.

At this point I felt I understood for the first time why the idea of *treachery* had been so totally *unimaginable* to Mia. In her unconscious fantasy she was repairing her mother *not only* for the abandonment by her husband but also for the abuse her mother had suffered at the hands of her own father. I understood more profoundly (as with everybody's fantasy concerning the underlying significance of their love relations) that this double aim of reparation in Mia's love-life was her lifetime ideal.

Mia then went on to say that she had been trying to gather her history together and to understand the role of the women lovers in her life. Looking back on what she still referred to as Claire's "treason" or "treachery" she added that she now understood very clearly what she should have known before—namely the role that she had played in *Claire's* inner psychic world—and how it was almost predestined that the relationship would end in catastrophe for Mia, as well as recognizing that Mia's suffering would be incomprehensible to Claire who had endured much pain in her own life history, but could never accept that she was now wreaking vengeance on Mia for the pain of the past.

Mia: But what is less clear is what Claire represented for *me*. Anyway, thanks to her treachery I've had the experience of my analysis. In a sense, she could not have brought me a greater gift. [Long silence, before she continued talking]

Mia: I felt totally destroyed—it was much more than the loss of the person I loved and the person I thought loved me. You told me when I first came to see you it was as though I'd lost a vital part of myself, as though I'd left so much of myself with Claire that it would take time to recover these lost parts. Yes, I felt broken in two, like the plate in my dream. [Long pause] That makes me think of my mother's death. Was I looking to Claire to give me something my mother withheld from me? [Another long silence] I don't know why, but I'm now thinking about the new novel I'm writing . . . or rather the novel is writing itself—I don't even know where it is taking me.

[Thinking to myself that this new novel might lead us to what she was searching for in order to possess more profoundly her feelings connected with the loss of Claire, I asked her if she felt like talking about the new novel . . . a thing I would not usually do regarding creative work.]

Mia: I'd love to tell you about it . . . as far as it's gone. Well, for the moment it's called *Le Sosie*. [In English this would translate as "The Double" but includes the idea of an exact or almost mirror image of oneself. The word is derived from the character Sosia in

Molliere's *Amphytryon.*] In Mia's new novel the heroine has heard that she has a sosie and she decides that she will try to find this person, get to know her, see whether they have something in common, or whether there's some mysterious link between them. The heroine follows many divergent and dead-end clues but eventually meets the other woman. To her astonishment the sosie is quite *unlike the heroine* in temperament in that she is a very sad woman; her life has been filled with tragedy of every kind, beginning with the dramatic loss of both her parents. The heroine decides she must try to help her sosie find some fulfillment in life. [Mia stopped suddenly, then said] Well, I don't know where it'll go from there . - . . [pause] Does this novel have something to do with my relationship with Claire? She was in no way my double!

[I found it interesting that Mia made no link with her earlier association to what I had told her six years ago: that in losing Claire she seemed to feel *she had lost a vital part of herself.* Her novel could well be taken to mean that the heroine was searching for her own lost, sad, and orphaned self. But I didn't mention this since I never interpret the underlying significance of a piece of creative work—unless of course the analysand has come to treatment because of a severe block around this particular work.]

Mia then suddenly recalled a dream she'd had earlier in the week.

Mia: I had gone to what was my mother's apartment but strangely enough I realize that my old lover, Claire, is living there. I don't see her anywhere—but I see all the books, paintings, and furniture that belonged to my mother. I'm afraid Claire may not know how to look after these things properly or not know how the household runs, so I begin leaving her a number of written messages to explain what she must do. [The only associations she could find were that she avoided visiting the apartment because of her sadness over her mother's death.]

JM: You were writing something . . .

Mia: Yes, the words—I was telling Claire through my words what she needed to know. Has this something to do with my writing?

JM: It seems that Claire was to take over in some way from your mother—and perhaps the "messages" were to tell her how to do this?

Mia: Oh yes . . . as though she was to fulfill what my mother *should have done*. It suddenly occurs to me that what I wanted from Claire was all that I was unable to take from my mother—I was trying to recover something I had lost. [Pause] I believe I'm trying to recreate, through my writing, some lost parts of myself.

That was the end of the session.

The "Spasme de la Memoire"

In the year that followed the publication of her first novel, Mia was invited to Nice to participate in a colloquium on "The Novel Today." She prepared her contribution with great care, tracing the history of the novel in France from its beginnings. As she took her place at the table with the other presenters, she discovered she was sitting next to Felician Marceau, a well-known French playwright. She felt proud to be seated beside him and thought to herself, "My father would be about the same age as Felician Marceau if he were still alive."

The woman-president of the roundtable introduced the presenters one by one and when she came to Mia, to her great surprise, the president made lengthy reference to Mia's autobiographical novel in which she recounted her lesbian tragedy. From that moment on Mia remembered nothing. In reaction to her strange and sudden amnesia she tried to figure out where she was and what she was supposed to be doing there. She looked at the other participants at the table including an old gentleman next to her, but she recognized nobody. The only thing she retained was that a woman who seemed to be in charge had announced that there would be a break for coffee. She waited and as soon as the coffee break was announced she told a kind woman whose name she no longer remembered that she was feeling ill. Two women immediately offered to take her back to her hotel. She was unable to remember the name of her hotel; after asking the organizer for the name of Mia's hotel they were distressed when Mia could not remember her room number. A doctor was called immediately and gave her an injection which put her to sleep. When she awoke several hours later her memory was completely restored. With shock she realized that the time for her talk had passed, and she found a letter under her door in which the organizers proposed that she give her presentation the following day.

She phoned Florence to tell her of the tragic incident and said she was returning immediately to Paris. Florence said, "No you don't! You will stay there and give your talk and I shall arrange for you to see a neurologist as soon as you get back to Paris." She did as her partner insisted, and her presentation was received with great acclaim.

Extensive neurological examinations revealed no anomalies, and the neuropsychiatrist, somewhat at a loss to answer Mia's question about the cause of her strange experience, said, "Well—uh—you have suffered a memory spasm."

At our next session I encouraged Mia to recount every detail of her weekend in Nice and we were finally able to conclude that her hysterical loss of memory was linked to her thoughts about the aging playwright. She had supposed that he was of the same generation as her own father and she had also thought that her father, had he been present, would have been proud of her and her lecture on the history of the novel. But instead he was to learn that his beloved daughter was a lesbian! I reminded her of the circumstances surrounding her father's death shortly after she had finally accepted her homosexual orientation. Mia replied spontaneously—"Oh, that would have killed him!" From there we were able to construct the hypothesis that her "memory spasm" served to protect her father against a revelation that would have been mortally dangerous for their relationship accompanied by intolerable feelings of guilt. Later, Mia associated to the city of Nice a further revealing element that she had never mentioned in the past six years, namely that her mother, after the death of the father, had a lover and they often spent weekends together in Nice. At this point both the homosexual and the heterosexual oedipal couples occupied the psychoanalytic stage.

And from there on we were able to elaborate a vitally important dimension in Mia's internal reality that had never been put into words before, and which until now had exercised a severely inhibiting effect on her creative activity. In a sense she was blocked in using both her masculine and her feminine identifications to create literary children.

I shall conclude by quoting the opening lines of Mia's autobiographical novel since they express, metaphorically, some of the contours of our analytic voyage. Before quoting these lines I should mention that I obtained Mia's permission to use this fragment of her analytic adventure. After reading my clinic notes she wrote back:

I would never have permitted myself to write an authentic autobiography of this period of my life nor would I have known *how* to write it without the insights that analysis had brought me; I believe that the courage to do so came from the feeling of being understood and totally accepted by you. I would be very happy for you to make use of these notes in any way you wish. And by the way, I wish you could be my translator if ever this book is accepted for an anglo-saxon edition!

Her novel begins with these lines.

Paradise lost haunts the history of humankind. A thousand times Adam and Eve are banished from their protected space radiated with warmth and friendship, a place where time is immobile and the infinite arouses no anguish. I can see them, gasping feverishly and filled with fear, seeking everywhere for the entry way that has become forbidden, certain that they will find it again and convinced that their creator could never have treated them so unjustly. They penetrate many a secret cave with the hope of discovering their lost vision of the absolute; they climb incredible mountains in the attempt to catch a mere glimpse of the Eden they once had known, with its streams, its little decorative gardens set about with statues, water basins, hidden hedges, and sweetly scented plants. Often, in the midst of an arid desert, impregnated with thirst and death, the mirage reappeared. When they had not the strength to continue, when hatred turned them one against the other and weariness banished their desire, suddenly they would believe that they had found it once again. But it was never more than an oasis, a tamed volcano, violet-hued water haunted by sharks. Ersatz. . . .

In turn, I have followed in their footsteps. I had never suffered such treachery. At least that is what I believed . . . but the anxiety that had been with me ever since my childhood, my raging need to exist, and my terror of death were already the trace of some bygone, unknown treachery. . . . When, years later, the same thing happened to me, leaving me from one day to the next in the black hole of nothingness, I refound my childhood anguish. . . .

And the little girl who sleeps in my memory has taken the same pathway. No one had explained anything to her. Of course. Does one ever explain such things? Can one ever truly know what one is seeking?

Reference

McDougall, J. (1980), The homosexual dilemma. In: *Plea for a Measure of Abnormality*. New York: International Universities Press, pp. 87–139.

2

Exiled Desire: The Problem of Reality in Psychoanalysis and Lesbian Experience

Sandra Kiersky

> Real isn't how you're made. It's a thing that happens to you [Margery Williams, *The Velveteen Rabbit*].

The nature of the individual's relationship to reality has always been central in psychoanalysis. This is hardly surprising, for how we conceptualize what is real in human experience actually defines for us how we conduct an analysis and how we understand its therapeutic value. With this in mind, I would like to draw some connections between trauma and reality and a persistent assumption in psychoanalytic theory that lesbian desire is illusory or somehow unreal.

We find this skepticism about lesbian subjectivity as early as Freud's well-known paper, "The Psychogenesis of a Case of Homosexuality in a Woman" (1920). In it, he describes the dreams of a young girl who has fallen in love with a "disreputable" woman as "hypocritical" and "false," and this image of the deceitful dreamer is echoed by Melanie Klein (1957) when she cautions "the fact that such . . . women can have good object relations is deceptive" (p. 200).

This notion that a woman's desire for another woman is never authentic and must be indicative of something else originates in a Darwinian emphasis on procreation and genital difference as the hallmark of sexual authenticity and reflects a long-standing hermeneutic suspicion in psychoanalysis that has been seriously questioned in recent years (see Dimen, 1995; Mitchell, 1996). It remains implicit, however, in most theories of same-sex desire, though often embedded in discussions of developmental arrest, defense, or compensatory structure (Socarides, 1978; Siegel, 1988; Goldberg, 1995). It is clearly articulated in the work of Joyce McDougall (1979)[1] who writes that a woman who becomes homosexual has acquired a fictitious sexual identity and adds, "how is it possible to maintain the illusion of being the true sexual partner of another woman?" (p. 207).

Reality Known and Imagined

As O'Conner and Ryan (1993) point out, McDougall takes for granted that what she describes as reality and truth are incontestably that. Her perspective implies a hierarchically ordered, two-reality view of the psychoanalytic process in which one reality, the analyst's, is taken to be more objectively true than the patient's (Schwaber, 1983).

What is the reality that emerges in the psychoanalytic situation and who in the analytic dyad is in a position to claim this reality as their own? For Freud (1923), reality was a given. It was something the infant must discover, and despite his natural tendencies to the contrary, accommodate. If reality was in some sense lost, it was restored in analysis through the interpretation of unconscious distortions and desires which blocked the patient's experience of what was actually out there. In other words, like McDougall, Freud believed that the analyst "knew" and the patient "learned" what was real.

---

[1]Unlike many theorists, Dr. McDougall has changed her position regarding the illusory nature of same-sex desire in women. The interested reader will find her current position on this issue in chapter 1.

An increasing interest in interaction and relational experience, however, has brought other perspectives into view. Stolorow, Brandchaft, and Atwood (1987), for example, argue that the only reality that is relevant and accessible to psychoanalytic inquiry is subjective reality. As Schwaber (1990) notes, "There is no way we can extricate ourselves—our own theories, values, life experiences from our understanding of the patient's communications. What we can know of the world is from our own ways of seeing it" (p. 237). Analysts who are sensitive to loss due to some combination of their own experiences and notions about how children grow up, will respond with particular feeling and resonance to a patient's experience of loss and this becomes a significant organizer of the emotional atmosphere, narrative, and relationship that emerges. Similarly, analysts who cannot imagine or feel moved by love between women, will hear conflicts and anxieties around intimacy and sexual experience as evidence of its regressive or illusory quality. In this sense, as Orange (1996) suggests, experience is always both "given and made," and the reality that emerges in the analytic process is a shared reality, coconstructed and mutually transformational.

This is not to suggest that the problem of reality and desire is less important than history implies, simply that the experience of reality is far more important than history has acknowledged. Many patients, and certainly many lesbian patients, come to analysis, not because their desire is unreal, but because it feels unreal. As analysts, we need a perspective that deepens our understanding of this lived experience and our therapeutic possibilities. For this reason, I would like to explore briefly how the reality of desire is sometimes lost in childhood and adolescence and how it can be recovered in the analytic relationship. Along the way, I hope to raise some questions about the meaning and the effect of theories that label some desires unreal.

For the moment, I will ask readers to conceive reality in an uncommon way—not as something fixed and "out there" but ongoing and dynamic, continually transformed in our relationships with others, and vulnerable to disruption throughout life. This way of thinking about what is real in human experience has a long history in philosophy and science (Orange, 1996), but has found its way into analytic discourse only recently. It reflects a new paradigm which reframes psychoanalysis as a theory of meaning and authenticity rather than illness and cure (Mitchell, 1988). Stolorow and Atwood's intersubjectivity, Mitchell's relational psychoanalysis, Aaron's mutuality, and Beebe and Lachmann's theory of mutual influence all suggest, in some way, that reality is intersubjectively organized in childhood, sustained in interaction with others, and vulnerable to disruption throughout life.

Shadowland

Like Winnicott (1971), these theorists recognize that when a child looks into his mother's face, he sees himself. For some children, however, the reality discovered in this mirror of relatedness is too painful to integrate and constitutes a trauma which exiles them as children, and later as adults, to a land of shadows. In this shadowland, the color and clarity of experience are lost and a sense of belonging feels out of reach. Life simply does not feel real or vivid or immediate. It is shadow rather than substance, creating a painful sense of strangeness in even the most familiar landscape. One patient described this as a feeling that she had grown up sitting before a window watching other children play but was never called out to join them. This shadowland is not exclusive to any particular group, but it often has special significance in the lives of lesbian women, and to understand why this is so, we must first understand the kinds of responsiveness that children need to hold fast to the reality of their experience.

A growing body of literature on infancy and the organization of affects (Stern, 1977, 1985; Field, 1981; Beebe and Lachmann, 1988; Kiersky and Beebe, 1994), suggests that all subjective experience is intersubjectively organized. Though these authors are not explicitly concerned with how experience comes to feel real, they offer a useful paradigm for understanding how this probably occurs and how it is sustained throughout life. It emerges, I would suggest, in a child's first social dialogues. Central to these are affect attunement and "matching," moments in which a mother reflects back or "matches" her infant's feelings in different ways. These seemingly ordinary moments in which a mother mirrors her child's excitement, or soothes intense distress, are actually extraordinary moments in which, over time, the infant locates herself and the emerging contours of her inner world. It is as though the infant would say, if she could speak, "Oh, here I am. Mother feels what I am feeling. My experience is real."

As the child matures, different forms of attunement and validation become important—an approving glance when the child presents a proud accomplishment or empathy and articulation if a child is humiliated at school. With each interaction, affects are evoked and must be responded to in a way that facilitates their elaboration and integration into the child's increasingly rich subjective universe. This is essentially the relational matrix in which a child's belief in the validity and the value of her inner world is organized. *Put simply, we feel real because our experience is responded to as real and because we are not left alone with our feelings.*

The Crisis of Adolescence

Though space does not permit a thorough discussion of the sense of reality as a lifelong, relational process, adolescence is a critical period in which a sense of the real with regard to desiring and being desired is richly elaborated or traumatically disrupted. For a lesbian who becomes aware of an interest in women in latency or adolescence, this process is precarious. It is difficult for her to locate herself and the emerging contours of her desire, without that validating mirror of relatedness that reflects, and in which she can reflect upon, the meaning and authenticity of her experience. Her confusion, which often includes concern about her body and her adequacy as a woman, may never be shared or clarified, and her desire, if it finds a voice, is generally met with anger, rejection, or disgust.

During adolescence, all women undergo a dramatic shift in their sense of themselves and in their relationships with others (Galatzer-Levy and Cohler, 1993). They become more compliant and less assertive. Girls who do not follow this pattern may be labeled unnatural, something less than women. Perhaps most important, girls describe themselves in adolescence as living in connection with others (Gilligan, 1982; Miller, 1986). Anything that threatens connection is potentially traumatic, and most lesbians fear that any expression of their desire will cut them off from family and friends. In order to fit in, they may pretend interests and involvements they do not feel, further increasing their sense of isolation and unreality. Often, these women leave adolescence with an organization of experience that Lachmann (Panel, 1993) describes as characteristic of trauma: that the world is dangerous and experience cannot be shared.

Though women negotiate this period in a variety of ways, the result can be a sexual identity imbued with guilt and shame, a fear that intimacy leads to rejection, and a lack of clarity with regard to subjective experience that has been hidden from those they love. This is the loss of the real that sometimes occurs in a lesbian childhood and it can be easily misunderstood by analysts who seek confirmation that this particular form of desire is inauthentic.

In general, I am proposing a model of trauma and reality which looks something like this. A sense of reality is organized in a child's meaningful interactions with others who validate, elaborate, and mutually regulate the child's inner experience. When this kind of developmentally requisite responsiveness is absent, a critical certainty about the truth of the child's perceptions and feelings is never adequately established. Self and mutual regulations are impaired and conflicts are structuralized, usually around attachment and loss. As a consequence, the child is thrown back on whatever means of self-regulation and connection to others is available and walls off feelings and memories that threaten her psychic integrity. Though a sense of continuity and self-cohesion are preserved, important aspects of the child's inner experience, including the feelings this experience evoked, are lost. Ultimately the child feels alone and without access to important dimensions of her own subjective world. One dimension which is often lost for lesbians, is the sense that desire is real and valuable to oneself and to others.

How this loss of the real can be restored is best understood if I describe a young woman who came to analysis for depression and a sense that she had created "a life that did not feel real." I have not chosen to speak about her because she is a typical lesbian, for there is no such woman. Desire of any sort is unique, contextual, and relationally configured. It emerges throughout the life cycle in different ways for different women. I have written about this woman because the problem of reality and desire was central to the early phase of her treatment and because she is an articulate young woman who can speak for herself about her experience.

The Analytic Discourse

When I first met Kate, despite her many accomplishments, she was painfully unsure of her personal choices. Deeply unhappy, she feared that she would never be able to say to herself, this is me, this is my life, and these are the people I love.

Our first interaction was important, for it was one of those ordinary moments that evoked a number of fears and feelings that had been walled off in childhood and were suddenly available for exploration. I had a free hour before the time of her consultation and, though it is not part of my usual routine, I came out of my office and up to the front door of the building, to be sure that she found her way down to me without mishap. Kate was disoriented by this gesture, a reaction we only came to understand fully some time later. During our first hour, I learned that Kate had completed a lengthy analysis in which she never felt a willingness on her analyst's part "to meet her halfway" and this, she imagined, was part of her surprising reaction.

During this first analysis, Kate explored what she described as the problematic aspects of her relationships with women which had been brief and unsatisfying. They were bright beginnings that ended in despair. She lost herself, she said, in these relationships—an experience she found frightening and unhealthy. Eventually she entered a relationship with a young man whom she liked and admired. When this occurred, her analyst suggested that she was ready for termination. She felt less clear about this, but left the analysis, she said, with a stronger sense of herself than when she had entered it. Soon after termination, her relationship ended, and she found herself increasingly depressed and unsure where she was headed. "Nothing feels real to me," she said, "I just can't imagine any future."

I commented how painful this must be, and Kate was suddenly filled with emotion. "I don't see how I can be in therapy with you," she said, "the moment I saw you, I felt an attraction. I could never be honest in that situation. I would be too worried about your feelings and what you thought of me. I feel anxious just telling you this and I don't need any more practice in wanting what I can't have. I'm already an expert in that area."

Here, in our first meeting, Kate's sense that her desires made it impossible to be herself and her fear of falling into a state of unmet longing was in the foreground of our relationship. When I suggested that we might try to understand this together, Kate recognized that her feelings were not entirely new and, despite her anxiety, we began. During the early months of treatment, Kate was preoccupied with a sense of hopelessness about her feelings toward me and a wish for our relationship to be different. "I can't stop wanting us to be lovers," she said, "and my feelings are so inappropriate and unreal. I want to touch you and I find this humiliating.'' I asked her how she wished to touch me and what seemed shameful about this. ''You seem so clear about sexual things,'' she replied, ''and I feel so unclear and unformed. I must seem ridiculous. And my wanting to touch you doesn't make you pull away. That's the most shocking thing.'' ''Why would I pull away?'' I asked. ''Because I can't imagine that you could even entertain such ideas. It just wouldn't be possible.'' ''You can't imagine,'' I reflected, ''that I could feel about you the way you feel about me.'' ''Exactly,'' she responded. ''Though, when you put it that way, I don't really know why.''

As our sessions continued, it became clear that although Kate was an exceptionally attractive and intellectually lively young woman, she felt completely lacking in any qualities that might draw others to her. In the transference, she experienced herself as a troublesome child and her analyst as the dazzling center of a universe she could never enter. In this particular configuration, Kate felt unable to connect to me or to her own experience. As these feelings were delineated, they were represented in the following dream which also contained a beginning hope that a connection might be forged:

> I was in a house. It was cold and not entirely mine, as though I had never come to inhabit it. I was waiting for someone to make this possible and I thought of you. Then the scene shifted and I was having intercourse with a man against a wall, but there was no emotional connection, as though being with him was another place that didn't feel like home. I think that this dream is about my feeling that I can never find what is really mine. And I'm starting to wonder what that means. It's something about my image of myself and this feeling I have that in your eyes, I must seem like nothing.

Together we focused on the unbridgeable gap Kate felt between us. ''Why,'' I asked her, ''do I seem so completely out of reach?''

My question reminded Kate of growing up with an anxious mother and busy father who seemed often otherwise engaged. The youngest of five, with a considerable age difference between herself and the rest of the children, Kate felt inadequate and exiled from the interests and activities of her older brothers and sisters. ''Their doors were closed to me,'' she recalled, ''I had to ask permission to join them, and I never felt they really wanted me there. You know how much trouble a younger sister can be when you're a teenager and caught up in your own world.''

Soon we understood that Kate's sense of herself as dull and trouble-some was organized in her early experience with her exciting but unavailable siblings. Love felt conditional for this tiny girl who had to knock before entering a room and be quiet if she wished to sit with her sisters and brothers and listen to their conversation. We also saw how my coming to open the door at our first meeting had stirred up long forgotten, painful feelings of exclusion and insignificance, which had never been shared and so had undergone little transformation.

As these connections were integrated, Kate began to feel that her inner world was really welcome in our relationship, something, she said, she had never felt before. When our tie was secure, she imagined that I understood her sense of despair and wish to be valued. When ruptures occurred, she feared my indifference and that others were more important. As ruptures were analyzed, a sense of hopefulness filled the sessions. Though little changed outside the analysis, with me, she said, she felt more alive and of interest.

It was in this atmosphere of greater safety in our relationship, that Kate experienced an upsurge of love and sexual desire that left her feeling lewd and ugly. She imagined that she seemed, physically, more like a child to me than a woman, and that her "lesbian body" could never evoke "real" desire in another person. It was, she believed, awkward and unappealing and she felt, in my presence, grotesque and inexpressibly vulnerable. She wished desperately to please me and feared my contempt. "I don't want to worry all the time about how you see me," she lamented, "but I want so much to be loved and special, I really have no choice." She worried, was she interesting? Was she a good patient? Did I find her disgusting? Could I be satisfied? "This is how I lose myself," she said sadly. "Everything I am and feel depends on how others see me. And that's what I feel with you."

Soon Kate brought a second dream that reflected her deep sense of defect and the danger she felt in this highly charged relationship with me. In the dream, she was visiting friends and an infant was crying and in pain, but no one noticed. Feeling that someone must help the child, she picked her up and carried her up the stairs. As she made her way, the baby turned in her arms and she saw, with horror, that she had no spine, her back was a gaping hole. Kate panicked, but reached the bedroom where she laid the child on the bed. She felt terrible, she said, for she knew the child would never find a comfortable position without that crucial part of herself.

We now focused on Kate's sense of irreparable damage and her feeling that she must handle her problems alone. She recalled being constantly afraid, in adolescence, that she would do or say something that would drive others away. "I never expressed my feelings," she said, "I was never myself." I commented how difficult it must have been that she could not be herself as a child and how important this is to feeling "real" with those we love.

"I was a tomboy," she continued, "even in high school, and it seemed like my father was so disgusted with me. He never looked at me with pride or admiration. He never touched me. He still doesn't." For the first time in the analysis, Kate cried, "I feel so completely rejected by him and sort of mutilated. It has something to do with how powerful he seems to me, and that if I'm not doing the right thing, I'll be punished for it. And that reminds me of wanting to know you physically, it isn't right, I shouldn't have these feelings." "You'll be punished for it," I added. "Yes, because I'm not the girl he wanted, and there's no place for me anywhere. You know my father is so disgusted by homosexuals, that he will leave the room if a lesbian comes on the TV. I feel paralyzed in his presence, like that baby, I can't find a comfortable position."

Kate was quiet for awhile and I asked her what she was feeling. "Lonely," she answered. "I'm thinking how I'm paralyzed here too. I'm so anxious around people that I disgust myself. I can't reach out and make contact." "Why?" I asked.

Because I feel they couldn't want me as I am and closeness is so painful if you aren't really yourself. It's so unreal and unrelated. And I'm realizing how I've always felt this in relationships. Though I don't feel it with you. I just feel scared all the time that it's going to happen. I looked at my body after my shower this morning and I was surprised how fit and toned I am. I liked the way it looked, which, for me, is unbelievable. And then I felt a wave of shame because I wanted you to know my body. Not just sexually, but to really know me.

"You want to be completely yourself with me," I added, "and still be cared about."
Kate was quiet for awhile and then responded.

You see there was only one point of view in my home and that was my father's. If you didn't adopt it, you just weren't connected. When

I told my father that I was gay, he said, "That's it then, if you do that, you have no future." He was willing to write me off so quickly, it sort of broke my heart. I guess I've adopted his point of view about me, too. You know I've always known that being different is a problem for me. But to realize that deep down, I'm feeling with you, these things I feel with my father—that I'm someone who can't love or be loved because I'm a monster. Someone unnatural who doesn't have a future. It's so jolting.

Suddenly Kate stopped and said, "God, why do I feel so anxious saying this to you?" "Are you afraid," I asked, "that I'll write you off, too?" "Sometimes, but it's something more. I think I make it happen. Like right now, I know the session is ending and I'm angry. I don't want it to end. I'm sitting here feeling this but not saying anything and that does disconnect me. I hate the separations." "You don't want to be left alone with your feelings," I added. "Exactly," Kate sighed, "even knowing I'll be back."

With Kate's growing sense that she often placed herself outside relationships in order to avoid being pushed out, she felt more relaxed with me and with friends and colleagues. She began to wonder about her intense wish to touch and be touched and its various meanings. Together, we discovered that this important desire carried not only sensual and sexual longings but a desperate wish to disconfirm a grim belief that she was untouchable, a fantasy apparently organized in her relationship with her father. Memories returned of being in his presence always "at arms' length" and longing to be asked about her day at school or her opinions of a current event. A successful and active man, he had little time for Kate and was apparently unaware of her need to be acknowledged. "Sometimes," she whispered, as though she were revealing a terrible secret, "I feel this longing for you to take care of me and keep me from being lonely. That really is shameful. It makes me feel so infantile."

"We don't stop needing to be held," I suggested, "or touched, or understood just because we grow up." Kate was shaken by this exchange. "It's confusing," she said, "because my whole first analysis was about learning not to need people. I see, in a way, how I'm always diagnosing myself as bad or childish and the fact that you don't do this, it feels so important to me, it's almost overwhelming." Kate smiled, then, and added, "I feel really touched by it."

Not long after this session, Kate visited her parents for a week because her father was ill. She said when she returned:

I was shocked to see how frail he is and he was panicked that I was back in therapy. It was hard for me to see him that way, but, for the first time, I felt more normal and he didn't seem so powerful. I could see how frightened he is for me and I was able to reassure him that I'm all right. I didn't feel that I had to make things okay for him by not being myself. You know when I woke up this morning, I saw that headline about the guy who devastated the British stock market, and I thought, at least I'm not the guy who brought down Barings—that would really be monumental.

Kate's newfound conviction that her shortcomings were not monumental, marked a shift in our relationship which brought with it a greater sense of mutuality and exchange. She felt, she said, "in a new place," a place of greater clarity than she had felt before. Her sexual feelings for me no longer felt frightening or disruptive. She noticed that I was quite a bit older than she, though she reassured me that I was still attractive. In the transference, she no longer experienced me as the center of the universe and herself as a minor planet. For the first time, she imagined our mutual pleasure in ideas, and events, and conversation, thoughts that had been unimaginable at the beginning of analysis. Kate pictured my life, now, as full of experiences that were familial and satisfying, but did not feel excluded by this. She began to wonder exactly what she wanted for herself and how she might secure it. It seemed, to me, that Kate's desires, in all their complex and varied manifestations, had finally taken center stage.

"You know," she said one day, "I seem to know more women than I thought. I kept running into them all weekend. As though it were suddenly okay to notice them. I went to a movie with a woman I met recently and I'm going to see her again. Of course, I'm afraid that when she gets to know me, she'll be disappointed. But not so afraid that I won't try."

Kate's increasing interest in the world outside the analysis, brought with it a fear that this would somehow damage our relationship. She wavered between newfound pleasures in intimacy with others and concern that I would be angry or jealous. "Or worse," she said, "you might not care either way." These feelings reminded her of how impossible it seemed to go her own way in adolescence and not lose the people she loved. Then, she had retreated, to her room after school. "I was always alone," she remembered, "always waiting for my real life to begin." She felt, now, she said, suspended between hope for a future and fear that everything would be lost. She reflected on a part of herself that she believed she had rediscovered. "I have so much missed women," she told me. "Something about just holding Lee is so nice. I feel so completely myself with her and it's very intense sexually, too. She doesn't seem to want more than I can give and I don't feel afraid that I'm going to lose myself just by caring about her."

During this period, Kate occasionally missed sessions or arrived late having been caught up with something that felt too important to leave. "In a way," she laughed, "I know I'm testing the waters but it's not fair for you to make all the rules." My continued interest in her activities but firmness that her sessions were important, helped her feel that I was not indifferent to her presence, though I understood that there were times when rules were made to be broken. This metaphor for Kate's desire was not lost on either of us.

Soon Kate brought another dream. It contained many of the themes and feelings we had explored in our work together in the preceding months:

> I was coming to see you. There were a number of routes to get there and I was worried about finding my way. A man followed me who, at first, didn't seem dangerous but then turned evil and frightening. When I arrived, there were two small children playing in your office. I was upset at the thought that you were married but then I felt all right, because it didn't change anything. You were concerned about the route I had taken and said there was a nicer one. I was surprised that you cared about my route being pleasant. Then you turned to write directions for me—you wrote them carefully and for a moment we were turned in the same direction looking at them together and we were very close. It was wonderful and I felt overwhelmed by this feeling that I wasn't alone. And even though the man was there, I realized he wasn't menacing.

"What comes to mind?" I asked.

"The dangerous man reminded me of a friend's therapist who gave me a referral when I first came to see you. I saw her once and my friend said that his therapist was disappointed when I chose you instead."

"Ah," I said, "a dangerous man who doesn't approve of your choices."

"My father," Kate nodded. "But the danger faded in the dream and the biggest feeling was this feeling of being close to you and your care about my finding my way."

Kate fell silent for a few moments, then said, "You know, you did turn in the last session to write an appointment for me, you may not remember, but your skirt slipped up and I saw a lot of your leg. I wondered if you were aware of it?"

"Did you wonder if I was being seductive with you?" I asked. "No," Kate laughed:

> The main thing was that I could imagine that you were. It wasn't ludicrous to me that you might find me sexy or interesting—someone worth seducing. And that makes me feel like the world is full of possibilities. I was remembering how afraid I was that being attracted to you would close me down and, somehow, it opened me up. I don't want to make this an ode to you or anything, but I am really grateful.

At this point in the analysis, the particular transference configuration in which Kate connected desire and despair had been fairly well delineated, and many of the feelings that had been walled off in childhood had been recovered. She no longer experienced herself as irreparably damaged and permanently exiled from the world of intimate relationships and adult desires.

The Restoration of the Real

From my perspective, Kate was a child whose experience was pushed into the shadows until only a shadowland remained. A cumulative trauma of nonresponsiveness to her emerging sexual feelings in adolescence, left her feeling, not only bad and ugly, but unsure of the reality of her own experience. In the transference, these desires and the fear of repeated nonresponsiveness were evoked, allowing shame ridden and conflictual experiences of self and other and their related affects to finally be articulated, mutually regulated, and transformed. This fragment of her analysis illustrates, I believe, the crucial role of the analytic relationship in restoring a sense of reality to past and present experience. As Stolorow and

Atwood (1992) note, it is not so much the specific trauma which has such far-reaching consequences for a child, it is the fact that the child's reaction to the trauma, which includes overwhelming affect, is not met with any attuned responsiveness from others. Lost as a child, in a world of older children and adults, Kate felt left behind and closed off from those she loved. This early experience of self and other became the template through which her emerging sexual feelings in adolescence were organized. She feared again being outside and cut off from those she needed. Her sexual feelings toward women were clearly unacceptable to others, evidence that she was monstrous and undeserving of the love she feared to lose. As is often the case, her body and her sexual longings became the site of defect and irreparable damage—a concrete expression of a grim belief (Weiss and Sampson, 1986) that she had failed as a woman and as a person. During adolescence, the fantasy emerged that if she acted on her desires, her father would never touch her again. In this way a sense of herself as untouchable came to organize her experience of herself as a desiring but undesirable woman.

What is it that helped Kate recover the reality of desire in her relationship with me? I would emphasize my belief in the authenticity of her experience and an integrated approach in which an "optimal responsiveness" (Bacal, 1985) is provided, on the one hand, and a consistent exploration of the analytic interaction, on the other. We see in Kate's treatment a series of moments with me in which desire and its associated affects of guilt and shame are evoked and can be identified and understood. My response to her sexual feelings, which I did not find infantile or inauthentic, disconfirmed the expectation, organized in a lonely adolescence, that she would be ridiculed and abandoned should she go her own way in matters of the heart. When she expressed a desire to touch me, I did not interpret this as an unmet need to be held by her mother or a repudiation of her father. Rather, I tried to maintain an attuned responsiveness to her inner experience. Essentially, I invited her to tell me more about this wish, making it possible to explore over time *all* the memories, meanings, and feelings contained in this "touch" that she imagined. There were times, of course, when countertransferentially my responsiveness was less than optimal. Early in the analysis, for example, Kate asked me how old I was. Anxious about her fear that sexual feelings for me would make it impossible for her to make use of the analysis, I answered, "I guess I'm about the same age as your mother." Patients, however, are very forgiving, and she came to the next session pointing out that my discomfort with her desire had caused me to push away her feelings and make them about someone else. I acknowledged the truth of this and we were then able to explore the meaning of her question and its relevance to our relationship. Over time, Kate knew that she would not be left alone with her feelings, despite lapses on my part. In this relational context, her exiled desires were finally shared, elaborated, and intersubjectively reorganized. Kate came to feel that she was "someone worth seducing" and that her ways of being had a validity and value of their own.

To return to my original question about the meaning and the effect of theories that label lesbian desire unreal, I would suggest two things. These theories actually exile desire theoretically, just as it is exiled in the family, culture, and community. It is made incomprehensible in traditional psychoanalytic theory, just as subjectivity is incomprehensible in women (see Orange chapter 7) and tenderness and intimacy in men (Kaftal, 1991). The effect in analysis is far reaching, for it replicates an original trauma by creating a significant relationship in which, as Kate described it, there is one point of view and, if you don't adopt it, you just aren't connected. One analysand, speaking of her prior analyst, described this effect in the following way: "He treated my relationship as though it were a dream, so after awhile, I just stopped talking about it."

In my view, what distinguishes sexual desire from sexual impulse is the longing for a particular person who is felt to be irreplaceable. If desire is exiled, so is love. Butler (1995) captures this complex relationship between lesbian love, desire, and exile quite well. She writes about the uncertainty with which homosexual love and loss are regarded, "is this regarded as a 'true' love, a 'true' loss, a love and loss worthy or capable of being grieved and, in that sense, worthy or capable of ever having been lived? Or is this a love and a loss haunted by the specter of a certain unreality, a certain unthinkability, the double disavowal of 'I never loved her, and I never lost her.' " These are questions we must ask ourselves, as analysts, if we are to help our patients overcome the sense of exile which is part of lesbian experience.

References

Bacal, H. (1985), Optimal responsiveness and the therapeutic process. In: *Progress in Self Psychology,* Vol. 1, ed. A. Goldberg. New York: Guilford Press, pp. 202–226.

Beebe, B., & Lachmann, F. (1988), The contribution of mother-infant mutual influence to the origins of self and object representations. *Psychoanal. Psychology,* 5:305–337.

Butler, J. (1995), Melancholy gender. *Psychoanal. Dial.,* 3:170–171.

Cohn, J., & Tronick, E. (1983), Three month old infants' reactions to stimulated maternal depression. *Child Develop.,* 54:185–193.

Dimen, M. (1995), On our nature: Prolegomenon to a relational theory of sexuality. In: *Disorienting Sexuality: Psychoanalytic Reappraisals of Sexual Identities,* ed. R. Lesser & T. Domenici. New York: Routledge.

Field, T. (1981), Infant arousal, attention and affect during early interactions. In: *Advances in Infancy Research,* Vol. 1, ed. L. Lipsitt. Norwood, NJ: Ablex, pp. 31–36.

Freud, S. (1920), The psychogenesis of a case of homosexuality in a woman. *Standard Edition,* 18:145–172. London: Hogarth Press, 1955.

———— (1923), The Ego and the Id. *Standard Edition,* 19:1–59. London: Hogarth Press, 1961.

Galatzer-Levy, R. M., & Cohler, B. J. (1993), *The Essential Other.* New York: Basic Books, pp. 166–196.

Gilligan, C. (1982), *In a Different Voice: Psychological Theory and Women's Development.* Cambridge: Harvard University Press.

Goldberg, A. (1995), *The Problem of Perversion.* New Haven, CT: Yale University Press.

Kaftal, E. (1991), On intimacy between men. *Psychoanal. Dial.,* 1:305–328.

Kiersky, S., & Beebe, B. (1994), The reconstruction of early non-verbal relatedness in the treatment of the difficult patient. *Psychoanal. Dial.,* 4:389–408.

Klein, M. (1957), *Envy and Gratitude and Other Works 1946–1963.* New York: Free Press.

McDougall, J. (1979), The homosexual dilemma: A clinical and theoretical study of female homosexuality. In: *Sexual Deviation,* ed. I. Rosen. Oxford: Oxford University Press.

———— (1980), The homosexual dilemma: A study of female homosexuality. In: *A Plea for a Measure of Abnormality.* New York: International Universities Press, pp. 87—139.

Miller, J. B. (1986), *Toward a New Psychology of Women.* Boston: Beacon Press.

Mitchell, S. (1988), *Relational Concepts in Psychoanalysis.* Cambridge, MA: Harvard University Press.

———— (1996), Gender and sexual orientation in the age of postmodernism. The plight of the perplexed clinician. *Gender & Psychoanal.,* 1:45–73.

O'Connor, N., & Ryan, J. (1993), *Wild Desires & Mistaken Identities.* New York: Columbia University Press.

Orange, D. (1996), *Emotional Understanding: Studies in Psychoanalytic Epistemology.* New York: Guilford Press.

Panel (1993), On trauma. 13th Annual Spring Meeting, Div. 39, American Psychological Association. New York.

Schwaber, E. A. (1983), Psychoanalytic listening and psychic reality. *Internat. Rev. Psycho-Anal.*, 10:379–392.

———— (1990), Interpretation and the therapeutic action of psychoanalysis. *Internat. J. Psycho-Anal.*, 71:229–240.

Siegel, E. V. (1988), *Female Homosexuality: Choice without Volition.* New York: Analytic Press.

Socarides, C. W. (1978), *Homosexuality.* New York: Aronson.

Stern, D. (1977), *The First Relationship, Infant and Mother.* Cambridge, MA: Harvard University Press.

———— (1985), *The Interpersonal World of the Infant.* New York: Basic Books.

Stolorow, R. D., & Atwood, G. E. (1992), *Contexts of Being.* Hillsdale, NJ: Analytic Press, pp. 51–61.

———— Brandchaft, B., & Atwood, G. (1987), *Psychoanalytic Treatment: An Intersubjective Approach.* Hillsdale, NJ: Analytic Press, pp. 1–14.

Weiss, E., & Sampson, H. (1986), *The Psychoanalytic Process.* New York: Guilford Press.

Winnicott, D. W. (1971), *Playing and Reality.* New York: Basic Books.

3

Body Language: Reflections on the Homoerotics of the Female Dyad in Psychoanalysis

Edith Gould

If we consider the possibility that all women—from the infant suckling her mother's breast to the grown woman experiencing orgasmic sensations while suckling her own child, perhaps recalling her mother's milk-smell in her own ... to the woman dying at ninety, touched and handled by women—exist on a lesbian continuum, we can see ourselves as moving in and out of this continuum, whether we identify ourselves as lesbians or not [Adrienne Rich, 1980, p. 82].

Introduction

From a postmodern, relational perspective, the myriad experiences of the body evolve out of interactions with primary caregivers. The body is a coconstructed experience, carrying the imprint of primary aspects of the family and the culture. The psychological encoding of these relational exchanges coalesce as central aspects of the body self. Traumatic aspects of primary relationships can be exiled from conscious awareness and exist in muted and deadened forms as components of the body self. These deadened and disavowed aspects of the body self come into being and can be revitalized in the psychoanalytic relationship (Parlow, 1998). The literature on the power of the psychoanalytic dyadic experience to alter and revitalize the body self has been relatively sparse. In particular, there is a paucity of erotic material in the clinical reports of the transference–countertransference relationship with both heterosexual and lesbian patients, and women therapists (O'Connor and Ryan, 1993).

Not long ago, a supervisee related a vignette about a female patient who maintained the fantasy that her analyst was a lesbian. This transference belief remained unshakable, over a number of years of treatment, despite the fact that the analyst practiced in her home, where the patient had opportunities to observe the comings and goings of a heterosexual family life. This patient remembered a close physical relationship with her mother until she reached puberty, at which point her mother rebuffed her affectionate overtures and expressed repugnance in regard to further physical contact with her daughter. From her mother's perspective, physically affectionate relating had to come to an end because "only lesbians touched each other." Thus, years later, the patient's transference longings for sensual contact with her analyst could only be placed in the context of a dreaded and prohibited homosexuality, her own and her analyst's.

Four years into her analysis, a patient of mine, Rebecca, expressed in dreams and associations her longings for physical closeness with me. She spoke of hugs and prohibitions against hugs in our relationship. She brought in what she called a "strange dream," in which she was a naked infant, held and rocked by her mother. In the dream, her mother's arm brushed against her genitals and she experienced a frisson of sexual pleasure. She was frightened of the dream. Did it mean she was a lesbian? Such an idea was terrifying to consider and she avoided further inquiry into the subject. Rebecca's mother, cold and aloof, had never caressed or held her. She seemed to prefer affectionate contact with the patient's younger brother. She illustrated her mother's discrepant attitudes toward her and her brother by pointing to the fact that his genitals were named by her mother, whereas her genitals were referred to as "between your legs." Rebecca had sought treatment because her erotic desire was in a state of exile (Kiersky, chapter 2). She had disowned her sexuality and her sexual body, neither seeking nor responding to sexual contact with either men or women. It wasn't until her analysis was well underway that she could bring herself to touch her vagina, to wash herself, or to pleasure herself. But her dream proved to be too anxiety provoking. Fleeing from the emerging homoerotic transference, she precipitously took a "break" from analysis to travel around the world. During her travels, she engaged in sexual encounters with exotic men to prove to herself, and to me, that she was not a lesbian.

A different patient, Deena, steadfastly maintained that she was "really a heterosexual" despite the fact that her most sustained and fulfilling sexual relationships were with women. She used her recurrent dreams of having violent sexual intercourse with men, where her body was "pounded" as evidence of her "primary heterosexual orientation." In her analysis, Deena connected these dreams to her being beaten up, "pounded" by her four brothers, when she was growing up, something her father thought "toughened" her up.

Embedded in these vignettes are reflections of the ways in which representations of the body self and desire emerge out of the relational matrix. The contemporary divide between heterosexual and homosexual sexualities is also implicit in the clinical material. Same-sex physical contact is condemned and stigmatized. Yet for human beings, touching and the desire to be touched is bred in the bone.

Societal prohibitions against sensual and sexual experiences between women are internalized and become an aspect of the rules governing women's relationships with one another. These prohibitions are passed from mother to daughter. Women's normative promptings to bond with other women in sensual and affectionate ways are muffled and prohibited because such forms of relating have come to be viewed as deviant. Kiersky (personal communication, 1997) points to the "paradox" inherent in women's views of themselves as more affectionate by nature and, at the same time, anxious about affectionate feelings and behaviors experienced toward one another.

Throughout the history of psychoanalysis, theories of female sexuality have been based upon the assumption of discrete and unitary categories of heterosexuality and homosexuality. Today, psychoanalytic writers are forging a new theory of desire. Calling into question the primacy of the biological determinism of the Freudian model, contemporary theorists assert the necessity of including sociocultural and relational forces along with biological factors in the organization of desire. New psychoanalytic theories of desire embrace definitions of desire as fluid and diverse rather than static and binary. Expanded perspectives on sexuality move away from the construction of discrete categories, toward a view of sexuality and desire as existing along a continuum (Rich, 1980). Symptoms expressed by the body, as well as subjective constructions about the body self, can symbolize a diverse array of psychological themes, such as wishes for fusion, separation anxiety, abandonment fears, strivings for autonomy, gender conflicts, gender inadequacy, disruptions in sexual desire, and conflicts over sexual and aggressive wishes. In this chapter, I will discuss the case of a patient whose desperate strivings for, and conflicts over, separation and independence from her mother, were primarily expressed in somatic terms. This chapter is a contribution to the new literature that presents a more expanded picture of female desire. Departing from the constraining vise of the Freudian model of female psychology, I will propose a model of female desire that is more variable than has been conceptualized in the traditional psychoanalytic canon. A model of female desire as existing along a continuum is suggested as an alternative to the binary constructions of defining sexuality in terms of an either–or sexual orientation view. Following a brief literature review, I will turn to an illustrative vignette of clinical work with a woman who experienced intense fantasies, desires, and conflicts in relation to her own body and the body of her analyst. These desires were expressed in the transference and represented central organizing aspects of our analytic work.

Lesser (chapter 8) has stated that categories such as *homosexual* and *heterosexual* "are historical and cultural constructions which create boundaries between what is forbidden and what is acceptable, defining both deviance and normality" (p. 127).

The rigid adherence to the gender polarities of masculine-feminine and the homosexual-heterosexual binary in regard to "sexual orientation," serve defensive functions in our culture. "Mutually exclusive categories of (gender) and sexuality rule out other possibilities that may engender anxiety" (Schwartz, 1995). Harris (1995, p. xv) calls for the "opening up" of the discourse on sexuality to embrace "more variegated experiences of sexual beings than the limiting binary category scheme of homosexual/heterosexual."

Psychoanalysts are made uneasy by the notion of desire as a mercurial force. Erotic transference "longings can evoke . . . a sense of disorientation and a narcissistic threat in the countertransference. Schuker advises that heterosexual analysts need to analyze their countertransference to understand and value homoerotic yearnings, including wishes for erotic pleasure and pride different from one's own manifest interests'' (Schuker, 1996, p. 504).

More often than not, psychoanalysts adhere to the ''idea of stable, coherent subjects and stable sexual identities'' (Lesser, chapter 8) and tend to strive toward the achievement of these goals with their patients. Analysts and patients alike attempt to maintain rigidly defined boundaries with regard to sexuality and sexual identity. The reduction of all desire to sexual desire, the enforcement and maintenance of the heterosexual–homosexual binary, and the male–female gender divide continue to exert a powerful and constricting influence on psychoanalytic theory and clinical work.

The demonization of homosexuality that preoccupied people in the twentieth century shattered the acceptability of a continuum of female desire, and changed the nature of women's relationships to one another. Alienation between mother and daughter is a familiar theme in our culture. Psychoanalytic theory and practice represent cause and effect in these ruptures. In Freud's conceptualization of the Oedipus complex, ''crucial derivatives of his unconscious hostility and other negative affects in relation to his mother can be found, not in his psychology of the boy, but rather in his description of the psychosexual development of the girl'' (Stolorow and Atwood, 1979, p. 67). Freud's defensively motivated view of the perfection of the mother–son relationship is reflected in his famous statement in ''Femininity.'' ''A mother is only brought unlimited satisfaction by her relation to her son; this is altogether the most perfect, the most free from ambivalence of all human relationships'' (1933, p. 133). In stark contrast, Freud's concept of the girl's oedipal drama is replete with devaluation of, and alienation from, the mother. Psychoanalysis, reflecting the culture within which it evolved, has marginalized women, mothers, lesbians, mother–daughter relationships, and the feminine. Women's nurturing capacities have been made short shrift of in psychoanalysis. The important ways in which women perform maternal functions of mirroring, soothing, comforting, and supporting one another, has never been taken seriously in psychoanalytic theory. Dimen and Shapiro (1996) urge the ''recuperation of the feminine'' in psychoanalysis and call for the recognition of women's unique strengths and capacities for intimate relating. Feminist writers have underscored ''the lack of maternal subjectivity in Freud in particular and psychoanalytic theory in general'' (Chodorow, 1994, p. 95). ''That Freud was not prepared to think about mothers very far is . . . evident from how little he said directly about them and relationships with them'' (Schafer, 1976, p. 346). In Freud's theory ''the maternal, as a strong, intense feeling, preoccupation, and identity in women, as subjects, is almost entirely absent, along with adequate recognition or treatment of infantile attachment to the mother'' (Chodorow, 1994, p. 4).

With the advent of relational and intersubjective models in psychoanalysis, the role of the mother moved to a more prominent position, though not always a positive position. Developmental theory has a special place for the child's disidentification from mother. Traditionally the references to disidentification in the psychoanalytic literature have been to the boy's need to disidentify from the mother in order to foster and maintain a masculine self (Greenson, 1968). It is now generally accepted that both boys and girls identify and disidentify in various ways with parents of both sexes (see Benjamin [1988], for a discussion of the girl's identificatory love for her father). Butler (1995) maintains that the girl must disidentify, that is, give up her primary attachment to the mother, in order to support female gender identity. Disidentification from mother involves an experience of early loss for both sexes (Chodorow, 1978; Pollack, 1995). In women, the buried, ungrieved lost mother may live on in a desire for physical contact with the comforting body of the mother-caregiver. The dyad of the female analyst and the female patient is ripe for the activation of the myriad permutations of the early sensual mother–daughter relationship. An illustration: Peggy, at the beginning of her analysis, reported a dream in which she and I are having a session in my bathroom. She notes that in the dream, the space between us keeps shifting. This is distressing to her. We are, in some moments, physically close to one another, in others more distant. She can't quite tell where she is standing in relation to me. Her associations to the dream are to the very pleasurable, sensual experience of bathing her daughter, and then to her relationship with her mother, who was always trying to perfect her own body through a fanatical regime of diet and exercise. Our dialogue about the dream led to a central concern of hers. Would I cherish her body self, could I ''touch'' the body she felt was ''yucky'' to her mother, the body she wanted to hide from view under baggy clothes? These inquiries inevitably led to Peggy's anxious questions about the nature of her sexuality. How can she desire physical closeness with a woman without being homosexual? From her point of view, everyone is either one or the other, homosexual or heterosexual.

In the analytic dyad the "maternal erotic transference," so vividly recognized and described by Wrye and Welles (1994), includes "all manner of sensual bodily fantasies in relation to the analyst's body" (p. 35). Whether avoided, disavowed, or actively desired, reverberations of the early, body-based experience with the mother, are universally evoked in the therapeutic situation. The manner in which this transference will be experienced and expressed is extremely variable. The analytic creation of linkages between the current body experiences and the original, body-based interactions between caregiver and child, provides the patient with a vitalized self, freer from the constricting effects of unmentalized themes. The analytic dyad of female analyst/female patient allows for the "recuperation of the feminine."

Case Vignette: Suzanne[1]

Early in a three times a week, six-year analysis, Suzanne reported the following dream:

> A young woman was leaning on a windowsill looking down onto the street. An older woman with "dreadlocks" was lying on top of her. The young woman commented on an attractive man who was walking in the street. The older woman ordered the young woman to shoot him, which she did.

Midpoint in her analysis, Suzanne related the following "disturbing dream":

> I was making out with my mother, kissing her on the mouth and mother said she wanted more, like she wanted sex with me. I thought, "I don't want to have sex with you," and she said, "But it's OK, you're supposed to. I'm your mother and I need more."

During the termination phase of her analysis Suzanne reported the following dream:

---

[1]The patient Suzanne described in this clinical vignette represents a composite picture drawn from women patients I have worked with over a number of years.

I was with a very attractive man, like Mick Jagger. We were at a party. I felt so desired by him, so attractive. Then we were in the house I grew up in, where mother and I lived. She used to sleep in a big bed in the bedroom, and I slept in an alcove between the kitchen and the living room. In the dream, she was going to sleep on the floor in the living room and let me and this man sleep in the big bed together. She did this begrudgingly.

Each of these three dreams encapsulates central organizing themes, core conflicts, and desires that pervaded Suzanne's intense struggle to resolve her powerful, ambivalent tie to her mother. To free herself from the "dread lock" of her mother's psychological grip on her, and go on to have an independent life, including a fulfilling relationship with a man, was the overall focus of our analytic work. Suzanne's connection to her mother was primarily experienced in body-based terms. Thus, when she was depressed she confessed to me that she wished she could curl up into a ball and be held and rocked by her mother. It was only with mother, and later transferentially with me, that she felt "totally taken care of." Significantly, her masturbatory fantasies of engaging in mutual oral sex with women were also described as blissful states of being "totally taken care of." She became aware that she was envisioning her mother's face when she masturbated. These fantasies were understood as transformations of her early sensual experiences with a mother whom she felt owned her body.[2] She was very distressed by the persistence of fantasies of having oral sex with women, when she was actually engaged in having intercourse with a man. She fretted about these fantasies, thought they meant she was a lesbian, and that would be "terrible" for her. In her mind, there was a strong demarcation between homosexual and heterosexual, so she tried to rid herself of the fantasies, but they kept haunting her. In the early years of her analysis, to have any kind of sexual experience without some reference (in fantasy) to her mother, represented an abandonment and betrayal of mother. To appropriate her own body and get her mother out of her sex life, became a therapeutic goal.

Suzanne grew up out west, with a depressed, anxious, and hypochondriacal mother, who turned to her daughter for the comfort and maternal nurturing she had been deprived of by her own mother. Suzanne's father

---

[2]The fantasy of the daughter's body belonging to the mother was dramatically illustrated in another patient's dream. The patient dreamed she was having sex with a man when she heard her mother's voice, sternly reprimanding her, "How dare you do that with *my* body!"

had never lived with them. Shortly after Suzanne's birth, he moved to a Hippie commune in Hawaii, where he went on to father six more children. After the age of 6, Suzanne spent summers with him and the extended family of the commune. She recalled being happy there, where she was "free to run around naked" with the other children. A particular sexual episode from that period of her life figured significantly in her analysis. When Suzanne was 16 her father told her that he used to shower with her when she stayed on the commune with him. He was amused by the fact that he would get erections, which she would become "very interested in." Suzanne had no memory of these bathing experiences with her father. The only thing she remembered about this period of her life was how much she worried about her mother's loneliness during her visits to the commune.

Later reconstructions in her analysis led to the interpretation that her guilt about her "oedipal victory" reinforced an already powerful identification and mergerlike relationship with her mother. These themes emerged in a recurrent transference fantasy. In the fantasy Suzanne tells me that she had fellated her father. In this fantasy, as she is speaking to me, she becomes intensely nauseated, gets up off the couch, runs into my bathroom, where she vomits. I run in after her and comfortingly hold her forehead, as she throws up into the toilet. Often this fantasy scenario would emerge in association to her recounting sexual experiences with her boyfriends. For years, all her relationships with men ended with her running back to the sensual comfort provided by mother and by me, in the transference. Her experience of lying on the couch, listening to my voice, replicated the "totally taken care of" experience she described having with her mother and in her fantasies of oral sex with women. She referred to "basking in the therapy." But the warm, holding aspects of the analytic space in time became a double-edged sword. At times, the therapeutic environment was experienced as dangerously constricting to her. When she had a new boyfriend, she was convinced I wanted her to leave him. That she is with "Mick Jagger" in the third dream is relevant here. He was her mother's favorite rock singer and "Jagger" suggests the jagged or potentially hurtful aspect of her having a love affair with anyone but her mother. She was caught between her intense body-based tie to her mother and her desires to be with men. Insufficiently consolidated capacities for self-regulation of intense affect states, kept her inextricably bound to her mother. Her mother's failure to sanction Suzanne's independent desire was an additional factor that prohibited separation/ individuation.

Suzanne's conviction that her mother owned her body, had its origins in her mother's failure to establish boundaries between her body and her daughter's body. The degree of psychological fusion between mother and daughter was dramatically represented by Suzanne's confession that hearing her mother's voice over the telephone prompted the urge to move her bowels, a remedy she would resort to if she was constipated. They bathed together until Suzanne rebelled against it when she was an adolescent. At home, there were no closed doors. The bathroom door had to be left open, at all times, therefore toileting activities were mutually witnessed. The smell of her mother's body soothed Suzanne. She spoke of "smelling her mother and knowing that she had had sex with a man." "In these moments," Suzanne said, "I'd lose her. She was no longer my mother." Her conviction that love relationships had to be exclusively dyadic was recapitulated in her transference fears of knowing anything about me, my personal life, or my other patients. She was terrified of finding out anything about me that could be construed as "losing" me. Suzanne's early and ongoing experiences of maternal and paternal "intrusion and boundary violation" traumatically compromised her ability to "feel safe if the other person . . . [was] known" to her (Orange and Stolorow, 1998). For a long time, Suzanne's emotional safety depended upon the maintenance of my complete anonymity to her. Not knowing anything about me sustained the necessary illusion that I was completely hers and there only for her.

The first dream of Suzanne's, referred to earlier, was a concretization of the suffocating, boundaryless, exclusive, symbioticlike "dread lock" relationship she had with her mother, a relationship that prohibited any sexual interest in a man. She came into analysis in a severely depressed and psychologically depleted state, desperately needing help with getting her mother off her back. Her homoerotic fantasies served multiple functions. They simultaneously connected her to, and distanced her from, her mother. By the time she terminated her analysis, when she moved out of the state to pursue her career, the range of her erotic fantasy life had considerably expanded. She no longer thought about whether she was gay or straight. The homoerotic fantasies took their place amongst a variety of other sexual scenarios that signaled increasing individuation from her mother. As expressed in the "Mick Jagger" dream, Suzanne was able to less conflictually engage in relationships with men. Her mother, though still close by, was now relegated to a more distant corner of her inner world. Now her mother was sleeping on the floor in another room, instead of lying on top of her, pinning her down, as in her dream.

Discussion

Viewing female desire as existing along a continuum, rather than dwelling within the confines of the discrete categories of homosexual and heterosexual, allows for greater flexibility in our understanding of the erotic life of women. "Butler suggests that gender identity might be more fluid, if social forces were less constraining. Might object choice be similar?" (Schuker, 1996, p. 500). Could it be that rigidly maintained, discrete categories of gender and sexual preference will ultimately give way to more fluid and inclusive views; just as the rigidly maintained notion of the vaginal orgasm as the sine qua non of femininity, collapsed under the weight of Masters and Johnson's research findings and the protests of thousands of women on the couch?

Schwartz (1995), cautioning clinicians, maintains that holding a sexual orientation view "shapes the manner in which its adherents listen to clinical material; because of their belief in a stable sexual orientation they would be unlikely to discover or be interested in same-sex desires in heterosexuals or other-sex desire in homosexuals" (p. 155).

What do we mean when we describe a woman as a lesbian?

[We could be] referring to a woman's sexual fantasies, to her sexual activity and responsiveness, or to her sense of self-identity and association with a social group or social role. These are not necessarily concordant. Homoerotic fantasies and a lesbian lifestyle are not the same thing. A same-sex object can be utilized (in reality or fantasy) in strivings for safety, intimacy, pleasure, power or other gratifications. Erotic fantasy itself may have been homosexual from early childhood, . . . may include varying degrees of bisexuality, may be absent, or may not be homosexual despite homosexual activity or a same-sex behavioral requirement for arousal. Should erotic fantasy itself define sexual orientation? [pp. 496–497]. . . .

[Like Suzanne], some women desire or need bodily intimacy with another woman for arousal. . . . This issue of behavioral vs. fantasy choice is also entwined with that of mutability vs. immutability of object choice [p. 497].

Suzanne's case illustrates the complexity and diversity of women's desire. Suzanne's homoerotic fantasies and transference longings had originally evoked panic over the possibility of her being a lesbian. Analytic work involved the uncovering and exploration of her rigidly maintained sexual and gender polarities. Suzanne experienced shame and conflict over her sexual identity and homoerotic desires, which were experienced as threatening evidence of her being a lesbian. For Suzanne "lesbian" meant being forever yoked to her mother, from whose grip she desperately struggled to free herself. The violation of the natural self–other boundaries by Suzanne's mother set up powerful, body-based connections to her mother that were relived in the transference relationship. Homoerotic fantasies were expressions of central organizing themes related to maternal misattunement, impingement, and loss, as well as containing Suzanne's strivings for individuation. As her analysis progressed, she grew to be more accepting of her sexual fantasies about women, viewing them as an expression of the diverse nature of her own sexuality. The homoerotic fantasies continued to be powerfully arousing, though less exclusive. Suzanne's homoerotic fantasies also served as self-vitalizing experiences that countered depression and feelings of emptiness. She was able to utilize me as a calming, soothing selfobject. She felt "totally taken care of" on the couch. Frighteningly intense affect states experienced somatically were calmed by my presence.

Conclusion

In this chapter, I have proposed and illustrated a continuum model of female desire. The goal is to unpack desire in order to avoid prepackaged assumptions about the homoerotic transference–countertransference material in the analytic situation. A woman who has homoerotic fantasies may not be a lesbian and a lesbian with heterosexual fantasies may not be heterosexual. Despite the widespread recognition today, on the part of psychoanalysts, that object choice involves "multiple determining factors, we still remain ignorant about key influences that open or close off possibilities in a given individual" (Shuker, 1996, p. 499).

The revival and integration of primarily unconscious dimensions of body-based aspects of the early mother relationship, provides the analytic patient with a richer, more expanded sense of her self, her sexuality, her relational options, and in the Loewaldian (1978) sense, the opportunity to "own" her history. Understanding the origins and meanings of her desires and placing them in relational contexts, helps to transform rigidly maintained ideas about one's sexuality. Attention to bodily themes in the psychoanalytic situation provides the patient with a vivid, metaphorical referent to subjective experience. The potential to work through conflicts and obstacles to intimacy and expand capacities for same-sex and opposite-sex sensual and sexual relating, is contained within the investigation of these dimensions of encoded early childhood experience.

References

Benjamin, J. (1988), Woman's desire. In: *The Bonds of Love: Psychoanalysis, Feminism and the Problem of Domination.* New York: Pantheon Books, pp. 85–132.

Butler, J. (1995), Melancholy gender: Refused identification. *Psychoanal. Dial.,* 5:165–180.

Chodorow, N. J. (1978), *The Reproduction of Mothering: Psychoanalysis and the Sociology of Gender.* Berkeley, CA: University of California Press.

——— (1994), *Feminism, Masculinities, Sexualities: Freud and Beyond.* Lexington: University Press of Kentucky.

Dimen, M., & Shapiro, S. (1996), Trouble between women. Paper presented at National Institute for the Psychotherapies Workshop, New York.

Freud, S. (1933), New Introductory Lectures on Psycho-Analysis. *Standard Edition,* 22:1–182. London: Hogarth Press, 1964.

Greenson, R. R. (1968), Dis-identification from mother. *Internat. J. Psycho-Anal.,* 49:370–374.

Harris, A. (1995), Foreword. In: *Disorienting Sexuality: Psychoanalytic Reappraisals of Sexual Identities,* ed. T. Domenici & R. C. Lesser. New York: Routledge.

Loewald, H. W. (1978), *Psychoanalysis and the History of the Individual.* New Haven, CT: Yale University Press.

O'Connor, N., & Ryan, J. (1993), *Wild Desires and Mistaken Identities.* New York: Columbia University Press.

Orange, D. M., & Stolorow, R. D. (1998), Self-disclosure from the perspective of intersubjectivity theory. *Psychoanal. Inq.,* 18:530–537.

Parlow, S. (1998), Suffering the body in the analytic situation. Paper presented at the 18th Annual Spring Meeting, American Psychological Association, Division 39, Boston.

Pollack, W. S. (1995), Deconstructing dis-identification: Rethinking psychoanalytic concepts of male development. *Psychoanal. & Psychother.,* 12:30–45.

Rich, A. (1980), Compulsory heterosexuality and lesbian existence. In: *Women, Sex and Sexuality,* ed. C. R. Stimpson & E. S. Person. Chicago: University of Chicago Press.

Schafer, R. (1976), Problems in Freud's psychology of women. *J. Amer. Psychoanal. Assn.,* 22:459–485.

Schuker, E. (1996), Toward further analytic understanding of lesbian patients. *J. Amer. Psychoanal. Assn.* (Suppl.), 44:485–508.

Schwartz, D. (1995), Current psychoanalytic discourses on sexuality: Tripping over the body. In: *Disorienting Sexuality: Psychoanalytic Reappraisals of Sexual Identities,* ed. T. Domenici & R. C. Lesser. New York: Routledge, pp. 115–126.

Stolorow, R. D., & Atwood, G. E. (1979), *Faces in a Cloud: Subjectivity in Personality Theory.* New York: Jason Aronson.

Wrye, H. K., & Welles, J. K. (1994), *The Narration of Desire: Erotic Transferences and Countertransferences.* Hillsdale, NJ: Analytic Press.

4

Transforming the Ties That Bind: Lesbians, Lovers, and Chosen Family

Ellen Shumsky

There is a relational phenomenon, common in the lesbian community, of ex-lovers who continue to remain vitally important in each other's lives. These women—who were once not only sexual partners, but best friends, "soul-mates," companions, or surrogate family—have ended their life as a couple, but maintain a significant ongoing bond. Though they may each go on to establish new primary partnerships, their tie to each other continues and is sought and acknowledged by both, as emotionally important. I will refer to this profound lesbian friendship as a family/friendship.[1] This type of separation is a very different phenomenon from heterosexual "divorce" where ex-spouses, especially if they remarry, often regard any loving feelings they continue to experience for their former partners as guilty secrets that are kept hidden with the force of a taboo.

---

[1]Dr. Ro King has coined the term gokwa—an acronym for God Only Knows What we Are—to refer to this anomalous relationship. There is a community of lesbians throughout the United States who use the word *gokwa* to refer to a family/friend.

Psychoanalytic theory, its Freudian origins firmly embedded in patriarchal culture, has, until recently, enshrined the masculine ideals of autonomy and independence as the highest expression of mature psychological development. In the traditional developmental model, the infant has been viewed as starting from a place of total merger, and, if all goes well, becoming increasingly independent (Mahler, Pine, and Bergman, 1975). Practitioners working from this model tend to implicitly support moves toward separation, which is seen as health, and to devalue needs for close attachment. The terms *merging* and *clinging* ring with pejorative regressive connotations. This theory has been informed by what Stolorow and Atwood (1992) refer to as "the myth of the isolated mind" (p. 7)—a defensive fantasy of the mature adult as someone who needs no one.

Contemporary relational paradigms such as self psychology and intersubjectivity theory are supported by infant research as reported by Beebe and Lachman (1988) and Stern (1985). These studies demonstrate that infants begin life with a recognizable subjectivity—a locus of independent initiative—which is reinforced or modified in the mutual regulatory system of the parent-infant bond. This subjectivity is influenced throughout life by all the relationships that sustain one's sense of self. An important measure of growth from this perspective is not autonomy or independence, but fluid self-expression within increasingly complex and flexible relational fields.

The Mahlerian construct of human development as a progressive move toward autonomy is also challenged by feminist theorists (Miller, 1976; Chodorow, 1978). These authors have addressed the significance of the gender asymmetry that characterizes the different separation experiences faced by male and female children in relation to a maternal primary caregiver. "From very early on . . . because they are parented by a person of the same gender . . . girls come to experience themselves as less differentiated than boys" (Chodorow, 1978, p. 167). This difference has been pathologized by theory that has normalized male developmental process and its inherent emphasis on individuation. Maturity has been equated with autonomy, and concern with relationships has been viewed as a weakness rather than a strength. The women of the Stone Center propose the notion of the "self-in-relation" which shifts the emphasis "from separation to relationship as the basis for self-experience and development." In this model, a basic goal of development is "the deepening capacity for relationship and relational competence" (Surrey, 1991, p. 53).

These new perspectives redirect the focus of psychoanalytic discourse from the study of intrapsychic mechanisms to more fluid and contextual relational concerns. The bedrock of psychoanalytic intersubjectivity theory, as explicated by Stolorow and Atwood (1992), is that psychological phenomena cannot be understood apart from the intersubjective contexts in which they take form. This is particularly salient in considering the phenomenon of the lesbian family/friendship which, to be understood, must be contextualized in the sociocultural matrix that has powerfully influenced lesbian psychology and its ensuing relational configurations.

Buloff and Osterman (1995) have detailed the process of the marginalization of the lesbian in a homophobic culture. When lesbianism is routinely demonized and pathologized by prevailing sociocultural institutions, lesbians are commonly estranged from, if not blatantly rejected by, their families, churches, affiliates, and communities. As a result, there is a particular hunger for belonging, bonds of acceptance and trust, and a vitally important sense of relational continuity. Kohut argued passionately that the most fundamental human need is for meaning and human contact (1981, p. 545). The family/friend tie reflects the preciousness for lesbians of relationships with a history of intimacy. The mutuality of falling in love creates the conditions for the development of intense closeness. When lesbians, who may otherwise be deprived of dependable, sustaining familial ties, fall out of love, they continue to need the deep knowing, the familiarity of one with whom they have shared their most exposed and vulnerable selves. The ongoing nature of the relationship, in a world of fragile connections, is something worth preserving. Becker (1988) captures this in her description of family/friends:

> [They] had shared an extensive emotional history and participated in each other's psychological, social and cultural growth, [they] . . . had a deep and broad understanding of one another. They viewed their current life events within an historical context of meanings, projects, conflicts and intentions. . . . They could rely on their family-like connection as a stable point to which they could return for validation of themselves and the continuity of their lives [p. 216].

Ironically, the same marginalization that has kept lesbians alienated and deprived of needed ties has also been a carrier of freedom—the space in which to evolve oneself and one's relationships in greater harmony with authentic needs. Because lesbian relationships have existed outside of the American cultural mainstream, they have not been explicitly regulated by the social and religious institutions of this culture. As outlaws, lesbians have been able to be more emotionally daring, with fewer sanctions, and the family/friend bond is an innovative reflection of this social reality.

Psychologically, the family/friend relationship can best be understood in terms of Kohut's ideas about selfobject ties. Kohut promulgated the existence of a lifelong need for connection to empathically responding others, as vital for psychological survival as oxygen is for physical survival (1984, p. 47). He saw such ties as necessary for the development and maintenance of a cohesive self throughout the life cycle and referred to them as "selfobject" bonds. The partner in such a bond provides "selfobject functions" which include mirroring responsiveness, an idealized source of greatness, calm and security, and a sense of an alike other. The good-enough provision of these selfobject functions creates a buoyant medium which holds, strengthens, and enlivens the unfolding self of the other. In the absence of this medium, an enfeeblement or fragmentation of the self may result which can reach terrifying proportions.

The family/friend bond can be seen as originating in a reciprocal selfobject tie. The couple who become family/friends have, as lovers, been mutually serving selfobject functions for one another—admiration, reassuring strength or calm, and/or a sustained experience of feeling known and understood. The buoyant medium generated by this relationship has supported the ongoing self development of both partners. Lesbians who transform their relationship from lovers to that of family/friends are determined to protect this nourishing bond and its self cohering functions.

There are many complex reasons why any primary partnership—homosexual or heterosexual—ends. The commitment may have been made prematurely before the individuals knew themselves or each other well enough to have made such a lifelong decision. Lesbians, estranged from their families of origin and needing a sense of secure belonging, may be especially eager for selfobject connection and prone to precipitous couplings. Individuals commonly commit to one another without the ability to emotionally manage vulnerability, closeness, difference, or conflict—the ingredients of intimacy. They may blame their partner for the couple's problems and proceed through several repetitions of relational failure before they will be ready to accept responsibility for their difficulties with intimacy. This is true of heterosexuals and homosexuals. What seems to distinguish some lesbian breakups from heterosexual divorce is not a particular kind of lesbian-specific problem with intimacy, but the psychosocial reality that lesbians, as members of a stigmatized and marginalized group, need to salvage and protect the intimate ties they have created even when they don't lead to lifelong primary partnership.

For some couples, the mutually nourishing selfobject tie itself, fueling increasing self development, can move the relationship into an emotional crisis. Stolorow, Brandchaft, and Atwood (1987) have written that "derailment of the self-differentiation process occurs in an intersubjective situation in which central affect states associated with the development of individualized selfhood are consistently not responded to or are actively rejected" (p. 52). They are referring to the psychological dilemma of individuals who have sacrificed self development in order to protect needed ties with parental selfobjects, a not uncommon lesbian experience. When a lesbian's "hope for a new beginning" (Ornstein, 1974)—a new selfobject tie where she will be freer to express herself—is realized with a lover, previously hidden dimensions of her personal idiom emerge and flourish. The self expansion of both partners set in motion by a reciprocally nurturing connection, may create profound dislocations and incompatibilities that can threaten and disrupt the new selfobject bond.

As self delineation proceeds and differences become exaggerated, conflict intensifies. The partners may each experience their self strivings as repeatedly rejected by the other and the selfobject tie falls under siege. Each rupture recapitulates the early traumatic parental negation of self development. Over time, a chronic erosive condition develops. When the intensity or constancy of this stress threatens to jeopardize the very survival of the bond, the lovers, in order to preserve their vitally needed tie, may break up and redefine themselves as family/friends—a relationship with fewer expectations.

Case Vignette

Susan and Ann met when they were in their twenties. They fell in love, became lovers, and remained in a primary relationship for ten years. Initially, they were enthralled with each other. Each idealized in the other qualities she lacked in herself. Ann was enchanted by Susan's sensual, intuitive, in-the-moment streetsmarts. Susan was in awe of Ann's articulate, intelligent thoughtfulness. Both had been feeling lost, misunderstood, insubstantial, and searching, until, discovering the other, they found a home. The admiration, support, validation, and emotional security engendered by their bond fueled their ongoing individuation. During those years, they helped grow each other up. They completed graduate and postgraduate training, chose and developed professional identities, created homes separately and together, built communities of friends as a couple and individually. In their relationship they were lovers, best friends, "soulmates," companions, colleagues, and chosen family.

As each grew, new conflicts emerged in their relationship. Although in the same profession, their interests and affiliations, initially similar, began more and more to differ. Always city dwellers, they bought a country home for weekends. As Susan found herself increasingly attracted to life in the country, conflict within the relationship escalated further. Ann preferred an urban life-style and had discovered a love of travel. Negotiating shared time was proving increasingly difficult and more of their shared time was spent fighting. They were both frequently feeling disappointed, frustrated, thwarted, and angry. When Ann cultivated a new friend—a single gay woman who was available to be her travel companion—Susan was beside herself with feelings of jealousy and threat. This new ingredient of Susan's jealousy was more than Ann could emotionally handle. After years of intense struggle around seemingly irresolvable conflicts, Ann decided to break up with Susan. What this meant was that she would pursue her life independently of Susan, including the possibility of sexual and romantic interests. Their life as a couple in primary partnership was over.

Ann did not, however, wish to completely discontinue a relationship with Susan with whom she had shared the most intimate, enduring bond of her life. Though no longer lovers, they were still friends, companions, colleagues, and chosen family to each other. Susan, too, though in great pain over Ann's decision, had an investment in maintaining a significant tie. They had officially parted ways, but were nonetheless continuing a critically important relational drama. In changing the shape of their relationship to one that made fewer demands for sharing and joint decision making, while at the same time, refusing to disavow their reciprocal selfobject tie, they were embarking upon the transformational process of becoming family/friends.

This process can be best understood as a preservative maneuver to restore the buoyant medium in which both partners have been securely held and supported in their individual growth. The breakup of the relationship is an acknowledgment by the couple that their plan of moving into the future in primary partnership is stressing their needed connection beyond endurance. A change in the nature of the relationship is psychically lifesaving. No longer primary partners, there are fewer demands to tax the bond, but there is an implicit assurance that a necessary surrogate family tie is in place.

There are an indeterminate number of factors that influence whether a primary relationship can grow and survive, must end, or is best transformed. Variables that come most immediately to mind include the degree of self development of the partners at the inception of the bond; the intensity and chronicity of conflict; the capacity and willingness of each partner to tolerate difference and separateness; the capability of the partners to psychically manage and endure the stress of change; the presence and nature of social and cultural supports, rewards, and sanctions.[2] It is beyond the scope of this paper to consider all of these variables in depth or detail. But it is out of this mix of considerations that a resolution will be generated.

Clinical Implications

When a lesbian seeks help to determine the direction of her growth in what she perceives as a confusing, anomalous relationship, the theoretical bias of the therapist she chooses can be a determining factor in the treatment outcome. Ann consulted with me when she was struggling with her decision about ending her primary relationship with Susan. She had recently left a therapist with whom she had worked for several years. This therapist, working from a Mahlerian model, had unequivocally supported the separation as a healthy step in the direction of independence and autonomy, but she questioned Ann's continuing involvement with Susan in ways that suggested disapproval. She referred to the "blurred boundaries" of their relationship as if blurring were synonymous with pathology. The emotionally complicated nature of Ann's continued attachment was seen as regressive and was labeled as "resistance" to

---

[2]In this regard, lesbian coparents, like their heterosexual counterparts, may struggle to make the relationship work for the sake of the children.

healthy separation. The battles the couple waged in their war to both hold on and move on were interpreted as a rigid defense against a necessary loss. Ann was left with a queasy feeling that there was something wrong with her for working on the transformation of the relationship. The implicit value judgments of her therapist were undermining her effort to protect and restructure a vitally needed tie. The experience distant, shame inducing interpretations contributed to an unsafe ambiance that ultimately drove her from that treatment.

Viewed from a self psychological perspective, Ann and Susan were struggling to find a form in which they could continue to serve reciprocal selfobject functions. Ann's ongoing claim to a vital bond with her former lover, though no longer in primary partnership with her, was understood and explained as an entitled and forward moving consolidation of expanded self experience. From this empathic vantage point, a collaborative effort to understand and unravel the complex nature of their bond was set in motion. Ann was helped to identify and negotiate comfortable boundaries with Susan. At the same time, she was supported in claiming and protecting close ongoing family ties with her.

In order to help a lesbian patient work through conflictual issues in a dissolving relationship it is important that the therapist approach the situation with an open mind—the possibility of ongoingness as real as the possibility of a clean break, and everything in between. For only if the family/friend tie is viewed as valid and meaningful as a marriage or a clear parting of ways, is the patient truly free to explore all of her conflicted feelings to determine the direction of her growth in a transforming/terminating relationship.

The evolution of a relationship from lovers to family/friends can be a years long process that encompasses numerous developmental achievements. The family/friend bond has the emotional significance of a nuclear family connection. As such, it will evolve through the full range of developmental sequences that characterize leaving home, establishing life on one's own, and creating a new family centered around a primary partnership. It will most probably evoke earlier separation issues within one's family of origin. Powerful dramas of loss and celebration, attempted possession and loving letting go, jealous rage and soothing reassurance, annihilating replacement and secure belonging, will be enacted. The adult child does not renounce her bond with the parent. Rather, she integrates that bond into a new life that at some point will include the primacy of her tie to a lover.

Just as some adults may cling to the parent and have difficulty negotiating a separation that frees them to establish new significant ties, some lesbians may use the family/friend relationship to defend against unbearable loss. These individuals may be unable to risk the terrifying states of disintegration that could result from disrupting the selfobject bond which has been supporting their sense of self cohesion. A lesbian, who has had to sacrifice sustaining ties to family and community-of-origin in order to claim her sexual identity, may be traumatically vulnerable to loss. It is understandable that separation, associated with forced repudiation of life supporting bonds, might be dreaded and resisted.

Very often, the breakup that begins a family/friend transformation is precipitated by the appearance of a third party to whom one of the lovers is in some way attracted. This triangulation, as in the case of Ann and Susan, becomes the destabilizing straw. Whether it happens before or after the breakup, negotiating a triangular relationship will at some point become a major feature of the transfigurational drama. One of the partners will take a new lover, an event which easily triggers a recapitulation of early experiences of sibling rivalry, or the dysfunctional aspects of being a child of two parents. This problematic triadic relationship is often prominent in the treatment of lesbians who are struggling with family/friend bonds. For those dealing with the competing demands of a lover and family/friend, unconscious organizing beliefs about relational requirements and outcomes in systems larger than a dyad will be in the therapeutic foreground.

The defensive aspect of triangulation in lesbian relationships has been touched on by Burch (1987). In elaborating some of the issues that may create barriers to intimacy for lesbians, she calls attention to the nature of the female-to-female bond—its powerful evocation of the earliest mother–daughter relationship with all its resonances of unconscious identification and union (p. 132). She speaks of the boundaries in lesbian relationships that are "doubly permeable, more fluid on both sides" and the resultant possibility of increased threat of loss of self (p. 134). Viewed from this perspective, the lesbian couple's shift away from primacy and exclusivity toward a family/friendship, with the possibility of taking a new lover, may be seen as providing a buffer against engulfment. It can be understood as an adaptive exogamous move toward a broader, more expanded, less threatening relational universe.

Case Vignette

Elaine, a woman in her forties, married, divorced, and the mother of three grown children, was befriended by a woman who lived in her neighborhood. They grew closer and closer, eventually becoming lovers. This was a truly shocking, though in profound ways fulfilling, turn of events for Elaine who had no previous experience with or knowledge of the gay lifestyle. Her lover, Bea, had been intrigued by her and focused attention on her in a way that made her feel, for the first time in her life, very special and cared about. Bea mentored her as Elaine began a vigorous informal study of lesbian culture and feminist social criticism and the two women enjoyed an exhilarating intellectual companionship. Elaine grew to care deeply for Bea, though she reserved commitment and was ambivalent about their sexual relationship, which eventually ended. However, though no longer her lover, Elaine continued to feel very loving toward and attached to Bea in a deeply connected way. It was important for Elaine that I as her therapist support this anomalous relationship. She had never known anything like it before and did not know what to make of it. Her mother had been a cruel and controlling woman who, through vicious verbal and physical attack, had attempted to appropriate her daughter as a self extension. Elaine had "sleepwalked" through much of her life, inured to the aliveness that would threaten the maternal bond. Now that she was awakening, she was excruciatingly prone to shame. She needed her feelings about her new tie to a loving partner mirrored, not analyzed.

As her initial fascination with the new world to which Bea introduced her began to wane, she felt that she was neglecting interests of hers that Bea did not share. She began to join women's activity groups that reflected her enthusiasms. In setting out on her own she discovered that she was quite attractive to women, several of whom were very open about her appeal to them. She, however, felt strongly connected and loyal to Bea. As she pursued one friendship in particular, Bea—apparently very threatened by Elaine striking out on her own—became increasingly critical, attacking, and rejecting. This was in stark contrast to the support that Elaine was getting in therapy and from friends for expanding her world, but it resonated with an organizing belief that an intimate bond required submission and exclusivity. Bea's accusations and condemnations continued to escalate, until Elaine felt so assaulted, misunderstood, and unable to cope, that she was relieved when Bea, in a fit of rage, departed from the relationship. It was unclear whether the departure was temporary or terminal, but for Elaine, who missed Bea terribly, it was of utmost importance that all outcomes feel equally acceptable.

Shortly after the breakup, Elaine began a sexual affair with her new friend. She frequently spoke of missing Bea painfully, but remained steadfast in her unwillingness to accept Bea's emotional battering about which she felt helpless. After a ten-month separation Elaine and Bea tentatively reconciled. At the time of the reunion, Elaine, still in her new relationship, was in a stronger place where she could more firmly challenge and disallow Bea's attacks. She was immensely relieved to be reconnected to Bea, with the understanding that she wanted a close enduring friendship even as she pursued her relationship with her new lover.

Elaine was particularly pleased when I introduced the designation *gokwa* (see footnote p. 57) to name her relationship with Bea. It offered a gift of language to refer to a particular lesbian relational experience for which mainstream culture has had no name. The word *ex-lover* is an inadequate depiction of the family/friend bond, referring as it does to a relationship in the past. "Ex-lover" specifies nothing about the current relationship or even residual feelings from the former relationship. Ex-lovers might or might not have a current relationship. They might hate, love, or be indifferent to one another. Ex-lover may as readily refer to fond feelings as to an emotionally dead relationship.

By contrast, family/friend (or gokwa) refers to a relationship of ex-lovers that is in an active process of transformation with the potential of becoming chosen family. It is very alive, carrying resonances of rich emotional vibrancy—of passionate attachment and a commitment to its preservation. By definition it cannot be dead. When family/friends first discover a designation to speak of their important tie, they experience enormous relief and gratitude at being given a name for a vital relationship that up until then had been nameless. Language validates experience by facilitating the creation of a shared reality and reassuring sense of belonging. "Other people know this relationship and there is a name for it." It removes a painful and lonely stigma of anomaly.

I have encountered the phenomenon of family/friends in my own clinical work, the work of students, and in workshops and discussion groups I have led about this experience. The creative permutations and combinations of this relational form are myriad and far-reaching. There are family/friends who, each with a new partner, co-own and live in a two-family home; a woman who travels as a way of life and has family/ friends to make her feel at home in every port; family/friends who are raising their children as extended family; family/friends ministering to their ex-partners who are terminally ill; family/friends who have relocated and vacation with one another. The possibilities are as varied as all the different ways that parents and grown children, or adult siblings find to keep their intimate familial connections protected, vital, and flourishing. In essence, family/friends names the bond of chosen family.

References

Becker, C. S. (1988), *Unbroken Ties: Lesbian Ex-Lovers*. Boston: Alyson.

Beebe, B., & Lachman, F. M. (1988), The contribution of mother–infant mutual influence to the origins of self and object representation. *Psychoanal. Psychol.*, 5:305–337.

Buloff, B., & Osterman, M. (1995), Queer reflections: Mirroring and the lesbian experience of self. In: *Lesbians and Psychoanalysis: Revolutions in Theory and Practice*, ed. J. M. Glassgold & S. Iasenza. New York: Free Press, pp. 93–106.

Burch, B. (1987), Barriers to intimacy. In: *Lesbian Psychologies: Explorations and Challenges*, ed. Boston Lesbian Psychologies Collective. Chicago: University of Illinois Press, pp. 126–141.

Chodorow, N. (1978), *The Reproduction of Mothering: Psychoanalysis and the Sociology of Gender*. Berkeley: University of California Press.

Kohut, H. (1981), Introspection, empathy and the semicircle of mental health. In: *The Search for the Self: Selected Writings of Heinz Kohut: 1978–1981*, Vol. 4, ed. P. H. Ornstein. New York: International Universities Press, pp. 537–567.

——— (1984), *How Does Analysis Cure?* ed. A. Goldberg. Chicago: University of Chicago Press.

Mahler, M. S., Pine, F., & Bergman, A. (1975), *Psychological Birth of the Human Infant: Symbiosis and Individuation*. New York: Basic Books.

Miller, J. B. (1976), *Toward a New Psychology of Women*. Boston: Beacon Press.

Ornstein, A. (1974), The dread to repeat and the new beginning. *The Annual of Psychoanalysis*, 2:231–248. New York: International Universities Press.

Stern, D. N. (1985), *The Interpersonal World of the Infant: A View from Psychoanalysis and Developmental Psychology*. New York: Basic Books.

Stolorow, R. D., & Atwood, G. E. (1992), *Contexts of Being: The Intersubjective Foundations of Psychological Life*. Hillsdale, NJ: Analytic Press.

———— Brandchaft, B., & Atwood, G. E. (1987), *Psychoanalytic Treatment: An Intersubjective Approach*. Hillsdale, NJ: Analytic Press.

Surrey, J. L. (1991), The self-in-relation: A theory of women's development. In: *Women's Growth in Connection: Writings from the Stone Center*, ed. J. V. Jordan, A. G. Kaplan, J. Baker Miller, I. P. Stiver, & J. L. Surrey. New York: Guilford Press, pp. 51–66.

5

A Barrenness of Body and Theory: An Analysis of Infertility

Donna Bassin

> [T]here, where the one who speaks is no longer the
> mouth-piece of a school, but the patient on the couch
> [Michele Montrelay, 1978].

T his essay describes Sally's endeavor, in her own words, "to become a real mother"[1] and considers her particular psychoanalytic
path toward maternal subjectivity. I track the vicissitudes of Sally's analysis from her miscarriage, through three years of subsequent
infertility, and the eventual birth of a healthy boy. Central to this phase
of Sally's analysis was her conflicted experience of her identity as a
lesbian who was seeking to become a mother. I present an aspect of
Sally's treatment to inform our understanding of infertility, sexual identity, and maternal subjectivity. But I also discuss my work with Sally in

---

A version of this paper appeared in *Studies for Gender and Sexuality*, January 2001.

[1]Schwartz (1993, 1998) has noted that the concern over being a "real woman" arises for
some homosexual women. However, this question of legitimacy of womanliness is one that many
heterosexual infertile women ask as well.

the spirit of Crespi's (1994) suggestion that we begin to pay attention to the actual "phenomenological experiences of lesbian patients and their analysts in doing the day-to-day work of analysis" (p. 19).

Psychodynamic treatment with infertile women who are pursuing medical interventions is a new task bringing with it a unique set of concerns and therapeutic responses, as well as new transference–countertransference configurations. The current psychodynamic literature about infertility is sparse, and the little that has been published is about heterosexual women. I gave up the "logic" offered by any cohesive school of thought regarding the origins and development of maternity as I followed Sally into her experience of barrenness, uncertainty of outcome, and the discomfort of departure from the known. Instead, I describe the theoretical organizers we considered during her treatment, along with my subsequent reflections on our work together. I do so without any claims to generality or consistency. The theoretical organizers that proved most helpful in our work were Loewald's (1979) reconfigurations of the oedipal task and a reconsideration of the fantasy of heterosexual completion.

Sally's desire for a baby followed the death of her father. She pursued this wish with curiosity and excitement. Sally and her partner set out to conceive through alternative insemination. They garnered support through a group for lesbian couples pursuing parenthood. Sally soon became pregnant. However, eleven weeks into the pregnancy, it ended in miscarriage. Despite this miscarriage and three subsequent years of infertility, Sally persistently pursued her wish to become a biological mother. She relied on her treatment to help her through the physiological, social, and psychological obstacles. Her particular struggle with biological infertility ended with the birth of a healthy son after three years of medical intervention. Despite her biological success, her struggle with the realness and legitimacy of her maternal subjectivity persisted.

In an earlier phase of her analysis, Sally had resolved some of her presenting anxiety around loss of control and her infantile belief in the dangers of the external world. Be that as it may, her inability to produce the wished-for child reactivated some of those older psychic organizers. She experienced shame and doubt not only over her failure to perform a bodily function she assumed she could manage, but in many other aspects of her life as well. Her reproductive difficulties cast doubt on the functioning of her body and her state of mind and amplified old perceived inadequacies.

The "miracles" of modern science and advances in artificial insemi-nation became Sally's Trojan Horse (Bassin, 1989). The apparent gift of each new, unsuccessful medical procedure became a germinating medium for a variety of self-defeating theories regarding her sexuality. Numerous tests indicated that there was nothing physically wrong with her. Sally was left with only the realization that frozen sperm was not the easiest way to get pregnant.

In the throes of her anxiety, she began to imagine that her reproductive difficulties were a punishment for her homosexuality: infertility became divine retribution. Her fear of punishment echoed the damning authority of the divine—a collection of fears and beliefs that are often enacted through incantations, prayers, dances, and sacred dramas. Her fears also meshed with the ideas of psychoanalytic theorists who had suggested in the 1940s and '50s that infertility might be psychogenic. Repudiation of femininity as well as hostility to men were used to explain infertility as well as difficulties during pregnancy (Deutsch, 1945; Benedek, 1952). It was argued that conflicts and fantasies repressed from thought were expressed through the body. The hysterical female mind would use the body to give voice to what it did not know or could not say. Belief in the power of the right frame of mind to induce fertility suggested that the infertile woman was consciously or unconsciously responsible for her situation.

These early psychoanalytic assumptions came under scrutiny and cri-tique with the advent of modern medical diagnosis and new knowledge regarding the range of hormonal and structural problems contributing to infertility. Current medical technology has revealed a range of hormonal and structural problems leading to biological infertility. Such informa-tion, however, does not necessarily mitigate the amount of anxiety and depression experienced by infertile women. Many women continue to blame themselves for their reproductive complications; they cite as the cause their sexual sins, including premarital sex, masturbation, and abor-tion (Keye and Deneris, 1983; Mazor, 1984). Further, when the process of becoming pregnant or carrying a baby to term is difficult or impossible, infantile fantasies and anxieties may erupt and lend symbolic meaning to the physiological processes. Although we no longer consider the repu-diation of femininity or hostility to men as causing infertility, many stud-ies indicate that the anxiety and depression that often accompany infertility may contribute to hormonally linked infertility and certain instances of spontaneous abortion (Domar and Seibel, 1990).

Sally's Fantasized Heterosexual Solution

Sally internalized her lack of success in getting pregnant as punishment—specifically, punishment for her lesbian identity. In response to these feelings, she began to fantasize about leaving her lover and finding a male partner. This fantasy served to organize her distress around her infertility and undo her helplessness. Only the (re)production of a healthy baby could reassure Sally that her wishes and sexual identity were legitimate. In contradiction to her identity, she began (paradoxically) to believe that she could legitimize her homosexuality only through the enactment of heterosexual coupling and reproduction. In further contradiction of her own political beliefs, she asked, "How can a lesbian woman come to want and expect a child when she is defying nature and the heterosexual way?" Sally anxiously questioned whether she was, in fact, a "real woman" who could produce a real baby.

Initially Sally experienced any intervention or interpretation regarding the connection she had made between her infertility and her lesbianism as my dismissal of her solution. Despite her intellectual acceptance of my attempt to challenge her fantasy, she felt she needed my understanding and compassion. It was crucial that I take her theory of infertility as real. She needed to experience a (m)other who was at least trying to be aware of Sally's experience, rather than superimposing on it what I (mother) thought was right or best for her.

With time, we came to understand how this fantasy expressed Sally's conflict with what she felt to be her oedipal transgression of the heterosexual imperative of the Oedipus complex. We began to examine how she was operating with a simplified and concrete notion of the Oedipus complex. We also began to look at how she might be enacting a simplified oedipal renunciation. I worked toward helping Sally deconstruct her fantasy and introduced doubt so that we could explore the deeper meanings of her experienced transgression.

Underscoring my efforts was my attempt to rethink along with Sally the classical psychoanalytic understanding of a girl's route to motherhood. We examined how her own fantasies matched the classical model and how that correspondence complicated the analytic task of listening for the defensive and symbolic aspects of her personal version of the oedipal transgression. We worked toward her giving up the fantasy of heterosexual completion in order (paradoxically) to be true to her own sexual desire, but what if reproductive privilege, she asked, required giving up much of what she was?[2]

The oscillation between the material resolution of her wish (a real baby) and a psychic resolution (a restoration of and confidence in an internal productive inside—her own subjectivity) was constant and hard to manage. I had to resist my own need for a concrete result and her insistence "that only a biological baby would undo her distress." It was difficult for me to accept my ultimate powerlessness. It was hard to resist her pleas to the imaginary fertile couple, embodied at times in her transference to me. Sally and I went through parallel cycles of hope and despair in the struggle to accept that the outcome was outside of our control. Our only solution was "to hold open" and "keep in mind" alternative possibilities to understand the defensive nature of Sally's wish for material heterosexuality. Like the painters Bonnard and Monet, whose multiple renderings of the same scene afforded more and more variation and thus more opportunity to catch what exists on the periphery, Sally and I had to look and look again at the same fantasy.

During the long, arduous years of her treatment, I often wondered what I could offer when society was on the side of her self-blame and quick to support her critical internal fantasies. The culture's intensely negative sanctions against lesbian motherhood left her with only a small peer group from which to find encouragement. I was relieved (in part) of the possibility of being the phallic father who could provide her with the magical interpretation in order to replace absence with presence. Yet, the continuous lack of fulfillment of this legitimate accomplishment of adulthood, and the duration of her experienced failure further stressed us both.

I also had to uphold the reality, however unfair or unjust, of loss and incompleteness. Doing so entailed "holding her" throughout her incessant rage and grief. Her categorization as a lesbian had to be understood, at certain moments, as a distraction from the necessary attention to her own particular resolution of, as McDougall (1995) would say, the inherently traumatic aspects of growing up human. While we were attentive

---

[2]Crespi (1995) has argued that although many homosexual women express their conflicts, pain, anger, and even grief about not being heterosexual, this should not be viewed as a desire to change. Crespi observes that when homosexual feelings emerge in a heterosexual patient the analyst most likely accepts these feelings as a component of heterosexuality without assuming that the patient will change her sexual identity.

to Sally's experience as a lesbian in a homophobic culture, we also needed to temporarily bracket such understanding. Clearly, managing the complexity of multiple identifications during an analysis and describing them in linear statements for publication are impossible tasks. My use of McDougall's understanding of "growing up human" includes coming to grips with the actual boundedness of the self, the differences between the generations, and our own inevitable death. Sally's fantasy of a heterosexual solution shielded her from enormous grief over the many losses in her life, some idiosyncratic and others part of being human. Over time, the meaning of a baby and its presence in absence confronted Sally usefully but painfully with other relatively unmourned losses.

Some History and a Dream

Before discussing Sally's struggle with fertility allow me to pause here to consider some relevant history and how it was expressed in a dream. Key to Sally's heterosexual fantasy was her belief that as a homosexual she was a disappointment to her parents. Despite her father's consistent support for her artist self, Sally felt that he rejected her identity as a lesbian. She could understand that perhaps he felt rejected by her decision to be with a woman. But she saw him as sealed off regarding her sexual identity, and she did not know how to reach him. In subsequent analytic conversations, we eventually understood Sally's wish to establish a relationship with a man as, in part, her last ditch attempt to reconnect with her father. She longed for her father's forgiveness and his loving approval, and she wanted to be the heterosexual daughter that Sally was sure he wanted. This mourning of her father's authority and love would occupy much of her treatment. Her mourning was magnified by the fact that her father had a life-threatening illness, then in remission. Sally was fearful that he would die before she could resolve her feelings toward him.

Sally perceived her mother to be extremely fearful of bodily harm and the dangers the world presented. Sally struggled with similar concerns and located their origin in her mother's communications. Unlike her mother, however, who submitted to these irrational fears, Sally relied on the strength of her will and her reason to overcome her phobic predilections. Sally also saw her mother as quite beautiful, self-absorbed, and too easily influenced by her father's interpretations of Sally's being and behavior. Sally had never felt truly understood by her mother, who, according to Sally, could only react to Sally's behavior narcissistically. Sally told many stories regarding her mother's difficulties in supporting her growth and individuation. Her mother was without agency, hope, self-awareness, and courage and could respond to Sally's strong-willed moves toward independence and individuation only by withdrawal. Sally had a younger sister who she perceived as being less able and successful in the world, but a more acceptable daughter for her parents.

Her father died without accepting her sexuality. Cleaning out his workspace and taking home the tools he had bequeathed for her left Sally feeling somewhat like his son. The tools she spoke about were real but also symbolized her many useful identifications with her father. These tools of competency, problem solving, autonomy, and power were also a necessary protection from the helplessness and anxiety she perceived in her mother. These skills clearly made her different from the devalued mother. Along with her grief and sadness over the loss of her father, Sally also felt relieved by his death. She hoped his death would afford her a much-desired opportunity to work out a new, independent relationship with her mother. Her mother would be free of her father's influence, and perhaps now Sally could have more direct access to her.

In the earlier phases of her analysis Sally welcomed the opportunity to report and discuss her dreams. During her infertility dreams were sparse and when recalled suffered a barrenness of association. Eventually, one significant dream made its way into a session. She felt it was very important, and she continued to refer to it and unravel its significance for some months:

> I was pregnant. I am going to get an abortion by my father. He is handy and can do anything. I was stopped by the reality, and realized the absurdity of this fantasy even in the dream. I thought, why didn't I go to the doctor's office to do this? I am in the doctor's office with my mother. The nurse is going to give me an injection on the top of my arm. It was almost deliberately painful. My mother had arranged for this. The last thought I had was that my mother had told the doctor to do something so that I couldn't have children.

Her dream, as we gradually understood, suggested regression from the path she had begun to take before attempting pregnancy. In her struggle to assert the separateness of her sexuality and her life, she had begun to recognize her parents' genuine differences and limitations. But her dream and subsequent associations revealed her sense that her parents would not accept their symbolic death and instead would render her physically and psychically infertile.

Her first association was a memory from when she was a young girl, a memory that related to her mother's reluctance to accept Sally's independence and bodily self-control. Sally was 8 years old and desperately wanted her ears pierced. Her mother protested, and seemed to do so for irrational reasons. Sally compared her feelings from childhood and her remembrance of her mother's arbitrary power to her current thoughts about her mother. Once again, her mother was protesting Sally's independent rights to her own body, pleasures, and wishes. She believed that her mother was preventing her from having the child she wanted. Such feelings coincide with Klein's (1928) suggestion that a girl's deepest anxiety is not castration anxiety, but, rather, a female-specific anxiety that the mother has destroyed the girl child's insides in retaliation for the girl child's envy of the mother's body.

The production of a "real" baby would be reassurance that such retaliation and destruction had not occurred. A well-meaning friend suggested adoption as an alternative and viable route to motherhood. This prospect was unacceptable to Sally because she feared that her mother would reject an adopted baby as not real or legitimate. Sally's refusal to consider adoption alerted her to the pressure she felt to fill the gap that was increasingly growing between herself and her mother. Perhaps she thought the baby would console her mother in mourning the loss of her husband as well as replace the little girl that Sally had long since left. But only a "real" biological baby would suffice.

Sally's ongoing envy of her mother, sister, and all potentially fertile heterosexual woman (with their competent bodies and their social acceptance), along with her protective devaluation of them as a defense against the envy, was eventually accepted by Sally with new understanding of its origins. This shift from self-hatred to self-understanding enabled Sally to reconceive her mother's so-called hatred of her and denial of her maternal wishes. She began to consider her mother's behavior as a function of her mother's overall ambivalence and fear of anything new. Conversations with her mother furnished her with a new understanding of her mother's concern for Sally's physical health and the problems of lesbian motherhood. These were concerns that Sally harbored and could now discuss. In fact, when Sally finally became pregnant her mother was of great help, offering money and emotional support.

Our apprehension of Sally's anxiety that she would not be a real mother related partially to her aggression and envy. But her memory of her frustrated 8-year-old self having to wait for pierced ears and earrings evoked in me memories of my frustration and self-doubt while waiting to grow up and get breasts like my mother had. Despite our attention to "what we as women have rather than what we don't have," the little girl does have to wait to see and experience her body as she sees and experiences the body of the mother. Oliviere (1989) has imagined what the impact of beginning as a little girl may have on an adult woman's sense of womanliness. She argues that there is an area of real darkness for a little girl, a body-specific void that has to wait for confirmation of the same breasts and reproductive capacity as her mother.

Sally began to speak more openly about her regret and her relief that her father was no longer alive. She thought he would be appalled at the prospect of her pregnancy. Recalling her dream, Sally reflected on her father's role in taking away her baby. Perhaps, as the dream suggested, he was punishing her for getting pregnant without his permission, and without a man in her life. She remembered being surprised in the dream that he did not perform the abortion. She associated to her father as handy, able to do anything. This thought led to Sally's contemplation regarding her own work and creativity.

Sally ran a very successful business as an artisan, and she was generally secure in her competence as an artist. She related her gifts to her father's skills with his hands and his generally imaginative problem-solving abilities. He had been supportive of her work and the development of her business. Her work as an artist did not make her feel masculine, but it did make her feel competent and powerful like her father. In this realm she could feel the pleasure of mastery and pride.

In her art-making space, Sally allowed for some relatively comfortable identifications with the power of both parents. Her identity as an artist not only allowed, but also required, a space where she could imagine having and holding all she needed inside. I viewed Sally's ability in this regard as the enactment of the complementary sexual functions of her parents. In this way, Sally could manage some of her physical noncomplementarity to her mother and, in the process, enhance her own agency.

Milner (1952) has suggested that tolerating states of emptiness, necessary for true creativity, depends on a child's experience of separation from mother (maternal holding environment). A good-enough holding environment provides the confident expectation that barrenness will eventually be replaced with something or someone. Sally's experience of her ungiving body reactivated old frustrations and disappointments with the body of (m)other.

Sally's talents and creative process had previously allowed her to bypass some of the frustrations of her early holding environment. This earlier capacity, however, was gradually diminishing, along with her confidence in her biological fertility. Intense anxiety over her ability and wishes for artistic productivity took pleasure's place. The frustrated wish for a real baby, and the attendant fantasies that both mother and father had destroyed the creativity-making space, led to more massive inhibitions of her creativity. Sally the artist could make many beautiful things. Her creative gifts and her competent symbolizing mind had enabled solutions in the past. Yet Sally the ordinary citizen could not make the wished-for baby nor restore her dead father with her creative activity.

Sally's earlier sense of herself as an active agent and transformer had shifted to an image of an inert container, passive and given over to her gynecologist and the monthly engagements with technology. Her attempt to appease the punishing godlike father and mother by giving up her ability to create art was articulated as her own form of a reparative magical sacrifice. Sally had to give up her belief in the power of her parents to give or take away. Killing them off in this way evoked guilt and required a painful mourning for childhood's security and protection. She had developed a new awareness of her genuine powerlessness to impact on the outcome of her conception attempts.

An important illustration of this occurred in the transference. The dollhouse in my office had always held great interest for Sally. In contrast to other patients, who assumed I worked with children, Sally thought it represented the playful parts of myself. She made a gift to me of two pieces of doll furniture she had found at a flea market. The miniature chest of drawers and a desk were for the dollhouse bedroom; she wondered and worried about how I would feel about her putting her gift in my house. Sally would occasionally look at the dollhouse before lying down to start her sessions. Some weeks later, she questioned my selection of doll figures, which were a mother, father, daughter, and son. She was confused and questioned my support of a pregnancy for a lesbian woman. On the one hand, the doubt I had cast on her fantasies of retaliation (through her pregnancy) was perceived as encouragement and permission. On the other hand, she thought that perhaps my selection of a typical heterosexual family to occupy my house was a truer indication of what I really believed was normal and correct. This transference crisis became an opportunity for Sally to separate from me, her mother and father, and the heterosexual community of parents. Sally was going to have to become a mother in her own way distinguishing herself from her parents, and most of the social world she lived in. Sally's acceptance of her own particular path, as well as her resolution of her history, had to be supported. In addition, her independent solution had to be distinguished from her fear that separation would lead to the retaliation she had experienced in the past. Sally had to give up her belief in the power of her parents to give or take away. Killing them off in this way evoked guilt and required a painful mourning for childhood's security and protection.

Attempts to Conceive

Sally's miscarriage caused her great grief, and, as is usual in our culture, was barely acknowledged. Unlike the death of an existing child, a miscarriage calls for practices, if such they can be called, that offer little accommodation for this invisible personal loss, let alone for unfulfilled fantasies. Mourning is particularly difficult for the infertile patient, given the illusive nature of the loss and the lack of community reactions to the loss. Mourning for infertile women occurs in relation to a fertile peer group who are experiencing the vitality and richness of pregnancy and childbearing. But perhaps even more difficult is the reevocation of grief at the beginning of each menstrual cycle. This reevoked grief is then simultaneously intermingled with renewed hope and possibility during ovulation.

Sally experienced her three years of continuous attempts to conceive as the roller-coaster ride of her life. A two-week period of hope and joyful anticipation after each insemination was inevitably followed by two weeks of loss and mourning after menstruation. Every menstrual period, seen as the sign of her failure, was experienced with shame and humiliation. She fled from her bodily sensations, which she felt as persecutory or as sadistic false signs of conception. Gradually, the two weeks of Sally's grief and her attempt to articulate and manage her mourning became replaced with hardness to her own experience. She felt closed over and raged at me for my attempts to articulate or understand her grief. Sally's grief bled into rage, self-hatred, envy, doubt, and helplessness.

Sally's infertility required that she rely on others, including her lover, her doctors, and me. She felt forced back to an early relationship of dependency on a weak, incompetent, and narcissistic mother. Her fear of dependency exacerbated her difficulty in getting necessary support and comfort during her crisis. Her response, quite organic to her history, was to deny any need for nurturance and to disconnect from mother and her mother's representatives. To rid herself of her feelings of dependency and fragility, Sally turned to obsessional mental gymnastics, which provided a semblance of mind control. She would use her own mind to replace (m)other's care. The "mental tools" on which she had always relied provided a fantasy of self-sufficiency.

As the months of infertility turned into years, Sally could no longer contain her sadness and her feelings of rage about her deprivation. She began to withdraw from family celebrations of engagement, marriage, or birth. She avoided all situations where she would be in the presence of pregnant women or families with young children. Not a day went by that she did not experience anxiety in going outside where she might be confronted with pregnant women. They seemed to fill the streets. Sally experienced her anger as irrational, but she felt unable to control herself and suffered terribly from the realization of her old worst fears. Her inability to control and contain her bad feelings made her feel as if she had an inadequate mind that mirrored her body, an inner self that could not hold its contents or take care of its productions. Fearful of negative repercussions for the expressing of her depression, despair, and anger, she attempted to bury them deeper. She withdrew even more from the usual supports in her life. Even the most supportive friends criticized her for her withdrawal. I attempted to help her understand her wish to find a place where she was comfortable and protected from celebrations of pregnancy, childbirth, and heterosexual life, and from the critical inner voice that punished her for her infantile solution of hiding.

Sally's rivalry with her younger sister intensified around this latest challenge in the "better daughter competition." She was fearful that her sister would marry and get pregnant before she would become pregnant. She could not bear the possibility that her sister would win again, by providing the valuable son-in-law and grandchild. With great shame, Sally shared her hope that her sister's relationship would fail. Confronted with the extent and toxicity of her deepening envy and her guilt-ridden wishes to have her sister suffer as she was suffering, Sally began an earnest pursuit of some historical understanding. She remembered brutally attacking a doll given to her by her mother at the time of her younger sister's birth. Recalling her childhood rage at her mother for not only abandoning her for the new baby, but also trying to comfort her by leaving her with a fake plastic replica, dissipated some of her current intolerance. The separation of her old rage/envy over her mother's reproductive capacity, in the light of her then immature body, provided some solace and a different perspective regarding her current barren body.

However, Sally remained concerned that her evil and envious thoughts toward fertile women would bring her harm. Although her medical team was uncertain about the exact reason for her infertility, they suggested medications to facilitate and support conception. Sally feared long-range damage to her body or to the child she might conceive in this chemically induced environment. In addition, Sally believed that she needed to produce this child by herself and that to take more medication was to cheat. She felt that the use of fertility drugs by a lesbian would be a further assault on Mother Nature. On the other hand, if she were indeed being punished for the fact and fantasy of her self-sufficiency, perhaps assisting Mother Nature would be acceptable and even productive.

After three years, Sally finally became pregnant again. There was much understandable anxiety about miscarriage, which oscillated with her protective magical doubt that perhaps she really was not pregnant. She was particularly concerned about what she perceived as the small size of her pregnant belly. Comparing herself with other pregnant women, she thought her belly was too tiny and her naturally thin, angular body not female enough to hold a baby. In an attempt to hide what she thought was an inadequate sized belly she wore maternity clothes before they were actually necessary. Alternatively, she wore very tight, clinging clothes to augment what she did have and demonstrate her progress. "I want people to see my pregnancy, how big and full I am. On the other hand, I feel embarrassed. I feel like I have fooled someone. I didn't need a man to get pregnant. I feel powerful doing it by myself. And fear that I will be punished for trying to have a baby without a man." Sally's old pride and pleasure in her strong, thin angular body devolved into new thoughts about being inadequate as a female who could hold and nourish a baby. Pregnancy, Sally claimed, is invisible until you show.

After her amniocentesis, the technician indicated that she knew the sex of the baby and asked Sally whether she wanted to know the results. Sally declined and then spent the week discussing her wish that it would be a boy. This wish surprised her, as she thought she had wanted a girl. She questioned what two women would do with a little boy. When she finally requested the information and found she was to have a boy, she was very pleased. It was hard for her to believe, however, that she actually had a boy growing inside. She could not really imagine being a female and having "a little thing coming from inside with a penis between his legs." She spoke with her lover, and they decided to name the baby after Sally's deceased father. In Sally's mind, having a boy child was like having the father's love and support in some indescribable way. She anticipated the delight in teaching her son what her father had taught her. After all, as Diamond (1997, 1998) has argued, the categories of mother and father are only gendered categories for object relational, care-giving capacities.

The birth of her baby took Sally only part way into the acquisition of her maternal subjectivity. Sally spent many sessions discussing situations where her identity as the real mother was uncertain. She internally raged at strangers who questioned who the mother of her child was when she and her partner were out. It was crucial that others recognize her as the "real mother," and she often went to great lengths to establish the fact of her biological motherhood. Sally craved an environment where she could be alone with her baby without anyone challenging her competency or her legitimacy. Although she understood her son's need for two parents, she had difficulty accepting her partner as the baby's mother as well. Her ongoing need for recognition of her "real" motherhood spoke to the fragility of her own internal acceptance, as well as the relative isolation of lesbian motherhood in a heterosexual society. But she had glimpses of another world, internally as well as socially, where diversity and choice existed with bearable guilt.

Reengaging Oedipus

The vicissitudes of Sally's infertility and her attempt to articulate her lesbian sins and to redress them through the fantasy of heterosexual union, came to be seen as a diversion from the more difficult task of reengaging with her oedipal dilemma. We had to return to her oedipal solution, not as she initially believed and feared, which was to shift the object of her desire, from mother to father, but rather, to reexamine the meanings of her internalizations and rework her identifications with all aspects of the oedipal constellation. Loewald's (1979) reformulation of Freud's articulation of the Oedipus complex rescues it from its presymbolic logic. While Freud (1925) relied on a castration model, Loewald saw the oedipal origin and motor in an "active urge for emancipation." As a new version of the "basic union-individuation dilemma" (Loewald, 1979, p. 404) there is never a final dissolution or resolution of the oedipal task, but, rather, a waxing and waning of an ongoing reenactment. Loewald's emphasis on the reconciliation of parricide with parental love as the vital gist of the oedipal task, focuses our attention on both the necessity for and possible outcomes of the lifelong renegotiations of the internalized parent–child relationships. Rather than the task being an ideal resolution of the problem of identity and desire, it may now, for any given subject, appear as repetitive reengagement with the dilemma of the Oedipus complex. Loewald argued that such reworking is necessary for a person's ownership of her history, present, and future.

Sally's initial fantasy of cure matched a simplified scheme of oedipal renunciation: following the rules of the reality principle and complying with the social order require renunciation of the primal object of desire. The outcome she imagined, her fantasy of compliance with a literal heterosexual solution, mirrored only the most concrete and limited interpretation of the oedipal task. As the lesbian daughter of heterosexual parents, Sally's emancipation from daughter to mother, and from little girl to woman, did, in fact, involve a transgression. This transgression, however, was not her sexuality; it was, rather, a necessary emancipation from and destruction of an internalized parental authority, an authority that in her mind demanded heterosexual behavior in order to have a child. From this position, her insistence on recognition as the "real mother" after her baby's birth was also a form of compliance with what she saw as a rejecting retaliatory social order.

The evolution of her autonomy required a symbolic killing of her parents and the usurpation of their power and competence (Loewald, 1979). As her dream suggested, she imagined her parents had already retaliated for her attempt at separation and usurpation by rendering her sterile. But the actuality of her mother's situation was quite different. Her mother had lost her husband, as well as her fertility, she was in menopause. Sally's father was dead and his own creative dreams gone with him. Her initial attempt at a remedy was to follow the rule(s) of the father. To become heterosexual would give her the love and acceptance of her parents and their societal representatives; but it would also preserve the inadequate infantile dependency coded by her as feminine. In this psychic space, her identifications with her father and her previous comfort with her creativity and competence as an artist were placed in doubt and considered fraudulent. She experienced this position as one of lack and it contributed to her belief that she was without a productive inside. In addition, the defensive flight into withdrawal and the hardness of omnipotent mind games protected her from the helplessness of what she had equated with femininity. These solutions, experienced for different reasons as humiliating and shameful, were her attempt to evade, as Loewald (1979) has suggested, the bearing and mastering of parricide guilt (see Benjamin [1999] for her observation that humiliation can be the flip side of guilt). For this solution there was parental and social approval and even encouragement. But motherhood for a lesbian remains a new path full of questions about the outcome of child development as well as the unconscious fears of women without male consorts or supervision.

We might begin, in our attempt to understand further and to support the varieties of any sexual solution (and their accompanying anxieties) in adult life, to reflect on the destructive aspects of the idealization of the inner heterosexual parental couple within the self. This unmourned idealization may contribute to the depreciated value many persons place on their own coupling regardless of the sex of their partners. The development of Sally's own moral authority, a necessary acquisition for every emancipated adult, had to occur outside of the perceived restraints and idealizations of her parents and the larger social order. She had to continue to recognize the limitations of nature and the social world without using them as standards against which to measure her own self-worth.

A Barrenness of Theory

O'Connor and Ryan (1993) have argued that classical psychoanalytic theory reduces lesbian motherhood to an evasion of the Oedipus complex. Perhaps, as Chodorow (1994) has written, we have viewed heterosexuality as a resolution because we link it with reproduction. However, our work with heterosexual women who present with marital or parental difficulties signals the limitations of our classical understanding of resolution of the oedipal processes in the female. For some heterosexual women, the seemingly necessary tasks of emancipation from the parental pull, the deidealization of the parental couple, and the integration of same and cross gender/cross-sex representations, may be temporarily bypassed or assuaged, but not resolved, with the behavioral accomplishment of marriage. Kestenberg (1956) suggests that the adult woman must establish a separation and privacy of the generative inner space from the biological functions of motherhood and childcare. But what exactly does that require? We do not understand clearly the relationship between the wishes for a baby in childhood and in adulthood, nor do we have a clear understanding of the development of maternal subjectivity. Certainly, as Kirkpatrick (1989) has noted, and Sally's analysis suggests, our understanding of maternal interest and capacity need to be separated out from identity and sexual orientation.

Coda

In the last section of Freud's (1933) paper "Femininity," he noted that women had made few contributions to the discoveries and inventions in the history of civilization. He did, however, grant women the discovery of plaiting and weaving. Speculating on the possible unconscious motivations for these activities, he suggested the concealment of the female genitals, the imaginary origin of women's sense of lack and absence. Pubic hair, the source material for the original weaving, emerges organically from the body, but the problem of making threads adhere to each other was left to the imagination. While Freud's speculation regarding the origins of weaving and plaiting may be more reflective of his own best, but nevertheless concrete, attempt to narrate over uncertainty, his observation suggests some appreciation of the anxiety of exposure and the role of imagination in mitigating that anxiety. It is my hope that, in our investigations into the female mind, we can learn to tolerate this anxiety without a pull to prematurely force a new coherence.

References

Aron, L. (1995), The internalized primal scene. *Psychoanal. Dial.,* 1:29–51.
Bassin, D. (1989), Women's shifting sense of self: The impact of reproductive technology. In: *Gender in Transition: A New Frontier,* ed. J. Offerman-Zuckerberg. New York: Plenum, pp. 189–202.

Benjamin, J. (1999), Women's oedipal conflicts and boys' oedipal ideology. In: *Female Sexuality: Contemporary Engagements,* ed. D. Bassin. Northvale, NJ: Jason Aronson, pp. 87–95.

Benedek, T. (1952), Infertility as a psychosomatic defense. *Fertility & Sterility,* 3:527–537.

Breen, D. (1993), *The Gender Conundrum.* New York: Routledge.

Chodorow, N. (1994), *Femininities, Masculinities, Sexualities: Freud and Beyond.* Lexington: University of Kentucky Press.

Crespi, L. (1994), Some thoughts on the role of mourning in the development of a positive lesbian identity. In: *Disorienting Sexuality: Psychoanalytic Reappraisals of Sexual Identities,* ed. T. Domenici & R. Lesser. New York: Routledge, pp. 19–32.

Deutsch, H. (1945), *The Psychology of Women: A Psychoanalytic Interpretation,* Vol. 2. New York: Grune & Stratton.

Domar, A., & Seibel, M. (1990), Emotional aspects of infertility. In: *Infertility: A Comprehensive Text,* ed. M. Seibel. Norfolk, CT: Appleton-Lange, pp. 30–44.

Diamond, M. (1997), Boys to men: The maturing of masculine gender identity through paternal watchful protectiveness. *Gender & Psychoanal.,* 2:443–468.

——— (1998), Fathers with sons: Psychoanalytic perspectives on "good enough" fathering throughout the life cycle. *Gender & Psychoanal.,* 3:243–299.

Freud, S. (1933), New Introductory Lectures on Psycho-Analysis. *Standard Edition,* 22:112–135. London: Hogarth Press, 1961.

——— (1925), Some psychical consequences of the anatomical distinction between the sexes. *Standard Edition,* 19:241–258. London: Hogarth Press, 1961.

Kestenberg, J. (1956), On the development of maternal feelings in childhood. *The Psychoanalytic Study of the Child,* 11:257–291. New York: International Universities Press.

Keye, W., & Deneris, A. (1983), Female sexual activity: Satisfaction and function in infertile women. *Infertility,* 5:275–285.

Kirkpatrick, M. (1989), Women in love in the 80's. *J. Amer. Acad. Psychoanal.,* 17:535–552.

Klein, M. (1928), Early stages of the Oedipus complex. *Internat. J. Psycho-Anal.,* 9:167–180.

Loewald, H. (1979), The waning of the Oedipus complex. In: *Papers on Psychoanlaysis.* New Haven, CT: Yale University Press, 1980, pp. 384–404.

Mazor, M. (1984), Psychosexual problems of the infertile couple. *Med. Aspects of Hum. Sexuality,* 14:135–143.

McDougall, J. (1995), *The Many Faces of Eros: A Psychoanalytic Explanation of Human Sexuality.* New York: W. W. Norton.

Milner, M. (1952), The role of illusion in symbol formation. In: *The Suppressed Madness of Sane Men*. New York: Routledge, pp. 83–113.

Montrelay, M. (1978), Inquiry into femininity. In: *The Gender Conundrum,* ed. D. Breen. New York: Routledge, pp. 145–165.

O'Connor, N., & Ryan, J. (1993), *Wild Desires and Mistaken Identities*. New York: Columbia University Press.

Olivier, C. (1989), *Jocasta's Children: The Imprint of the Mother,* tr. G. Craig. New York: Routledge.

Schwartz, A. (1993), Thoughts on the construction of maternal representations. *Psychoanal. Psychol.,* 10:331–344.

——— (1998), *Sexual Subjects: Lesbians, Gender, and Psychoanalysis*. New York: Routledge.

6

Across the Great Divide: Gender Panic in the Analytic Dyad

Jack Drescher

> The term Lesbian ... has gained considerable usage within recent years ... Although there can be no objection to designating relations between females by a special term, it should be recognized that such activities are quite the equivalent of sexual relations between males [Kinsey, Pomeroy, and Martin, 1948]

> According to [the separatist-feminist lesbian interpretative] framework [that emerged from the 1970s], there were essentially no valid grounds of commonality between gay male and lesbian experience and identity; to the contrary, women-loving women and men-loving men must be at precisely opposite ends of the gender spectrum [Sedgwick, 1990]

L ay people, psychoanalysts, biologists, and literary critics, to name a few, have made innumerable attempts to categorize the origins and meanings of same-sex attraction. In those attempts to do so, and within the cultural framework of male-female dimorphism, lesbians and gay men are frequently grouped *together* as minority members who live outside a more populous realm known as "heterosexuality." In the numerous attempts to classify human sexuality, we often find an underlying assumption of a directed sexuality, otherwise known as a "sexual orientation." In other words, these classification systems define their subjects on the basis of the object they find sexually exciting and toward which they presumably "point." One might think of Cupid's arrow symbolically condensed as both the source of sexual excitement and as a one-way street directing the flow of traffic.

Directional concepts have had a powerful grip on theorists in various disciplines both in and outside psychoanalysis. Within psychoanalysis, the concept of "orientation" derives from Freud's drive theory. Freud (1905) hypothesized a sexual force, libido, "directed" toward an "object." Masculine libido is "active" and seeks out objects. Feminine libido is "passive" and achieves satisfaction by being sought after. In this nosology, a homosexual man is loved passively as is a heterosexual woman (Freud, 1910a, 1914), and a homosexual woman loves actively like a heterosexual man (Freud, 1920). Even Kinsey's radical and inclusive taxonomy (1948), using a continuum of "orientations," assumed that male and female homosexuality did not require the separate linguistic usage of "lesbian." That is because, in the language of directions, homosexuality meant the same thing whether one applied it to men or to women: sexual attraction "directed" toward one's own sex. Similarly, "heterosexuality" is applied uniformly to both men and women: attraction to the other sex. And, by playing upon the multiple antonyms of "homo" or "same," a different sex is frequently referred to as its "opposite."

The cultural division of the sexes into opposites preceded Freud's bisexual directional thinking. However, the unquestioned acceptance of the equation that difference = opposite, even by nonclassical psychoanalysts, renders the psychoanalytic literature unhelpful in clarifying the nature of psychotherapeutic relationships between lesbians and gay men. Furthermore, the pervasive psychoanalytic tendency to pathologize both male and female homosexuality (Lewes, 1988; O'Connor and Ryan, 1993; Glassgold and Iasenza, 1995; Drescher, 1995, 1997, 1998) completely sidestepped the possibility that these relationships might exist at all. Psychoanalysis historically relegated all lesbians and gay men exclusively to the role of patients and denied them the possible role of analysts. In the language of that bygone world a "heterosexual analyst" was a redundancy and a "homosexual analyst" an oxymoron. That historic fact is changing as psychoanalysis assumes its rightful place among the humanistic disciplines and as it discards older, pathologizing models of homosexuality. New kinds of relationships in the psychotherapeutic dyad ultimately raise questions about many psychoanalytic assumptions regarding sexuality and gender, to say nothing of identity formation, transference, and countertransference.

Here, in this still evolving matrix of psychoanalytic theory, is presented an example of clinical work in the treatment of a lesbian patient working with a gay male analyst. This clinical vignette illustrates several points: first, directional concepts inadequately explain the full range of human sexuality. Second, sexuality can be seen as a continuum or mosaic, embedded in intersubjective and relational meanings, rather than directional ones. Third, a procrustean attachment to the concept of sexual orientation may actually hinder transferential and countertransferential understanding of the analytic dyad. Fourth, that attempts to understand a wider range of sexual feelings and possibilities may evoke gender panic in both the analyst and the patient. And finally, an analyst's openness and willingness to question deeply held cultural assumptions about sexuality can make it possible to allow other feelings and paradigms to emerge in both the analyst and the patient.

Jill

Jill is a gay woman in her midthirties who came into therapy for depression. She hoped, she said, "to get to the bottom of my problems." However, the opportunity to learn more about herself proved extremely anxiety-provoking because of strong childhood memories of physical and verbal abuse at the hands of her mother. She spoke of repeated beatings for minor infractions as well as interminable verbal assaults on her self-esteem from an early age. She did not believe she had ever been sexually abused. Her mother had died several years before treatment started but Jill had avoided all contact with her for many years before her death. Although her father is still alive, Jill has neither seen nor heard from him. Although he himself did not physically harm Jill, she holds him responsible for negligently allowing her mother to abuse her. She presents herself as having no regrets about the decision to cut off her relationships with both parents.

Jill has lived with her lover for a number of years and describes her as a "nice person." Early in treatment, Jill came into a session and mentioned an evening of exciting love making that she felt made it possible for her to "lower her guard" with her lover, Marcia. This made her feel closer to Marcia than she had ever felt before. Early on in the treatment, when she presented Marcia in an idealized way, I was aware of my reluctance to ask too many questions about their relationship. I felt she presented Marcia as a person whose faults were yet to be detailed, and that she was reluctant to explore her nonidealized feelings about her. It was my sense that Jill was overwhelmed by her circumstances at work and she needed her relationship to feel like a safe haven. She did eventually provide me with more details when Marcia lost her job and Jill asked me to find her a psychotherapist. This occasioned the first time I heard her describe Marcia in critical terms. Her criticisms centered around both her lover's naivete and a lack of assertiveness in the workplace.

Jill alternated in her presentation of herself as an extremely competent woman who was managing well professionally and at other times gave the impression that she was on the verge of collapse from the interpersonal difficulties at work. She evoked in me her intense feelings of uncertainty and lack of safety in the work environment. These are feelings with which she lives on a daily basis. She works in a highly charged, competitive sales environment. It is a field where men control most of the power and money. Greed, incompetence, nepotism, betrayal, helplessness, and anger appeared to be routine experiences in her accounts of working life. Although the reports of those feelings have somewhat diminished as her treatment has proceeded, her initial accounts of the relationships at work felt intolerable to me. I wondered to myself how anyone could tolerate working in that environment. This led me eventually to suggest to her that she thrived in that setting, perhaps in part, because it was reminiscent of her childhood. She replied that her job was, in fact, less stressful than her early home life because it was a place where people were honest about their selfish interests. *Selfish* is a word she angrily uses to describe her parents' attitudes and behavior toward her.

Her early family relationships led me to speculate about why a gay woman would come to see me for treatment. I found myself thinking about it because, in my clinical and personal experience, lesbians usually seek out women therapists. I thought that a caretaking relationship with a man might be less consciously frightening to her than one with a woman therapist. The latter choice might be more likely to evoke images of her abusive mother. Perhaps her coming to see me represented the wish for the father who would finally protect her. However, my formulations led me to remind myself that psychoanalytic theorizing is notorious for making unproved assumptions about how one chooses an "object." After all, her experiences of men were also highly charged. She experienced the men at work as either useless sons of bitches or as sons of bitches with whom one could deal. Because of some medical problems and her interactions with male physicians in other specialties, men were also presented as arrogant authority figures who thought they knew everything.

This latter image was reminiscent of her father, an educated man whose wide intellectual and cultural interests she held in contempt. She initially presented herself as assiduously uninterested, and perhaps even deliberately avoidant, of intellectual subjects because of their connection to her father. However, she did respond favorably to several "intellectual" comments I offered. As our work progressed, whenever I found myself in a didactic mode, attempting to explain a situation which she experienced as chaotic, she listened carefully and questioned me about the exact meanings of my words. She found these interactions comforting and reported how she used them outside the sessions as well. For example, once while describing the chaotic conditions in her workplace, I said something to the effect of "entropy rules." She had not heard the term *entropy* before, and when I explained the concept to her, she was quite taken with it. She laughed as she reported in subsequent sessions that every time she felt overwhelmed by the chaos at work, she would remember our discussion of entropy and feel calmer.

In the evolving context of our relationship, in which I began to represent her wish for the caretaking father she never had, she reported the following dream:

I had a dream about my father and it was very upsetting. He was in one room and I was in another. The rooms connected in this corridor and everything was really dark. Everything was in monochrome; it was dark gray and darker gray and black. There was never any light. It was always nighttime. He had his bedroom and I had my bedroom and my mother wasn't there. She was dead and it was just him left. It wasn't the present as I know it. I was living in a house with him again. Everything that came out of his mouth I hated and there was practically no contact. At night, when it was dark out and he was in his bedroom sleeping with the door closed, I peer in and I look to see if he was dead. I was hoping I would find him dead. When I found him breathing, I would go back into my room and close the door.

The "monochrome" house reminded her of an old movie version of *A Christmas Carol* and she associated her father to Scrooge's miserliness. She talked about her early memories of wishing both parents dead. She described a desperate preadolescent attempt to run away from home in her parents' car. As she backed the car out of the driveway, she became anxious about how she would survive on her own. She pulled the car back into the driveway and her parents never noticed. She said she experienced less pain than she had in the past because her mother was dead and imagined she would feel even less pain when her father eventually died. She then associated to having recently made love to her lover:

Jill: Though we were both tired from the day, it didn't matter. When we made love that night, I was so happy, it was as though I had this out-of-body experience where I felt like I gravitated out of myself and I was watching me in a really happy movie.
Therapist: When you are happy, you can't imagine it's happening to you.
Jill: That was definitely a big feeling. It's so stupid (she laughed) to have to adjust to that feeling. It's ridiculous. It's like I'm coming here and I'm paying you money because I'm having a hard time adjusting to feeling good. It's pretty fucking sad. (She became tearful) It really is.

The dream and her associations to it illustrate a complex relationship between her hatred, her anxieties about the dead mother within her, and the internalized father who will not die, her desire for safety within a relationship not to mention her ability to locate herself and her feelings within her own body. The dream is monochrome because she believes she only wishes her father dead and is not sure what to make of her longing for him. The dissociative phenomena she experienced during intimacy are not unusual in those who have been severely traumatized. These intense interrelated emotions within the patient generated equally complex responses within the therapist. I was keenly aware of an uncharacteristic reluctance to inquire too deeply about the sexual details of her relationship despite her references to them. For example, I might have asked what physical act was she engaged in when she felt herself leaving her body. Although not asking may have been technically correct during the early part of her treatment, I repeatedly wondered to myself how comfortable I was asking for descriptions of physical intimacy in a lesbian relationship.

I contrasted my tentativeness with Jill with the ease I felt in asking about intimate sexual details in the lives of the numerous gay men I have treated. Patients often find it therapeutic, despite feelings of shame and embarrassment, to speak aloud the intimate thoughts and feelings that emerge in their real and fantasied relationships. Jill was holding back and yet I uncomfortably did not feel an eagerness within myself to explore too deeply. When she reported her evening of fabulous lovemaking leading to closeness with her lover, I had two reactions. First, I felt I understood exactly what she meant. My second reaction was both a combination of curiosity and aversion about what physical acts of intimacy they engaged in while Jill had this feeling. Could this aversive feeling exemplify the consigning of her experience to what Kiersky (1995) calls the Shadowland of "exiled lesbian desire"? I also found that these feelings evoked in me a questioning of my competence to understand her.

Part of my reluctance to explore Jill's subjectivity came from my sense of her vulnerability to intrusions. A woman who had been severely violated in childhood does not need an overly zealous inquiry about either painful or pleasurable subjects. In her case it may have been retraumatizing. Asking too many questions can be a double-edged sword. For some patients, it may be experienced as a relief to describe themselves to the curious therapist, an opportunity to be known for who they are (Winnicott, 1960). For others, a therapist's ignorance of some aspects of their experience may be felt as an enormous burden obstructing the work of therapy. It is worth keeping in mind that psychotherapy is sometimes enhanced by a shared cultural experience among therapist and patient. The desire for understanding without words leads many patients to seek out a therapist they imagine is like themselves. However, sometimes it is the differences between the therapist and patient that generate learning and growth. This is usually true when differences between a patient and therapist are treated respectfully rather than labeling them with hierarchical and/or developmental models, what Mitchell (1988) refers to as "infantilism." It is also worth noting that therapists can always learn something about themselves at the same time they are learning something about their patients.

It is an inescapable fact that most gay people first learn about male and female homosexuality through heterosexual stereotypes rather than from actual experience. Gay men and women in my clinical practice frequently internalize denigrating, stereotypic beliefs of the larger hetero-sexual culture. Some people are fortunate enough to overcome deeply held stereotypical beliefs about homosexuals of their own sex through hard-won experience. However, stereotypes about homosexuality in the other sex may persist. How might these persistent stereotypes play them-selves out between a gay man and woman, not only in therapy, but in the innumerable settings in which lesbians and gay men interact? This is a dangerous territory fraught with numerous opportunities for gay men and women to both understand and offend each other as they wrestle with their own cultural and personal stereotypes about men and women, homosexuality and heterosexuality, gender identities and sexual activities.

Jack and Jill on the Slippery Slope

One day Jill came into her session extremely anxious and tearful because she was preparing to undergo a minor surgical procedure. The impending surgery evoked frightening memories of childhood doctor visits and she was panic stricken in my office. Her distress was quite palpable and I was aware of feeling anxiety myself as I tried to help her contain her fright. I sat closer to her than I usually do, leaning forward in my chair, establishing direct eye contact and trying to present a reassuring presence. Throughout most of the session I felt a recurring desire, which I sup-pressed, to hug her in order to calm her down. She was, in fact, calmer by the end of the session. As she was leaving my office, I again felt the desire to give her a physical reassurance; this time I felt like tightly holding her hand. Instead, I decided I would shake her hand. As she was walking out the door of my office and into the waiting room, I reached out and brushed my fingers against hers when Jill suddenly grabbed me and hugged me tightly. I responded by awkwardly patting her on the back.

Afterwards, when I was alone in the office, I thought about the impli-cations of what I had done. I am not in the habit of hugging patients and Jill's hug made me anxiously remember a paper that described how sex-ual boundary violations in psychotherapy often begin with a hug (Gab-bard, 1991). I thought, "how could hugging ever precipitate a sexual boundary violation between a gay man and a gay woman?'' Part of me wanted to take cover behind the concept of sexual orientation. Had I done so and dismissed the possibility of crossing a boundary, I might not have been open to the communications from Jill that followed. However, I chose to discuss what happened with several professional colleagues in an attempt to make sense of the possible meanings of that encounter to both Jill and myself. Most of them saw it as a nonsexual, compassionate response to her anxiety. I was not entirely convinced and wondered about its other meanings.

Jill began a subsequent session talking about her friend Bob and about not wanting to see him as often as he wished. She thought she was behaving ''selfishly'' and felt guilty about her wishes to avoid him. The marked intensity of her guilty feelings and what I knew of her relationship to Bob led me to interpret that what she referred to as her ''selfishness'' reminded her of her mother's ''selfishness.'' She had somehow connected her ''selfish'' desire to regulate contacts with Bob as equivalent to her mother's ''selfish'' abusive behavior. This made Jill laugh anxiously and she then took that opportunity to tell me that Bob and his male therapist were having sex during their sessions. I asked about her feelings regarding that. She felt fearful for him and talked about his bad judgment and his capacity for self-destructiveness. I openly agreed with her reactions but in addition I also had an internal response to the possible meanings and implications of our earlier hug. My initial, private association to doctor–patient sex was now being followed by the patient's story of doctor–patient sex. I now found myself increasingly questioning my earlier belief about the unlikely possibility of sexual feelings emerging between a gay woman and a gay man. Again, I did not address the issue directly with Jill. I thought about it privately and continued to discuss my own feelings with colleagues in an attempt to make sense of what was happening.

My openness to talking about Jill's feelings apparently reassured her of the safety in our relationship, and in a later session she began talking about her interactions with a man she recently met at work. She found him attractive in many ways: his looks, his style, his culture. She felt they had many things in common. She reported a sexual fantasy in which she desired him. She recalled a similar erotic feeling when she was 16 with a particular boyfriend, the only other time she had been sexually attracted to a man. She became anxious as she told me about her feelings for him in the session, and said she felt a tightening in her chest. I contrasted her feelings for this man with those she sometimes expressed about Marcia. In the relationship with Marcia, she felt she had to be the giving one and the caretaker. This man appeared capable of giving to her. I pointed out that her sexual feeling for him made her anxious because it did not fit in with her definition of who she was. *She told me she was anxious that she might act on the feeling because doing so might destroy the way of life she had created for herself.*

I emphasized to her that she could have this feeling and not act on it. She didn't have to do anything about it while she came to understand it. She associated to a movie in which Bette Davis played a governess; the governess and the father of the child she cared for fell in love without ever talking about it or acknowledging it. I pointed out that it was entirely possible to love another without ever having to consummate the love sexually. She still felt anxious at the end of the session. She said, "You are going to send me out with you feeling good and me still anxious." I suggested she try and see if she could tolerate the anxiety that came when she thought about this sexual image. In that way she could explore where it led her thoughts and feelings when she was on her own between sessions.

When she returned for her next session, she had given some thought to our last interchange and to my suggestion that her sexual attraction to this man could, in part, be understood as representing her desire to be cared for. She felt her attraction was related to the feeling that Marcia did not give her the things she gave in return. She felt she had to take care of Marcia but no one took care of her. When she thought about actually pursuing this man sexually, she felt "that is not me." She also reported that she felt less anxious because she was very comfortable about who she was: a woman who loved a woman.

Sexual Identity, Transference, and Countertransference

How does this brief clinical intervention inform us about psychoanalytic theories of sexual identity formation, transference, and countertransference? In the area of identify formation, Stoller's (1985) clinical work with transgendered individuals led to his modification of earlier psychoanalytic theories that stated homosexuals were confused about their anatomical gender. He separated the then conflated concepts of "gender identity," the sense of being male or female, from "sexual orientation," the gender toward which one's attraction is directed. The uncoupling of these two concepts made some clinical sense since it was quite obvious to many that lesbians and gay men did not feel themselves to be a member of the other sex despite their attraction to members of their own sex. Stoller's view of homosexuality took issue with the prevailing views of his psycho-analytic contemporaries that hypothesized a gender confusion intrinsic to homosexuality (Socarides, 1968). Stoller, however, wrote within a psychoanalytic tradition that concretized psychological processes in the language of "mental structures," such as ego and superego. This led him to hypothesize a "core gender identity" as a stable structure of the mind. Presumably formed by the age of 3, it is responsible for how we feel ourselves to be men or women. In a continuation of that psychoanalytic tradition, Friedman (1988) suggested that a homosexual orientation arose as a result of a childhood gender identity disturbance based on prenatal neuroendocrine influences. This led him to conclude that a sexual orienta-tion, grounded in a concrete or physiologically induced "structure," was biologically fixed and immutable and that analysts should not try to change it.

Writing from an entirely different tradition than Stoller and Friedman are Butler (1990), Harris (1991), and Schwartz (1995). They, among others, see gender identity and sexual orientation more as processes and products of interaction with a gender-coded environment, rather than a fixed biological structure that determines one's adult sexual fantasies and identities. Their work draws upon feminist theory, gay and lesbian stud-ies, and what is sometimes referred to as "constructionism" or "decon-structionism" or "postmodernism." This approach makes the case that sexual orientations may be a comforting myth, yet one incapable of ex-plaining the full range of human sexual expression. As was evident in Jill's case, unmasking a myth and exposing the wider range of her "orien-tation" generated great anxiety, both in her and the therapist.

Any identity is, in part, constructed of affectively laden markers that exclude from consciousness those words, symbols, or sensations that might induce anxiety. Sullivan (1953) called these markers that were capable of being acknowledged to the self as "good me" and "bad me." Those that were unacceptable to the self and dissociated were "not-me." In this model, a "lesbian identity" like any identity, straight or gay, is not the same thing as a "sexual orientation." Magee and Miller (1995) make the point that the use of synedoche (linguistically, the part that stands for the whole) obfuscates the broader meanings of a lesbian identity. Jill's lesbian identity is a complex psychological construction that acknowledges one form of sexual attraction while it actively excludes the possibility of another. For many people, their sexual identity ("I am gay"; "I am lesbian"; "I am bisexual"; "I am normal") is composed not only of what they feel, but is also defined by how they distinguish themselves and their own feelings from an imaginary other ("I am not straight"; "I am not queer"; "I am not normal").

Working with Jill made me ask some questions about my own identifications and the impact upon them of her feelings toward me. My gay male identity may have been stirred by Jill's brief allusion to her lesbian lovemaking. My anxieties about competence led me to ponder how my capacity to enter into her sexual subjectivity could be restricted by several possibilities: the absence within me of a frame of reference to understand her desire; the image of lesbian lovemaking may induce feelings of anxiety or other uncomfortable feelings in me; the symbolic meanings of her sexuality may evoke meanings in me that I judged to be unacceptable. A patient's invitation to enter into her subjectivity may not always be emotionally welcome, regardless of the therapist's good intentions and intellectual preparation. This is likely to be true for lesbian and heterosexual therapists, as well as for gay ones.

Freud (1915) believed erotic transferences were an enormous obstacle to treatment, and that their emergence justified an analyst's decision to send the patient to another colleague. However, it is ironic to find that he dismisses a patient from treatment in his reported case of a "homosexual woman" and sends her to a female colleague. Interestingly, he did not do so because of her erotic transference to him but because "she transferred to me the sweeping repudiation of men which had dominated her ever since the disappointment she had suffered from her father" (Freud, 1920, p. 164). That is, it was her rage, not her love, that Freud could not tolerate. Harris (1991) suggests that it was his inability to tolerate her masculine identifications that made Freud send her away: "In Freud's language we can note that the oedipal blow of castration has been struck: 'I broke it off.' This girl must not dare to inhabit male space, to represent phallic desire. He recommends that she be dispatched to a woman analyst. And here is the complexity of the defeat/victory, for perhaps he has sent the fox into the henhouse" (p. 210).

Harris draws attention to how the patient's identity may determine the nature of the transference and the analyst's identity the nature of countertransference in the psychotherapeutic dyad. Jill told me early on that it was through lovemaking with Marcia that she was able to lower her guard. Transferentially, she was lowering her guard with me. But the implications of doing that were anxiety-provoking for her and for me as well. She experienced the transferential feeling as threatening to her identity as a gay woman. She found it necessary to push away the heterosexual feelings in order to reduce her anxiety and to maintain the stability of her identity. Butler (1995), provocatively drawing upon Freud's (1917) theory of depression, hypothesizes a parallel mechanism operating in the development of a woman's heterosexual identity through "melancholic identifications," that is, identifications that ensue from loss:

> Consider that [heterosexual female] gender is acquired at least in part through the repudiation of homosexual attachments: the girl becomes a girl by being subject to a prohibition that bars the mother as an object of desire and installs that barred object as a part of the ego, indeed, as a melancholic identification. Thus, the identification contains within it both the prohibition and the desire and so embodies the ungrieved loss of the homosexual cathexis. If one is a girl to the extent that one does not want a girl, *then wanting a girl will bring being a girl into question;* within this matrix, *homosexual desire thus panics gender* [p. 169; emphasis added].

Heterosexual desire may also panic gender. In an unconscious attempt to preserve my own gay male identity, I countertransferentially exclude the possibility of identifying with any erotic "heterosexual" feelings between us. I initially did this by trying to deny that the hug could be construed as having a sexual meaning. I later did this through interpretation and divesting her heterosexual fantasy of its sexual meaning. Although the interpretation may be correct, I labeled the feelings as defensive before we had an opportunity to fully explore and understand all their possible meanings, and by suggesting to Jill that they were a metaphor for a nonsexual aspect of relatedness. By taking the "sex" out of heterosexuality, both of us may feel safer with each other as we preserve our individual identities. Her association to the movie in which the governess and her employer never speak or act upon their love for each other is compelling. That she confirmed my interpretation in the subsequent session does not necessarily mean it was correct. It may simply mean that we were both unconsciously colluding to stay away from a difficult and anxiety-provoking subject (Levenson, 1995).

In reviewing the sequence of events in the work with Jill, I was struck by the parallels of my intervention with those of Trop and Stolorow (1992) in their heterosexually subjective report of Alan, a man conflicted about his homosexual feelings. After feeling pressured by a woman he was seeing who wanted him to perform oral sex on her, he left her and went to an area frequented by "male prostitutes." He became excited by this and then went home "and masturbated to a fantasy of holding a man who passionately desired him" (p. 431). Alan's sexually charged story of heterosexual defeat and homosexual desire evoked the following reaction in his heterosexual analyst who "commented that the homosexual fantasies and urges seemed to counteract the intense feelings of danger and self-loathing that were evoked when the patient felt unable to comply with the woman's wishes. The homosexual desires, the analyst further interpreted, represented the patient's attempt to restore a sense of himself as worthy and desirable, which had completely collapsed. With evident relief, the patient said he thought the analyst really understood him" (p. 432). Here, too, the analyst desexualizes the patient's sexual narrative rather than explore the possibility of sexual feelings between the two of them.

A therapist empathically trying to approximate a patient's subjective experience may encounter difficulties in the realm of the patient's sexual excitement. Both an inability to understand a patient's subjectivity, or taking that understanding for granted, often generates problems in treatment as therapists countertransferentially try to fill in "gaps" (Sullivan, 1950) in their own knowledge. Analysts and other therapists may often rely on interpretive stances as a way to reduce their own anxieties. That is, they may automatically assume a sexual pleasure is defensive before they have entered into the feeling and then prematurely interpret it that way to the patient. Making a defensive assumption about same-sex feelings would be consistent with the training of many analysts.

Another example of countertransference in the realm of sexual identity would be an analyst's assumption that a patient doesn't know whether the analyst is self-identified as heterosexual or what sexual activities the analyst values. This common, heterosexist presumption demonstrates a lamentable but frequently common lack of understanding and empathy for the way gay people are sensitized to "who is gay and who is not" in their environments. A patient will often correctly discern something about the sexuality of the therapist by the kinds of questions therapists ask. Some gay therapists ask deliberately naive questions and pretend they know nothing about gay life when working with gay patients. This is presumably out of a desire to maintain the facade of neutrality, but it often means they don't want the patient to know they are gay. Sometimes it means they don't want the patient to know they have frequented the same places the patient does. Although the phenomenon may be less common than in years past, I have both met and known of several married, gay analysts who live closeted public lives. And in this realm of countertransference and the analyst's identity, what interpretive tack should a lesbian or gay analyst take with a lesbian or gay patient if they experience their own homosexuality as something secretive and shameful? This question has led some analysts (Isay, 1991) to conclude that gay and lesbian analysts should always come out to their patients lest they perpetuate the feelings of secrecy and shame with which the patient lives.

Countertransference in the early psychoanalytic literature was treated as an unanalyzed aspect of the analyst that could generate problems in treatment (Freud, 1910b). Later theorists in the interpersonal and object relations schools (Racker, 1968; Levenson, 1983; Bollas, 1987; Ogden, 1990) took the position that countertransference is not only inevitable in the treatment, but a source of information about the therapist, the patient, and their relationship. In such a model, there is much to learn within the ebb and flow of transference and countertransference. However, working with this model requires an acknowledgment of the anxieties it may generate in a therapist. For example, part of my initial response to Jill's hug was to feel anxious about how it might have an impact upon my professional life. As I struggled with the impact she had on me and shared my responses with professional colleagues, the possibility of talking about these feelings remained open in me. My openness ultimately led her to say something similar to what I felt earlier: *She told me she was anxious that she might act on the feeling because doing so might destroy the way of life she had created for herself.* This is exactly what I had feared, that I had done something that might destroy my professional identity. In that respect, I may also have been made anxious by a transference paradigm in which I was identified as the violating, abusive mother; an identity at odds with my own gender and image of my analytic, helping self.

There is, unfortunately, a tendency within the psychoanalytic field to avoid talking about our own anxious feelings. There is a tremendous wish to avoid the appearance of being in error, as if psychotherapy were a smoothly running and efficient encounter. Ferenczi's (1932, 1933) insights, evolving from his innovative work in mutuality, are still relevant today. He wrote of the technical usefulness of admitting one's errors to patients, and mused: "It would almost seem to be of advantage occasionally to commit blunders in order to admit afterwards the fault to the patient. This advice is, however, quite superfluous; we commit blunders often enough" (1933, p. 159).

In exploring one's own subjectivity, broadly defined as countertransference, therapists, regardless of "sexual orientation," should be prepared to ask themselves some difficult questions similar to the ones I was forced to ask myself. How does any therapist imagine, identify, or empathize with the diverse sexual identities and roles of their patients, especially when they are working with someone whose sources of sexual excitement differ from their own? It becomes increasingly apparent as one pursues this line of thought that lesbians and gay men have different sexual "orientations." Furthermore, it is obvious that heterosexual men and women also differ from each other in their sexual "orientations." This raises the question of whether a "sexual orientation" as it is usually defined is a meaningful clinical concept at all (Miller, 1995; Schwartz, 1995). Magee and Miller (1995) suggest the use of "lesbian rules," defined as "a [flexible] principle that helps theory to accommodate to the individual variety of sexual possibilities, and to the effects of changing contexts."

As we enter the second century of psychoanalysis, we find ourselves on a new frontier. The traditional psychoanalytic paradigm was that of an analyst, interchangeably male or female, presumably heterosexual and capable of working with all patients from a neutral stance. The analyst was completely analyzed and prepared to deal with patient transferences and resistances. That mythic individual has been supplanted by new psychoanalytic paradigms that offer a wide range of potentially confusing, intersubjective possibilities. Transference and countertransference are stripped of their dry, technical meanings and represent human feeling and interaction. In this arena, we will find psychotherapeutic encounters between lesbian analysts and gay male patients, gay male analysts and lesbian patients, lesbian analysts and lesbian patients, and gay male analysts and gay male patients. There are also the uncharted and undocumented relationships between closeted and out lesbian and gay analysts and their heterosexual patients, male and female. As often happens in the exploration of unknown territory, the old psychoanalytic paradigms will be used to make sense of new experiences. Christopher Columbus comes to mind, labeling the place he "discovered" a "new world" and the indigenous peoples that he found there "Indians."

It is not yet clear what we should call the things we are discovering. It is not even clear if we are discovering or creating (Spence, 1982). This paper does not presume to contain the answers to all the questions it raises. The readers of this paper should think of it as a rough sketch of a "new world" whose boundaries are yet to be determined. One hopes that future explorers will think about what is said here as they make their own way in this territory. In this exploration, the psychoanalyst's navigational tools will include curiosity, an openness toward the patient, and the possibility of openness with oneself. In my work, I ultimately found the concept of a "sexual orientation" an obstacle to appreciating the wider subjectivities of both the patient and myself. Coming up against this barrier generated anxiety in both the patient and myself. Ultimately, as I became less anxious, so did the patient and the work proceeded and continues to proceed along interesting lines. In clinical settings, when we admit to starting out from a place of not knowing where we are, we often find ourselves taken to places we never expected to go.

References

Bollas, C. (1987), *The Shadow of the Object.* New York: Columbia University Press.

Butler, J. (1990), *Gender Trouble: Feminism and the Subversion of Identity.* New York: Routledge.

——— (1995), Melancholy gender–Refused identification. *Psychoanal. Dial.,* 5:165–180.

Drescher, J. (1995), Anti-homosexual bias in training. In: *Disorienting Sexuality,* ed. T. Domenici & R. Lesser. New York: Routledge, pp. 227–241.

——— (1997), From preodipal to postmodern: Changing psychoanalytic attitudes toward homosexuality. *Gender & Psychoanal.* 2(2):203–206.

——— (1998), *Psychoanalytic Therapy and the Gay Man.* Hillsdale, NJ: The Analytic Press.

Ferenczi, S. (1932), *The Clinical Diary of Sandor Ferenczi,* ed. J. Dupont, tr. M. Balint & N. Z. Jackson. Cambridge, MA: Harvard University Press, 1988.

——— (1933), Confusion of tongues between the adult and the child. In: *Final Contributions to the Problems and Methods of Psychoanalysis*. New York: Brunner/Mazel, 1980, pp. 156–167.

Freud, S. (1905), Three Essays on the Theory of Sexuality. *Standard Edition*, 7:123–243. London: Hogarth Press, 1953.

——— (1910a), Leonardo da Vinci and a memory of his childhood. *Standard Edition*, 11:58–137. London: Hogarth Press, 1957.

——— (1910b), The future prospects of psycho-analytic therapy. *Standard Edition*, 11:139–151. London: Hogarth Press, 1957.

——— (1914), On narcissism: An introduction. *Standard Edition*, 14:67–102. London: Hogarth Press, 1957.

——— (1915), Observations on transference-love (Further recommendations on the technique of psycho-analysis, III). *Standard Edition*, 12:157–171. London: Hogarth Press, 1958.

——— (1917), Mourning and melancholia. *Standard Edition*, 14:237–258. London: Hogarth Press, 1957.

——— (1920), The psychogenesis of a case of homosexuality in a woman. *Standard Edition*, 18:145–172. London: Hogarth Press, 1955.

Friedman, R. C. (1988), *Male Homosexuality: A Contemporary Psychoanalytic Perspective*. New Haven, CT: Yale University Press.

Gabbard, G. (1991), Psychodynamics of sexual boundary violations. *Psychiat. Annals*, 21:651–655.

Glassgold, J., & Iasenza, S. (1995), *Lesbians and Psychoanalysis: Revolutions in Theory and Practice*. New York: Free Press.

Harris, A. (1991), Gender as contradiction. *Psychoanal. Dial.*, 1:197–224.

Isay, R. (1991), The homosexual analyst: Clinical considerations. *The Psychoanalytic Study of the Child*, 46:199–216. New Haven, CT: Yale University Press.

Kiersky, S. (1995), Shadowland: Some thoughts on homosexuality and the loss of the real. Paper presented at a Panel, "Psychoanalysis and Homosexuality: A Contemporary View," American Academy of Psychoanalysis, December 10.

Kinsey, A., Pomeroy, W., & Martin, C. (1948), *Sexual Behavior in the Human Male*. Philadelphia, PA: Saunders.

Levenson, E. (1983), *The Ambiguity of Change*. New York: Basic Books.

——— (1995), A monopedal presentation of interpersonal psychoanalysis. *Rev. Interpersonal. Psychoanal.*, 1:1–4.

Lewes, K. (1988), *The Psychoanalytic Theory of Male Homosexuality*. New York: Simon & Schuster.

Magee, M., & Miller, D. (1995), Assaults and harassments: The violent acts of theorizing lesbian sexuality. Paper presented at a Panel, "Psychoanalysis and Homosexuality: A Contemporary View," American Academy of Psychoanalysis, December 10.

Miller, D. (1995), Why discussions of "sexual orientation" make my head swim. Paper presented at a Symposium, "Psychiatric Attempts to Change Sexual Orientation," American Psychiatric Association, May 23.

Mitchell, S. (1988), *Relational Concepts in Psychoanalysis: An Integration.* Cambridge, MA: Harvard University Press.

O'Connor, N., & Ryan, J. (1993), *Wild Desires and Mistaken Identities: Lesbianism and Psychoanalysis.* New York: Columbia University Press.

Ogden, T. (1990), *The Matrix of the Mind: Object Relations and the Psychoanalytic Dialogue.* Northvale, NJ: Aronson.

Racker, H. (1968), *Transference and Countertransference.* New York: International Universities Press.

Schwartz, D. (1995), Current psychoanalytic discourses on sexuality: Tripping over the body. In: *Disorienting Sexuality,* ed. T. Domenici & R. Lesser. New York: Routledge, pp. 115–126.

Sedgwick, E. (1990), *Epistemology of the Closet.* Berkeley & Los Angeles: University of California Press.

Socarides, C. (1968), *The Overt Homosexual.* New York: Grune & Stratton.

Spence, D. (1982), *Narrative Truth and Historical Truth: Meaning and Interpretation in Psychoanalysis.* New York: W. W. Norton.

Stoller, R. (1985), *Presentations of Gender.* New Haven, CT: Yale University Press.

Sullivan, H. S. (1950), *The Fusion of Psychiatry and Social Science.* New York: W. W. Norton.

———— (1953), *The Interpersonal Theory of Psychiatry.* New York: W. W. Norton.

Trop, J., & Stolorow, R. (1992), Defense analysis in self psychology: A developmental view. *Psychoanal. Dial.,* 2:427–442.

Winnicott, D. W. (1960), Ego distortion in terms of true and false self. In: *The Maturational Processes and Facilitating Environment.* New York: International Universities Press, 1965, pp. 140–152.

Part II

Theoretical: Deconstructing the Myth of a Lesbian Identity

7

Desire in Intersubjective Systems and Contexts

Donna M. Orange

"What does a woman want?" Freud's rhetorical query is perhaps the most notorious throwing-up-hands question in the history of Western thought. Within the context of his thought, it rested on a logical impossibility, a contradiction in terms. A woman, for Freud, was by definition the kind of being who could not want, a nonsubject. A woman with desires of her own was, exactly to the extent that she wanted, adopting a masculine identification (Freud, 1905, 1920). A woman could be only the passive object of wanting, not the possessor of wants or the one who wants, the subject or organizer of her own experience. Men were not only entitled to want, they were defined as those who want (Krafft-Ebing had also defined men as the only active subjects [Katz, 1995]), the sole possessors of true subjectivity.

Among the wants that "real women" cannot have, of course, are sexual desires. Not only are they confined to passivity in heterosexual relationships, in addition, their love for other women becomes theoretically impossible, or at best, bewildering. *No one is there* to want the other unless at least one partner, as Freud was sure she must, adopts a masculine way of loving, and thus a kind of quasi-subjectivity. (This problem does not exist, even for Freud, in the study of gay men, because two genuine subjects are involved.) His nameless patient in "The Psychogenesis of a Case of Female Homosexuality" had to be understood as rejecting womanhood, and as having been transformed psychologically into a man: "This girl had entirely repudiated her wish for a child, her love of men, and the feminine role in general. . . . She changed into a man and took her mother in place of her father as the object of her love" (Freud, 1920, p. 158).

Freud's more general account of homosexual orientation is helpful, but incompletely so, in understanding why he found baffling women who loved women. In spite of his lifelong belief in human bisexuality, he thought one could love only difference. In other words, a person who identifies as a man or a woman can love only a person of the gender opposite to that of the identification (Freud, 1905). But this account relies on a very concrete and dichotomous notion of gender, and does not explain why women who love women should be less comprehensible than men who love men. Only the complete reduction of women to passivity, to nonbeing as subjects, explains this discrepancy. (For a helpful discussion of the intellectual contexts of Freud's puzzlement, see Makari, 1991.)

There are, fortunately, loud calls in contemporary psychoanalysis to restore and reclaim the subjectivity of women, and implicitly, the full reality of women's love for women or men. I want to draw attention to these attempts, so we can be aware of their potential pitfalls and use them carefully.

Uses of "Desire"

Let us first look briefly at two contemporary discourses in which the term *desire* appears frequently: psychoanalysis informed by feminism, and lesbian and gay studies.[1]

---

[1]Desire is also perhaps coincidentally, perhaps not, an important term in the field of sex therapy, where it occurs most frequently in phrases like "disorders of sexual desire" (Leiblum and Rosen, 1988). Here desire, depending on the particular author's view, is a biological–psychological *something* that a patient can be said to lack, or at least to have in a small amount. How one understands whatever is missing determines the sort of treatment one believes necessary. A practitioner who sees the deficit as primarily biological may suggest a medical remedy. If the problem is thought to be cognitive, some variety of cognitive-behavioral therapy will be encouraged. An orthodox Freudian will see the patient as suffering from conflict-based inhibitions, or from defensive walling off of

Desire has become a popular word in current psychoanalytic conversation. We read of "woman's alienated search for her own desire" (Benjamin, 1988, p. 474), and of "the desire which constitutes the subject" (Kristeva, 1990, p. 383). Each writer's agenda in using the term varies, but there are common themes. Examples are the restoration of an active sexual experience to women, and the rehabilitation of sexuality in relational theories of psychoanalysis. These agendas and meanings are sometimes made explicit, sometimes left unarticulated.

Desire is also an important term in gay and lesbian studies. There this term is often used to specify what is thought—depending on the perspective of the speaker—to be deviant or special and important about a lesbian or gay person. The larger society, including the psychoanalytic world, has identified lesbians and gay men exclusively by their sexuality. At times, gay and lesbian theorists seem to accept this designation, as if sexuality could be divorced from the rest of life. To justify political aims—all people are created equal—the impression may be created that sexual attraction is a thing in itself, a pregiven characteristic, abstracted from psychological and relational context or from what Wittgenstein (1953) would have called "a form of life." Although these aims are understandable and necessary, as psychoanalysts we must ask further for meanings, intentions, and context.

The many uses of *desire* may have more in common than at first appears. First, speaking as if all desire were sexual (a relational theorist who resists this mistake, and always distinguishes, is Mitchell [1992]), analysts tend toward an often unintended reductionism. Addressing this tendency, and showing the difference a relational perspective makes, Reisner asks, "Is motivation irreducibly tied to a relational context, within which a self is constituted and differentiated? Or does desire arise from accessions of internal tensions, biological in origin, seeking relief?" (Reisner, 1992).

Second, analysts may thus eliminate subjective experience by making a desire a thing. We probably ought to ask ourselves what we mean

---

sexual wishes felt to be impermissible, and will prescribe a traditional psychoanalysis. A relational psychoanalyst, thinking less concretely, may see the patient as repeating some relational pattern that shuts off access to sexual feelings. This analyst will want to engage the patient in a relational psychoanalysis that will engage the patient in new and freer relating. Similarly a self psychologically oriented analyst will see the problem as resulting from a fragile sense of self that finds sexual feeling overwhelming and fragmenting, and will expect a revived sexuality as part of the restored self. Intersubjectivity theorists, resisting the reduction of sexual desire to a *something missing,* will similarly attempt to understand and respond to the patient's organized *experience* of sexuality, especially in developmental and in treatment contexts.

when we use *desire* as a noun. Third, many analytic writers minimize or eliminate relational factors, or the intersubjective context.

Let us first consider the reductionism implicit in much talk of desire. Eclipsing the more general intentionality inherent in subjectivity—to be a subject is to have needs and wants—we may unwittingly use the term as equivalent to *sexual desire*. This usage isolates sexual experience from the rest of life and relatedness. The intent is often laudable, as if to say that we are all human, but just have different types, levels, or objects of sexual desire. No need for pernicious discrimination, or for pathologizing. The unfortunate and usually unintended consequence is, as Kiersky (1996) says, to reduce people to "body parts and sexual practices."

A second form of reductionism can be a dichotomous view of human nature that mimics the biblical "male and female he created them." Every activity or quality of a person then falls into sexual and gender categories. Androgyny would consist in having a good mix of qualities and activities predesignated, conceptually or culturally, as masculine or feminine. Desire then comes down to the capacity to want a sexual linkage with one category or the other, male or female, and therefore homosexual or heterosexual—a further rigid dichotomy. Even when a writer does not assume, like Freud, that all wanting is masculine, we may assume that healthy or normal desire is for coupling with the "other" sex. O'Connor and Ryan (1993) note that even as sophisticated an account as that of Benjamin (1988) does not consider the possibility of healthy lesbian or gay relatedness.

Another major problem with many current uses of the word *desire* is that they are too concrete, or as some would say, reifying. In some accounts, substituting the Freudian *libido* would be easy, and the meaning would be little changed. This is particularly true, and more understandably so, in the field of sex therapy, where patients frequently approach clinicians to be treated, or to have a partner treated, for lack of desire or deficient libido. Still, we can also recognize this concreteness in the writing of some psychoanalysts, who, having shifted to relational theories, and perhaps nostalgic for the embodied quality of Freudian psychoanalysis, begin to speak of desire as a noun.

I want to suggest that, to avoid the reductions and reifications noted above, we need to restore the notion and the experience of desire to larger contexts. I mean this on several levels. (The levels I will neglect are the cultural and religious contexts, a set of powerful influences too involved for inclusion in this article.) First, sexual desire of any sort is inseparable from a person's capacity to want anything at all, one's experience of being a subject. Survivors tell us that the extremely dehumanizing conditions of the concentration camps, including the scarcity of food, led to a complete disinterest in things sexual. Second, the capacity to want or desire forms and develops in the context of specific relational experience, especially of early and important emotional bonds. Third, the emotional atmosphere of the family, that larger intersubjective field, significantly shapes a person's wanting, including sexual desire. Finally, the emotional climate of the treatment, especially including the attitudes of the analyst, significantly influences the development of a person's capacity to experience and appropriate her own desiring. Let us consider each in turn.

Desire and Subjectivity

Sexual desire forms an integral part of a person's capacity to want anything at all, of one's experience of being a subject. This claim has two parts. First, it denies that sexual desire can be isolated from the larger context of a person's life, or can develop apart from the larger contexts of desire. This denial requires a distinction between compulsion and desire. Compulsions, sexual or otherwise, are rigid and automatic and experienced as unwanted. Desiring, on the contrary, is precisely integral to the experience of subjectivity. It acknowledges that sexual desire, while not the whole extent of desire, can be understood only as part of the whole category.

Second, this claim, owing much to the work of Benjamin (1988) and other feminist writers, highlights the crucial—I hesitate to say essential—connection between desire and subjectivity. By subjectivity I mean the experience of organizing, making sense of, one's own experience. By a subject I mean an organizer of experience. One common way to organize experience is to feel that we want something or someone, that something or someone "calls out to us." Conversely, we commonly observe as clinicians that people in states of depression are unable to want anything, even things they previously enjoyed. They are disconnected from their own subjectivity, unable to feel it. When the clouds lift, they can want again, can allow things or people to call out to them.

Such losses of subjectivity show that we must expand, not reduce, our understanding of desire. A person whose sense of self is whole and robust will be able to want, and can want relatedness, including sexual relatedness. Difference in sexual desire, with such desire no longer seen as a thing-in-itself, will no longer be construed as pathology, but simply as difference.

Desire and Attachment

The ability to want or desire forms and develops in the context of specific relational experience, especially of early and important emotional bonds (cf. Orange, 1995). This means that while a rudimentary capacity to want is probably innate, the form in which we experience wanting or desire develops in relational experience. Specifically, I believe early attachment experience powerfully contextualizes our sense of ourselves as desiring subjects. Do we find it safe or unsafe (anxiety-producing) to feel and acknowledge our own wants? Must certain forms of wanting be excluded from the organization of experience because they threaten important emotional ties? Have certain kinds of wanting—physiological comfort, sexual desires, intellectual curiosities, for example–simply been unable to find any validating responsiveness from the attachment figures, and thus failed to become fully real for the child, adolescent, or developing adult (cf. Stolorow and Atwood, 1992)? All these questions illustrate the bearing that attachment context has on the development of a felt ability to desire.

The Family and Desire

Closely related is the influence of the emotional climate and attitudes of a particular family, nuclear or extended, on the development of desiring subjectivity. *The emotional atmosphere of the family, that larger intersubjective field, significantly shapes a person's wanting, including sexual desiring.* In some families and cultures, any desire is a probable source of shame. In others, sexual desire may be acceptable, but attributed only to men or restricted to heterosexual expression. In others, ambition—desiring to "be somebody" or do something—may be honored, disregarded, or scornfully dismissed. Some families honor artistic aspirations or intellectual curiosity, while others consider these forms of wanting "sissy." Each family has its attitudes concerning desire, what is honored, what is ridiculous or shameful—and importantly influences its children's sense of the meanings and ramifications of various experiences and expressions of desire.

Analytic Attitudes Toward Desire

Finally, *the emotional climate of the treatment, especially including the attitudes of the analyst, significantly influences the development of a person's capacity to experience and appropriate her or his own desires.* The system composed of the analyst's attitudes in conjunction with those of the patient supports and/or limits the reworking of desire. The patient, most often, arrives expecting the same attitudes and limitations she or he has always found, together with an inchoate hope for something new. The analyst brings a subjectivity formed by emotional and relational experience as well as by theoretical attitudes (Orange, 1995). This combination, or intersubjective field, creates an indefinite number of possible configurations, conjunctions, and disjunctions. Perhaps the patient is exquisitely sensitive to the physical environment, wanting a particular set of lighting, heating, and seating conditions, while the analyst cares little for physical comfort, or vice versa. Or suppose analyst and patient differ in sexual desire—extent, range, or orientation. Or imagine that the patient is an artist, finely attuned to nuances of sound, for example, and interested principally in music, while the analyst speaks in visual metaphors, or is theoretically interested in sexual desires or aggressive instincts. As Wittgenstein (1966) said of Freud's "free" association method, "The fact is that whenever you are preoccupied with something, with some trouble or with some problem which is a big thing in your life—as sex is, for instance—then no matter what you start from, the association will lead finally back to that same theme" (pp. 50–51). He might have noted that this is equally true for both analyst and patient.

Difference or similarity of desire, or a mixture of both, significantly form the context of treatment, and shape for both parties the sense of what is possible and desirable. The following story (which appears in an earlier version in Orange [1995]), only secondarily about sexual desire, but all about the desiring subject in context, may briefly illustrate the development of the desiring subject in a treatment understood through the lens of intersubjectivity theory.

A 40-year-old woman came for treatment because of intense anxiety and growing depression, with an alarming wish to be dead, that she related to her failing marriage. She had, out of deference to her parents' wishes, married a wealthy man, and had become a very competent servant, managing the home, and providing excellent care for their two daughters, now adolescents. (She reminded me of Stevens the butler in *The Remains of the Day.*) With no sense of a life, or preferences, or opinions, or purposes of her own, her only function was to make sure things ran smoothly for the nuclear and both extended families. In the culture of both families, this was the only role for a woman, even an extremely intelligent one.

For many years, by her original account, the system had run smoothly. Her family of origin had been "wonderful" and her marriage "okay." Only now, when she had developed a friendship with another married woman, had she begun to feel anxious and depressed. The company of this friend made her feel important in her own right, and comfortable and safe in ways she could never remember having felt before. Soon she began to realize what she had been missing. In addition, the contrast between her marriage and that of her friend brought despair over her own future life prospects, and anxiety at the almost inconceivable thought of her own freedom. She preferred not to discuss the loneliness of her own marriage, nor the anger she sometimes momentarily felt when her husband berated her or failed to volunteer any help at times when she was obviously overburdened. From me, she said, she simply wanted help with feeling better, putting options out of her mind, and with putting up with the conditions of her life.

My original sense was that I was both like and very different from her. She seemed to feel entirely trapped while I had, after all, left a troubled marriage. If she could just come to understand what I had come to understand and feel, she could be just fine. I, of course, could know what would be best for her. The intersubjective field formed by my agenda and sense of things, with her very strong tendency to comply with others' expectations of her, only heightened her anxiety. Torn between complying with her parents' expectations, with her husband's demands, and now with my program, she felt bound to lose someone. For all sorts of practical reasons, she became unable to keep regular appointments. The needs of others always intervened.

I had to shift gears. To do this, I needed to become aware of my own emotional organizing principles and needs, to see how similar these were to hers, and to recognize my own impact on the treatment. What helped me was noticing this patient's ways of taking care of me in the session—telling me she was fine, asking about my well-being, watching the clock—and remembering how I had been like that with my own analyst. This patient and I were very much alike in our compulsive caretaking, in our assumption that our only value as persons lay in our capacity and skills as caretakers, and in the underdevelopment of desiring subjectivity. So I was taking care of her, trying to fix her life—in proper analytic interpretive style, of course—and she was taking care of me, trying to establish her value in my eyes and to maintain her fragile sense of worth in her own eyes.

When we reflected together on our caretaking patterns, changes began. The need to be helpful and caretaking loosened its grip on me, and her freedom in relation to me very gradually increased. Our tie no longer depended on her divining and complying with my hopes for her. We began to talk more about the complexity of compliance, caretaking, and loss of selfhood required to maintain ties in her family of origin. I began to be more able to feel my way into her emotional predicament. Simultaneously she began to report more sustained frustration with her marriage and her family role, along with some efforts to tell her husband and children that she expected respectful treatment. She also began to ask them for help occasionally, and was surprised that they protested less than she had expected. She is working at perceiving and following her own feelings, interests, and wants, and is just beginning to sense that these will lead her wherever she needs to go. As a result, she feels less trapped. She does feel a new kind of sadness—less despairing, but full of mourning for the person she never had a chance to become.

This story illustrates, among other things, the intersubjective context of desire in psychoanalytic treatment. Intersubjectivity theorists see transference as organizing activity. They often distinguish between the selfobject aspect of transference,[2] in which the analyst functions as support for the self-development and cohesion of the patient, and a repetitive dimension of transference. In this repetitive dimension, the patient may experience the analyst as the failing or abusive early caretaker. The analyst, no blank screen but a person with a history and emotional organization,

---

[2]This essay, written in 1993–1994, still uses the language of transference, which I now regard as a misleading remnant of Freud's atomistic notion of subjectivity (Orange, submitted).

recreates with the patient the intersubjective field of childhood. The memory of the pathogenic intersubjective field returns as transference. Selfobject transferences, or what Freud called the unobjectionable positive transferences, recede into the background, and can seem completely inaccessible. Depending, however, on the strength and reliability of the analytic bond, and on the analyst's capacity to reflect on her own contribution to repetitive intersubjective impasses, the process of working on the impasse may restore the selfobject transference to the foreground. It may even contribute to the usefulness of the analytic bond in restoring, integrating, or creating for what seems like the first time, a robust and full sense of the desiring subject.

To return to Freud's question, "What does a woman want?" we may respond that once we grant that women are subjects who *can* want, we will find them developing many desires, sexual and otherwise, in many emotional contexts. We will resist the reification and reduction of desire, and speak more frequently of the desiring subject. We may even find, to our amazement, that some perfectly ordinary women may want each other.

References

Benjamin, J. (1988), *Bonds of Love: Psychoanalysis, Feminism, and the Problem of Domination.* New York: Pantheon.

Freud, S. (1905), Three Essays on the Theory of Sexuality. *Standard Edition,* 7:123–243. London: Hogarth Press, 1953.

———— (1920), The psychogenesis of a case of homosexuality in a woman. *Standard Edition,* 18:145–172. London: Hogarth Press, 1955.

Katz, J. (1995), *The Invention of Heterosexuality.* New York: Dutton.

Kiersky, S. (1996), *Work in Progress.* Mahwah, NJ: Analytic Press.

Kristeva, J. (1990), Women's time. In: *Essential Papers on the Psychology of Women,* ed. C. Zanardi. New York: New York University Press, pp. 374–398.

Leiblum, S., & Rosen, R., Eds. (1988), *Sexual Desire Disorders.* New York: Guilford Press.

Makari, G. (1991), German philosophy, Freud, and the riddle of the woman. *J. Amer. Psychoanal. Assn.,* 39:183–213.

Mitchell, S. (1992), True selves, false selves, and the ambiguity of authenticity. In: *Relational Perspectives in Psychoanalysis,* ed. N. Skolnick & S. Warshaw. Hillsdale, NJ: Analytic Press, pp. 1–20.

O'Connor, N., & Ryan, J. (1993), *Wild Desires and Mistaken Identities.* New York: Columbia University Press.

Orange, D. (1995), *Emotional Understanding: Studies in Psychoanalytic Epistemology.* New York: Guilford Press.

———— (submitted), Why language matters to psychoanalysis.

Reisner, S. (1992), Eros reclaimed: Recovering Freud's relational theory. In: *Relational Perspectives in Psychoanalysis,* ed. N. Skolnick & S. Warshaw. Hillsdale, NJ: Analytic Press, pp. 281–312.

Stolorow, R., & Atwood, G. (1992), *Contexts of Being: The Intersubjective Foundations of Psychological Life.* Hillsdale, NJ: Analytic Press.

Wittgenstein, L. (1953), *Philosophical Investigations,* 3rd ed., tr. G. E. M. Anscombe. New York: Macmillan.

———— (1966), *Lectures and Conversations on Aesthetics, Psychology, and Religious Belief,* ed. C. Barratt. Oxford: Blackwell.

8

Category Problems: Lesbians, Postmodernism, and Truth

Ronnie C. Lesser

> Queer theory might better remind us that we are inhabited always by states of desire that exceed our capacity to name them. Every name only gives those desires—conflictual, contradictory, inconsistent, undefined—a fictive border, a definition that falsifies ... [Edelman, 1996].

Even though I've committed myself to writing a paper on lesbians for this book, something makes me balk at the task. Rather than try to sidestep this something (a strategy that has so far yielded no promising results), I want to give it a voice. By describing my reasons for balking, I hope to illuminate some problems faced by analysts who are trying to both critique and rethink psychoanalytic theory of lesbians.

The first source of my balking comes from my aversion to speaking about "lesbians" as a group. Speaking about such a broad group goes

My appreciation to Diane Burhenne and Erica Schoenberg for their help with this paper.

against a deeply engrained part of my personality that dislikes viewing myself or others as fitting into ready-made categories. Being pigeonholed as white, lesbian, woman, Jewish, all feel like attempts to force me into categories that don't feel like me. I dream of being a self-created individual who is outside of categories, theories, and fashions. I call this a dream because it is only part of a story which also includes the fact that I am constituted by the various categories that I find myself in and through which I understand and experience myself (including, of course, my thinking that I have a self to understand).

Thus, from my perspective, to speak about "lesbians" or a lesbian subjectivity violates the vast array of individuals united by the experience of lusting for women in cultures which stigmatize this experience (Butler, 1991). (Even this attempt to define lesbians fails because it excludes those who define themselves as lesbian but don't experience lust, and includes those heterosexual women who feel desire for other women.) What purpose does it serve to group together the vast experiences of those lesbians who are asexual, who have sex with both men and women, who have felt like lesbians since early childhood, or who experience lesbian love for the first time in middle age? Glossing over the differences among lesbians who are African American, Jewish, Hispanic, Catholic, Asian, upper class, lower class, is to treat sexuality as a category that is so essential that everything else can be reduced to it. To locate what is most essential about us in our genitals and what moves them has political consequences, since it leads us to treat class, racial, and cultural differences as insignificant. This pars pro toto schema is related to the way that writers in the social sciences have used a Western, male, white, middle-class model as if it represents everyone. To take a part as representative of the whole is to eradicate difference through an act of violence (Flax, 1990). This is something I don't want to recapitulate by using the term *lesbian*.

Writing about "lesbians" also recapitulates the tendency of psychologists to use socially constructed categories as if they are foundational. To write about lesbians in this way is to naturalize the homosexual-heterosexual binary so that it is accorded a universal, ahistorical status, removing it from politics and ideology. Yet our modern belief that people have defined sexual identities that can be divided into these categories is a historically specific production. The categories *homosexual* and *heterosexual* have existed for a relatively brief time in history, having been coined late in the nineteenth century, the term *homosexual* preceding the term *heterosexual* (Halperin, 1993). Until the last century, people's sexual behavior was not thought to define them anymore than their dietary preferences did (Halperin, 1993). In addition, since being coined, the meanings of the categories *homosexual* and *heterosexual* have changed. Prior to World War I in this country, the gay male world was not divided into homosexual and heterosexual the way it is now: men could have sex with other men and not consider themselves "queer" as long as they conformed to conventional stereotypes of masculine behavior. Many men who had sex with other men also desired women, and did not think that same-sex desire precluded opposite-sex desire. Only in the period from the 1930s to the 1950s did the now common conventional division replace this, and this change was uneven, marked by class and ethnic differences. The rigidly dichotomized distinctions between homosexual and heterosexual seem to have been adopted by the middle class at least two generations before they appeared in much of Euro-American and African-American working class culture (Chauncey, 1994). The categories *homosexual* and *heterosexual* are historical and cultural constructions which create boundaries between what is forbidden and what is acceptable, defining both deviance and normality (Domenici and Lesser, 1995). Because psychoanalysis treats these categories as if they're foundational, rather than embedded in history and politics, the status quo is reproduced rather than problematized.

To naturalize the heterosexual-homosexual binary is also to disregard the fact that it originated in a homophobic discourse. Consider, for example, the way that the terms are constructed: the first is unmarked and naturalized, conveying the idea that this is the category to which everyone belongs, while the second term is marked and problematized, conveying the notion that this category represents deviation from the norm. The fact that the unmarked term is dependent on the marked term for its definition (i.e., both logically and historically) gives the lie to the implication that the unmarked term represents lack of difference or abnormality. This analysis disorients our ideas about priority and truth by revealing that both homosexuality and heterosexuality are discursive and homophobic constructions (Halperin, 1995; Harris, 1995).

To naturalize the heterosexual-homosexual binary is also to assume that sexuality is stable and coherent. It is ironic that psychoanalysts freely use these terms, since the concept of stable sexuality is antithetical to the Freudian notion that the unconscious "undermines the subject from any position of certainty, from any relation of knowledge to his or her psychic processes and history, and simultaneously reveals the fictional nature of the sexual category to which every human subject is none the less assigned'' (Mitchell and Rose, 1982).

The ease with which some psychoanalysts have reproduced the idea of stable, coherent subjects with stable sexual identities is made more understandable when we consider that these views have been corner-stones of Western thought since the Enlightenment (Flax, 1990). Post-modern scholars have focused on the ways that Enlightenment metanarratives privilege unity, homogeneity, closure, and identity. For postmodernists, what is real is flux, and any appearance of unity and homogeneity can only be produced by erasing contradictory stories of others (e.g., non-Westerners, women).

Psychoanalysts influenced by postmodern critiques of sexual identity have tried to integrate these ideas into psychoanalytic theory of sexuality (Schwartz, 1995; Lesser, 1995; Schoenberg, 1995). Schwartz (1995) has emphasized that the sexual orientation view serves defensive purposes; conventionally masculine men are able to split off their passive same-sex longing by believing that only gay and bisexual men feel such desires. He has proposed that sexuality should be represented as fluid, contextu-ally influenced positions. I'd like to discuss this proposal and its ramifica-tions by examining Schwartz's paper in more detail.

Schwartz excavates the assumptions hidden behind our current tripar-tite sexual classification system (i.e., homosexual, heterosexual, bisexual), which he refers to as the sexual orientation view. These assumptions include the belief that these three types exhaust all possible permutations, that characterizing people on the basis of the sex of their eroticized object captures the most salient aspect of their psychoerotic system, and that these categories are stable within individuals. He cautions us that none of these should be taken for granted. He goes on to illustrate the ways that a sexual orientation view shapes the manner in which its adherents listen to clinical material: because of their belief in a stable sexual orienta-tion, they would be unlikely to discover or be interested in same-sex desires in heterosexuals or other-sex desires in homosexuals. Moreover, since sexual stability is viewed as a norm, it is taken to signify health, a view which leads to pathologizing those people whose sexuality is fluid. Schwartz takes issue with this view for important reasons.

According to Schwartz, the sexual orientation view is subverted by anthropological and historical findings (as well as midlife conversions) which point to sexual diversity and fluidity. Thus he concludes that we establish psychoerotic patterns suited to current conditions, including objects available, as well as other situational factors.

Clearly, there are important reasons for Schwartz to question the concept of sexual orientation and put it into a historical context, as I discussed earlier in this chapter. But is the notion of sexual fluidity a more accurate representation of how sexuality is? I believe that there are significant reasons to problematize this interpretation.

Although Schwartz does not cite specific cultures to support the idea that the sexual orientation view is contradicted by anthropological and historical findings, I assume he is referring to such coming-of-age rituals in some cultures as those in which young men fellate older men and then go on to have purely heterosexual relations. Other findings that would support Schwartz's argument are provided by Halperin (1990), who reported that in ancient Greece sexual desire for men did not seem to be based on the sex of the object but rather on power differentials. Free men were able to have sexual relations with male slaves, boys, and women, all of whom were deemed to be less powerful. Although these findings certainly demonstrate the plasticity and diversity of sexual practices across cultures, they do not necessarily demonstrate sexual fluidity within individuals. If we take seriously the idea that sexuality is shaped by culture, history, and power relations, then we cannot compare data across different cultures and historical periods to make generalizations about "sexuality." The fact that an adolescent boy fellates an older man as part of a coming-of-age ritual doesn't give us information about what that act means to him, how he feels when he does it, or whether he would even describe it as sexual. Thus to use the data to prove that sexuality is fluid is problematic. One could just as easily argue that sexuality is stable, because so many people in contemporary Western cultures experience it that way.

I agree with Schwartz that it is incumbent upon us to historicize our concepts of sexuality by noting the ways in which sexual categories are socially constructed and are not facts of nature. But in deconstructing this myth, Schwartz ends up reproducing the positivist fallacy by treating the notion of sexual fluidity as a more truthful descriptor of sexuality, thereby giving it a universal, ahistorical status. Now fluidity becomes what is essential about sexuality, and stability is merely a defensive maneuver.

Schwartz repeats this positivist fallacy when he describes how holding a theory of sexual stability means that an analyst will only pay attention to certain material and not other content, as though an analyst who holds a theory of fluidity will not similarly fail to attend to evidence of stability. Since neither has a claim to objectivism, listening will be constrained by either theory.

Although Schwartz says that he doesn't prescribe fluidity as a norm, I fear that one possible consequence of believing that we have found the truth of sexuality in the notion of fluidity is that we will view it as a new telos of development. Thus, those people who experience their sexualities as stable will be viewed as defensive and less developed than those with fluid sexualities. This would merely invert the traditional psychosexual model that holds that integration and coherence are more highly developed than fluidity. The unfortunate psychoanalytic propensity to equate difference with development would remain intact.

While the notion of sexual fluidity is part of an important effort by theorists to transcend the constraints of the homosexual-heterosexual binary, I wonder if it isn't a positivist dream in disguise. For how can we grant fluidity an ahistorical, universal status without believing that we have stepped outside of discourse long enough to have discovered it? This belief flies in the face of the poststructuralist view that science is a discursive enterprise. We as psychoanalysts are partially constituted by our involvement in these practices: we cannot stand back from them and analyze the social world in a detached way because we are that world (Morss, 1996). There is no discourse-free zone for determining which theory is better than another. Thus to hold that either sexual stability or fluidity is a truthful representation of sexuality, is to purport to stand outside of discourse. We might hold that the idea of sexual fluidity works better for some people in our present culture because it helps them be less rigid, or that we prefer it as a theory or way of life because it fits with our values, political beliefs, and aesthetics. But to laud a "passionate fiction" (de Lauretis, 1994) as a truth that's good or real for everyone closes off the possibility of dealing with difference in a nonhierarchical way.

The positivist dream that sexual fluidity is outside of ideology and that we are liberated if we experience ourselves in this way, distracts us from noticing that theories of sexuality are constituted within power relations. In a searing critique of sexual liberatory movements, Foucault described them as complying with the modern regime of sexuality (Halperin, 1995). While they have freed us to express our sexualities, they also require us to express them. While we can choose to be sexually free more easily, it is not so simple to choose not to be sexually free, or what to count as sexual freedom. We might be more sexually liberated, but are now enslaved to our sexualities since sexual expression is the sine qua non of freedom. Thus, we are enmeshed in a liberal concept of freedom as a regulative or normative ideal of what responsible human beings should do. Sexual liberation is part of power relations, and not outside of them. Are we "liberated" if we are sexually fluid, or does thinking this preclude our noticing the ways in which we are bound by culture and theory and not liberated?

Halperin (1995) has noted other problems with the concept of sexual fluidity: in particular, that deconstructing the homosexual-heterosexual binary causes homosexuals to disappear. Could our desire to deconstruct this binary represent both our hopes of transcending homophobic discourses, as well as destructive purposes of which we are not aware? I believe that these are important questions that require further attention.

At this point I want to come out as an analyst who, like Schwartz, prefers theories of sexual fluidity. I struggle with what it means to have theoretical preferences and to be open to surrendering them if an analytic encounter requires my doing so. Since my preference for thinking of sexuality as fluid affords me no neutral vantage point for listening to material, it seems to me that I have to keep in mind that fluidity is a fashionable fiction at the same time that I know I prefer it. T. S. Eliot's description of Henry James (cited in Ginsberg, 1995) as "having a mind so refined that no idea could violate it," seems to fit here, since having such a mind would mean that no idea or theory would solidify permanently. Such a state of mind would enable me to be open to listening to material in such a way that I could suspend my belief in fluidity long enough to acknowledge that stability might be preferable to someone else. When I am certain that an interpretation or theory is neutral and true, I am most vulnerable to not hearing what a patient is saying. I'd like to describe an interaction I had with a patient which enabled me to see the positivist fallacy in my theory of sexual fluidity.

Heterosexually married since her early twenties, B began a lesbian relationship in her fifties. She now defines herself as lesbian and is struggling to come to terms with this in spite of her Orthodox Jewish upbringing. Her identification of herself as lesbian follows a familiar, modern storyline; even though she was never attracted to women before K, and in spite of the fact that she was satisfied sexually by her husband, she feels that she has always been lesbian but wasn't aware of it before she fell in love with K. (I stress that this is a modern storyline, rather than a postmodern one that would explain the data as evidence that her sexuality is a fluid, changing position as a way to say that these are coequal narratives. Neither is a more truthful description of the data, and each can be utilized for defensive purposes.)

Several months ago B dreamed that she had passionate sex with a man. The dream made her extremely anxious; she felt that she didn't know who she was. Since I think of sexuality as fluid, I saw her problem as being due to her inability to reconcile having desires for both men and women. I dealt with her anxiety in a way that she experienced as flip: I tried to present the idea that being attracted to both men and women was an all right thing (and maybe the right thing) to feel. What I was unable to see was that for B this most certainly is not the case: she feels that she needs and wants a stable identity. Feeling that she is lesbian is like having both of her feet planted firmly on the ground. She was very disappointed that I didn't understand this and for many sessions afterwards tried to explain how defenseless she felt without an idea that her sexual identity was solid.

There are a variety of ways that I can understand this: I could conclude that B needs a sense of stability because her feelings about herself are fragile, and that when she becomes stronger she'll be able to accept the truth of her sexual fluidity. But note that this is advancing the idea of fluidity as a norm from which I judge her feelings of stability as defensive and less developed. An alternative reading is that B prefers a story of stability and that I prefer one of fluidity. From this vantage point one story is no more truthful or healthy than the other. Either story can be preferred for reasons that are defensive and personal. If B believed that her sexuality had changed and might change again, this could obviously serve defensive purposes. She might be afraid to accept her attraction to women because it makes her feel too alienated, different, or guilty. Or, it could be an expression of a wish to transcend her embeddedness in lesbian particularity, a defense against coming to terms with limitations and loss (Crespi, 1995).

What I've attempted to demonstrate in this paper is that the problems caused by thinking about sexuality in binary terms are not all solved by moving to a model of sexual fluidity. The idea of sexual fluidity is itself a fiction masquerading as a fact, and can cause problems for us in dealing with patients if we forget that it is a fiction.

What remains for us to work out is how we can incorporate the critique of the homosexual-heterosexual binary in a way that will lead us to describe sexuality without falling into the trap of reducing it to an essence (i.e., stability, fluidity, or a combination of both) and then generalizing it to everyone. How can we take account of historical, cultural, and interindividual variation without creating new norms and developmental trajectories which pathologize those who don't fit in? If we rewrite developmental theory and use sexual fluidity as a new telos, we erase the individual by prescribing standards for everyone and putting difference on a hierarchical scale.

Theories of sexuality are reflections of our own values and preferences for particular styles of sexual relating. We run into trouble when we think that they are more than personal preferences and begin to give them a foundational status. It is my hope that we can learn to withstand the uncertainty that would ensue if we were to stop believing that our theories are "true" and should be applied to everyone.

References

Butler, J. (1991), Imitation and gender subordination. In: *Inside Out: Lesbian Theories, Gay Theories,* ed. D. Fuss. New York: Routledge.

Chauncey, G. (1994), *Gay New York.* New York: Basic Books.

Crespi, L. (1995), Some thoughts on the role of mourning in the development of a positive lesbian identity. In: *Disorienting Sexuality: Psychoanalytic Reappraisals of Sexual Identities,* ed. T. Domenici & R. Lesser. New York: Routledge, pp. 19–32.

de Lauretis, T. (1994), *The Practice of Love: Lesbian Sexuality and Perverse Desire.* Bloomington: University of Indiana Press.

Domenici, T., & Lesser, R. (1995), Introduction. In: *Disorienting Sexuality: Psychoanalytic Reappraisals of Sexual Identities.* New York: Routledge.

Edelman, L. (1994), Queer theory: Unstating desire. *Gay and Lesbian Quarterly,* 2,4.

Flax, J. (1990), *Thinking Fragments: Psychoanalysis, Feminism and Postmodernism in the Contemporary West.* Berkeley: University of California Press.

Ginsberg, A. (1995), Spontaneous intelligence with Allen Ginsberg. *Tricycle: The Buddhist Review.*

Halperin, D. (1990), Sex before sexuality: Pederasty, politics, and power in classical Athens. In: *Hidden from History: Reclaiming the Gay and Lesbian Past,* ed. M. Duberman, M. Vicinus, & G. Chauncey. New York: Meridian.

————— (1993), Is there a history of sexuality? In: *The Lesbian and Gay Studies Reader,* ed. H. Abelove, M. Barale, & D. Halperin. New York: Routledge.

————— (1995), *Saint-Foucault: Toward a Gay Hagiography.* New York: Oxford University Press.

Harris, A. (1995), Foreword. In: *Disorienting Sexuality: Psychoanalytic Reappraisals of Sexual Identities,* ed. T. Domenici & R. Lesser. New York: Routledge.

Lesser, R. (1995), Objectivity as masquerade. In: *Disorienting Sexuality: Psychoanalytic Reappraisals of Sexual Identities*, ed. T. Domenici & R. Lesser. New York: Routledge.

Mitchell, J., & Rose, J. (1982), *Feminine Sexuality: Jacques Lacan and the Ecole Freudienne.* New York: W. W. Norton.

Morss, J. (1996), *Growing Critical: Alternatives to Developmental Psychology.* New York: Routledge.

Schoenberg, E. (1995), Psychoanalytic theories of lesbian desire: A social-constructionist critique. In: *Disorienting Sexuality: Psychoanalytic Reappraisals of Sexual Identities,* ed. T. Domenici & R. Lesser. New York: Routledge.

Schwartz, D. (1995), Current psychoanalytic discourses on sexuality: Tripping over the body. In: *Disorienting Sexuality: Psychoanalytic Reappraisals of Sexual Identities,* ed. T. Domenici & R. Lesser. New York: Routledge.

9

Revisioning the ''Fleshy Origins of Subjectivity'': De Lauretis and Grosz on Lesbian Desire

Erica Schoenberg

W e live in a time of vigorous intellectual upheaval in which old truths no longer make sense. The entire epistemological framework of intellectual life over the past hundred years is being interrogated and refigured. From assumptions and categories structuring our ideas about sex and gender to those with which we understand the very nature of our experience, our ways of knowing are up for grabs. This period may well be viewed retrospectively as one in which cherished epistemological paradigms sighed, shuddered, and died, exhausted and eviscerated by an inability to accommodate a mounting volume of increasingly incompatible ideas (Kuhn, 1996).

As private evaporates into public, depth reemerges as surface. In psychoanalysis, the forcible yanking into society of the personal, pristine unconscious replaces analysis of intrapsychic phenomena with consideration of intersubjective events. However they may reappear at some future date, claims to the presocial, the "natural," will never again assume the same naive shape they did before. Spawned by the technologies that surround us, the new epistemologies are startlingly and dramatically refiguring our entire view not only of "right" and "acceptable" ways to live, but even of possible ways. While at present we cannot imagine the choices that will be available to us, nor can we anticipate the modalities of understanding that will emerge from and give birth to these choices, we can be cognizant of some of the disruptive influences that are fomenting present unrest, those that will give form and shape to future frameworks of knowledge.

In this chapter I will consider the work of two theorists whose thought figures prominently in this disruption. Both Teresa de Lauretis and Elizabeth Grosz aim, albeit in quite different ways, to radically reconceive our views of subjectivity and desire. While the former seeks to revitalize established psychoanalytic discourse by resuscitating private life with the public breath that gives birth to it, the latter abandons psychoanalysis in favor of new analytic methodologies. The most cherished purpose for both, however, is to ensure the centrality of women's subjectivity—and, either implicitly or explicitly, lesbian subjectivity and desire—to these formulations.

The Practice of Love

> Identity at the level of the social may be oppressive, and identity at the level of the psychical may be fictional, but what about identity at the level of the political? One's identity as a feminist, for instance . . . Identities must be assumed, if only temporarily [Doane, 1989, p. 157].

In *The Practice of Love*, Teresa de Lauretis argues densely and meticulously for the "passionate fiction" of lesbian identity as the site of "actual" sexual differences between lesbians and heterosexuals. By this she means neither a psychic nor a social reality, but rather a "fantasmatic place and figuration in feminist theory: a place from where female homosexuality figures, for women, the possibility of subject and desire" (p.

156). It is this possibility of locating a place of subject and desire for women that causes de Lauretis to assert the paradox of identities that must be affirmed despite their being imaginary. In so doing, she positions herself solidly with those (e.g., Bersani, 1995) who believe that to deny a particularized gay subjectivity serves homophobic ends by erasing gay existence. And she positions herself vigorously against those (e.g., Sedgwick, 1990), who theorize a smooth, deeroticized continuum of female bondings, including mother-daughter, sisterhood, and other affiliative connections, of which lesbian bonds become only an example.

De Lauretis attempts to create this possibility of a specific erotics of lesbianism (and consequently of a place of female desire) by weaving together three threads of discourse: psychoanalytic views of lesbians, film criticism, and her own theory of lesbian subjectivity. She is devoted to Freud, attributing her allegiance both to the possibility his texts provide for women to be sexed and desiring agents (albeit only as either hysterics or deviants) and to her feeling that the Freudian canon speaks to her experience. I doubt, however, that Freud would have welcomed her into the fold of his followers after she spins his ideas through the revisions of Laplanche, Lacan, and the feminists, since her project here is, through the study of fantasy in lesbian sexual structuring and self representation, to provide a transition from the discourse of the couch to that of literature, criticism, and filmic texts, or from psychoanalysis to cultural analysis, from the first half of the century to the second, and from female homosexuality to lesbian subjectivity (p. 77).

Thus, while she retains conventional Freudian ideas like castration and perversion, they are elegantly and powerfully subverted. For example, de Lauretis maintains that Freud's theory of the perversions, as found in *The Three Essays* (1905), *is* his theory of sexuality. That is, noting Freud's belief that the existence of perversion "ends up by undermining and destroying the very notion of a biological norm" (de Lauretis, 1994, p. 12), she concludes that "normal" heterosexual and reproductive sexuality is not an actual state of being, but rather an approximation, a projection of historically constructed norms on our instinctual drives. Further, playing with Freud's description of neurosis as the negative of perversion, she infers that perversion is the positive. Thus, by unpacking the paradoxes in Freud's theory, she concludes that perversion and neurosis are the actual manifestations of sexuality. By stressing the "ambiguities, inconsistencies, and—in his own word—ambivalence" (p. 12) of Freud to his ideas about sexuality, she turns his phallocentric, reproductive, normative theory on its head and shakes free a perverse model of sexuality "as lived through fantasies and desire" (p. 26).

According to this reading, our fantasies and desires are products of culture rather than of intrapsychic or interpersonal conflict. Appropriating Deutsch's belief (1932) that it is the active consent of the analyst-mother that allows the patient to find sexual gratification, de Lauretis relocates the site of transforming dialogue from the private exchange of the consulting room to the public discourse of the cinema. It is film that produces the potential forms of identity and fantasy, defining "the conditions of the visible, what *can* be seen and represented" (p. 82). We cannot be or fantasize what we cannot imagine and we cannot imagine what is not available in the repertoire of social representations.

> [T]he figuration of the subject "caught up" in the sequence of images is an eminently cinematic trope; [and] the congruence between spectator and subject of fantasy, between film and fantasy, is no doubt one reason why [neo-]Freudian metapsychology has been so profoundly influential in the elaboration of the theory of spectatorship and of the cinematic apparatus . . . [p. 84].

Lesbian desire is created by being enunciated socially, specifically cinematically, by disrupting straight representational norms and constructing a space in which a specifically lesbian subject is presented to the spectator. For de Lauretis this involves a good deal more than merely substituting two women for a heterosexual couple in a standard romance. What lesbian films must do—and what in fact makes them lesbian films rather than heterosexually conceived representations of lesbian desire—is to theorize, articulate, and represent, "not only [lesbian] difference from heterosexual norms, its ab-normality, but also and more importantly . . . its own constitutive processes, its specific modalities and conditions of existence" (pp. 113–114). That is, if as Foucault (1980) argued, sexuality is produced, rather than repressed by society, then the creation of the lesbian subject on the screen, which publicly enunciates her in her specificity and difference, makes possible the conditions for fantasy and desire for the viewer. It is our spectatorship, our viewing of films, that makes available the structuration of the sets upon which our fantasies will be staged.

> How do I see—what are the modes, constraints and possibilities of my seeing, the terms of vision for me? How am I seen—what are

the ways in which I'm seen or can be seen, the conditions of my visibility? And more—how do I look *on*, as the film unrolls from reel to reel in the projector, as the images appear and the story unfolds up on the screen, as the fantasy scenario unveils and the soundtrack plays on in my head. For the question is, To see or not to see, to be seen [and how] or not to be seen [at all?]: subjective vision and social visibility, being and passing, representation and spectatorship—the conditions of the visible, what can be *seen* and eroticized, and on what *scene* [p. 85].

Thus, as conservatives fear, the more visible lesbians become, the greater the likelihood that a girl will become one.

De Lauretis explores the ways in which the specific modalities and conditions of lesbian existence are created by examining what she considers to be lesbian texts such as Sheila McLaughlin's (1987) film, *She Must Be Seeing Things*. According to de Lauretis, this film depicts a "primal" fantasy, the fantasy of lesbian origins that is simultaneously the lesbian fantasy of origins. It does this by taking on and disrupting the "ever-flaunted" (p. 103) assumption that sexual difference, represented by feminine and masculine gender positions, is the necessary condition of desire. In this girl-gets-girl film, McLaughlin creates a space for lesbian desire by scripting it as butch-femme, a mimicry of straight love that exposes our heterosexual iconography of desire as a masquerade of "penis related posturings, not a biological birthright" (p. 108). Thus, it is in butch-femme that de Lauretis locates the terms and signifiers of uniquely lesbian desire.

Psychoanalytic and feminist texts have undermined the power of such a uniquely lesbian iconography to disrupt conventional assumptions and to powerfully represent lesbian subjectivity, by interpreting it in one of two ways. The first, justified in part by butch, represents girls who want girls as thwarted men—or masculine women thwarted by men—envying or identifying with masculine desire. The second theorizes lesbians on the continuum of women, all of whom share a ubiquitous, nostalgic fantasy of remerger with the mother and her body as the "fleshy origins of subjectivity" (p. 164). While the first obliterates the very uniqueness of lesbian desire by heterosexualizing it, the second deeroticizes it, homophobically reducing it to an ambiguous "homomaternal" factor latent in all women. In both cases lesbians disappear, as the specific differences in subjectivity and desire which distinguish them from heterosexuals are erased.

De Lauretis, in contrast, seeks a theory of lesbian desire which inscribes its specificity and difference. She argues that while it may be true that all relations between women go back in some way to early relations with the mother, "surely they 'return' in different ways and, what is more, they 'return' to different mothers" (p. 195); these are differences which include race, class, and ethnicity. For lesbians, she maintains, there is a further difference. Theorists like Kristeva (1987) and Chodorow (1989) (from their heterosexual perspective) track female sexual difference as an identification with the maternal, the displacement of the unfulfillable nostalgia for fusion with the mother onto the fulfillable desire to be the mother. In lesbian texts, in contrast, while it is true that a "fantasmatic relation to the mother and the maternal/female body is central to . . . subjectivity and desire" (p. 171), de Lauretis believes that the main marker is maternal absence rather than unity. It is this absence or loss that marks lesbian desire. As the straight woman identifies with "the maternal phantasm as a memory of mother/daughter unity" (p. 200), and becomes a mother, the lesbian identifies with maternal loss, resulting in a loss of her own body image.

Continuing her gloss of Freud, de Lauretis represents this loss as castration, a term which she feels must be maintained in order to adequately represent desire.

> If the term *castration* designates the paternal [patriarchal] prohibition of access to the mother's . . . body, with its fantasy of unity and plenitude, and if the term *phallus* designates the sign that signifies the subject's desire to recapture that plenitude through [hetero]sexual union, then that notion of castration and some notion of *phallus*—some notion of signifier of desire—are necessary to understand the processes of subjectivity [p. 231].

What lesbians desire, and what their castration signifies, then, is not the lost maternal penis, but the lost female body "or something metonymically related to it, such as physical, intellectual or emotional attributes, stance, attitude, appearance, self-presentation. . . . [H]ence the importance of clothing, costume, performance, etc., in lesbian subcultures" (p. 228). Because they symbolize both the absence of and the wish for the object of desire, these function as fetishes, "fantasy-phallus(es)" (p. 224). However, it is precisely because such fetishes simultaneously represent loss and "disavow" castration in the heterosexual sense of a psychic relationship to the penis and the paternal phallus, that they mark the specificity of lesbian subjectivity. De Lauretis's choice of the term *fetish* rather than, for example, Butler's *lesbian Phallus,* is intended to avoid complicity with the penis while representing "the sign or signifier of prohibition, difference and desire, without which the lesbian lovers would be simply . . . two women in the same bed" (p. 232).

The frequent association of lesbian fetishes with masculinity (e.g., Steven in Radclyffe Hall's [1928] *The Well of Loneliness*) are therefore appropriations not of a missing penis, but of the most strongly culturally precoded symbols of sexual yearning and activity toward women and their bodies. Such signs deny the subject's female body while simultaneously signifying her desire for it. Similarly, femme represents the lost and desired female body via the reverse discourse of "quintessential, empowered, absolute femininity" (p. 264). The fetishistic scenario of butch-femme restages the subject's loss and recovery of her own libidinally lost body image through the narcissistic and libidinal reinvestment in the female body of the other woman. This then, is de Lauretis's theory of lesbian subjectivity as represented in our practices of love. Clearly she intends her text to be part of the representational project of inscription which consents to lesbian desire by defining these specific modalities and conditions of its existence.

This is a difficult and challenging book, the flavor of which has been conveyed, I trust, by my frequent use of quotes. While the language is daunting, de Lauretis raises several issues of importance on the contemporary theoretical scene. For one, in contrast to our conventional intrapsychic and interpersonal psychoanalytic and developmental psychologies, which theorize identity formation as a highly individualized process, de Lauretis replaces us in our society. From this Foucauldian point of view, the lesbian subject is a social production, emerging from the interplay of her own specific life experiences and circumstances with her participation in and identification with available public discourses. This radical shift has the potential to profoundly subvert all of our psychoanalytic assumptions, not just those about sex.

While I find this quite refreshing, there are other ways in which I find de Lauretis's argument rather problematic. Although I appreciate the considerations that led her to assert the "passionate fiction" of lesbian identity, I am not sure whether more is not lost than gained by it. Certainly, I do not advocate doing for the homophobes of the world what they themselves cannot accomplish, by erasing ourselves from view.

However, in what way can we assert the existence of lesbian identity without doing violence to those very persons whose safety we are trying to secure? Can we honestly maintain that lesbians form any sort of coherent group more similar to itself than to others? How can our economic, social, religious, racial, educational, and ethnic differences be so homogenized? How can the variety of ways in which we experience desire for other women be so leveled? What about lesbians who can't relate to butch-femme?

Further, while I also recognize her intention to profoundly subvert it, I seriously question de Lauretis's desire to retain the most patriarchal and homophobic aspects of Freudian theory. I believe that terms like *castration* and *perversion* should be retired from active duty. They can never be sufficiently rehabilitated from their oppressive connotations to be useful.

While de Lauretis intends her theory of lesbian subjectivity to subvert our assumptions and liberate us from the straightjacket of our normalizing beliefs, she ends up with a theory that is virtually indistinguishable from the most homophobic and oppressive theories in the psychoanalytic literature. Thus, for example, Elaine Siegel's (1988) theory, or perhaps better put, her prejudice masquerading as theory, posits the lesbian to be a woman who lacks an internal representation of her vagina, and whose involvement with other women represents her search for it in the other. (Of course Siegel does not explain why a little lost lesbian might not just as well look to heterosexual intercourse to find her vagina.) While de Lauretis is an immeasurably more complex thinker than Siegel, she too bases lesbian desire on our lack of a personal body-ego image. I recognize that for de Lauretis, absence is not damning, but rather is closer to the "real." However, in most people's minds, to locate our desire in deprivation while that of heterosexual women is situated in plentitude and abundance, again associates us with deficit. Nor can we be sorted and distinguished on the basis of our relations with our mothers; some women of all sexual persuasions have close or loving or enmeshed relations with their mothers while others of all persuasions hate or are distant or alienated from them. Furthermore, like those heterosexual women who ostensibly identify with the maternal, many lesbians want babies.

Finally, de Lauretis feels that there is, as yet, no resolution to the question of whether there is a "normal, inherited sexual instinct which pre-exists its possible deviations or whether instinctual life is but a set of transformations, some of which are then defined as normal" (p. 221).

I suggest that there will never be an objectively verifiable answer to that question. Rather, there will be a changing array of theoretical discourses that consider the problem from alternative points of view informed by different values and power relations. By posing the question as though it can be answered, de Lauretis positions herself within a positivist scientific model of thought that blurs the constructed aspect of our realities. I believe that a more useful approach would recognize both the need to consider the possibility of lesbian subjectivities and the positivist trap of passionate fictions that become confused with realities.

Volatile Bodies

Can it be that in the West, in our time, the female body has been constructed not only as a lack or absence, but with more complexity as a leaking, uncontrollable, seeping liquid; as formless flow; as viscosity, entrapping, secreting; as lacking not so much or simply the phallus but self-containment—not a cracked or porous vessel, like a leaking ship, but a formlessness that engulfs all form, a disorder that threatens all order? . . . The metaphorics of uncontrollability, the ambivalence between desperate, fatal attraction and strong revulsion, the deep-seated fear of absorption, the association of femininity with contagion and disorder, the undecidability of the limits of the female body . . . are all common themes in literary and cultural representations of women. But these may well be a function of the projection outward of their corporealities, the liquidities that men seem to want to cast out of their own self-representations [Grosz, 1994b, p. 203].

Elizabeth Grosz approaches the question of lesbian subjectivity from a radically different angle. Unlike de Lauretis—or Butler (1990) or Fuss (1995), for that matter—Grosz does not seek to revitalize Freud by reconceiving psychoanalytic concepts from a lesbian–feminist vantage point. Rather, she maintains that foundational tenets of the theory preclude its viability for the radical articulation of women's desire. These tenets involve two profoundly interrelated ideas: first, the implicit presumption in psychoanalysis of a masculine or neutral—read masculine here too—subject; and second, that the epistemology is based on lack and depth (1994a). Since many readers may be familiar with critiques of the masculinist bias in psychoanalysis (e.g., O'Connor and Ryan, 1993), I would like to briefly lay out the critique of lack or depth as the basis of desire. Grosz traces the foundational assumptions on which psychoanalytic views of desire are based back to Plato's concept of desire as lack, flaw, or imperfection. In the Freudian version, desire is the endless chain of substitution that creates a series of equivalent objects to fill a primordial lack.

> In seeking to replace an (impossible) plentitude, a lost completion originating (at least in fantasy) in the early mother/child dyad, desire will create a realm of objects that can be substituted for the primal (lost, forbidden) object. Desire's endless chain is an effect of an oedipalizing process that requires that the child relinquishes its incestual attachments through creating an endless network of replacements, substitutes and representations of the perpetually absent object [1994a, p. 71].

Profound problems are inherent in this conceptualization, Grosz maintains. One is the resonance of the notion of desire as absence or lack with capitalist ideology; when desire is "an abyss seeking to be engulfed, stuffed to satisfaction" (p. 71), the object of desire becomes yet another consumable commodity. Further, the metaphorics of this model inherently code desire as negative and insatiable, thus likening it to female sexuality. The resulting implication is that it is the masculine–feminine opposition and complementarity that fulfills the lack for both sexes. Thus, desire assumes a heterosexuality that "performs an act of violence" (p. 72) by precluding any possibility of female autonomy.

Having rejected psychoanalysis as a sufficiently recuperable basis from which to work, Grosz is free to engage an entirely different framework through which to approach the question of lesbian subjectivity. While like de Lauretis, Grosz seeks to integrate our psyches into their social worlds, Grosz locates society in our corporeal experience of the socially lived body. Her efforts to nondualistically imbricate psyche and soma in female experience puts quite a different spin on bodies, psyches, and subjectivities. Personally, I found the mix intriguing and surprising, albeit ultimately problematic and unsuccessful. Let us take a closer look.

Grosz turns for parentage to such philosophers as Spinoza (1986) and Merleau-Ponty, thinkers who did not privilege mind over body. For Merleau-Ponty, she states:

[C]onsciousness . . . is (always) incarnated; mind . . . is always embodied, always based on corporeal and sensory relations. . . . [T]he body is not an object. It is the condition and context through which I am able to have a relation to objects. . . . Insofar as I live the body, it is a phenomenon experienced by me and thus provides the very horizon and perspectival point which places me in the world and makes relations between me, other objects, and other subjects possible [p. 86].

In order to clarify and explore this idea of the interpenetration of biology and psychology in socially lived bodies, Grosz offers the example of body image. While body image is, on the one hand, the psychic representation of the lived experience of body, it is simultaneously the set of ideas and attitudes inscribed upon body that mediate its lived experience. Many women, for example, physically experience their bodies as too fat, regardless of the fact that a relatively objective outside observer might see them as average or even thin. Women's thinking, in this case clearly gender coded, affects their actual experience of their bodies, while their experience of their bodies, equally gender coded, affects their thinking. A parodic TV ad highlights this gendered aspect of our corporeal experience by showing men worrying about whether they look too fat in the outfit they're wearing and complaining about having thighs like their mothers. The perplexed, off-balance feeling one gets watching this ad highlights the socially mediated nature of the lived body and the impossibility of viewing it as a ''natural,'' presocial given.

Or consider the phantom limb experience. After the removal of functional extremities, close to 100 percent of patients (except for those who are mentally retarded or very young) continue to experience the amputated limb. This conscious, postsurgery experience is true not only of limbs, but has been noted in almost every part of the body, including eyes, breasts, larynxes, penises—which may experience phantom erections and phantom orgasms—and even internal organs such as appendixes. The experience of the phantom changes dramatically with the period of postsurgery time. The closer in time to the amputation, the more realistic the perceived appearance of the limb and the more painful the sensations emanating from it. This experience obviously has both physical and psychological components. Both the mind and the body memorialize the missing limb, striving to maintain meaning and continuity in the face of the current disruption.

Interestingly, hysterectomies are not usually followed by a phantom experience. Grosz hypothesizes that this may be because women's internal and sexual organs such as the cervix and the vagina are already paradoxically coded as missing. What might this tell us about differences in the ways that women experience their bodies compared to men? In addition to mourning the lost freedom, devalued status, and other social meanings of fantasy castration, do women code themselves as castrated, either psychically or physically? Do some then represent the lost phallus psychically?

These examples introduce Grosz's argument that the body is a "threshold concept that hovers perilously and undecidably at the pivotal point of binary pairs" (1994b, p. 23). Body and psyche are not independent entities, nor even mutually interacting entities, but rather continuous aspects of nature and culture, inside and outside. Since biology's psychological meaning is pliable, not fixed, bodies are indeterminate. They must therefore be understood historically, rather than concretely.

> [T]here is no body as such: there are only *bodies*—male or female, black, white, large or small—and all gradations in between. Bodies can be represented or understood not as entities in themselves or simply on a linear continuum with its polar extremes occupied by male and female bodies (with various gradations of "intersexed" individuals in between) but as a field, a two-dimensional continuum in which race (and possibly even class, caste, or religion) form body specifications [1994b, p. 19].

This field is not characterized by independent vectors intersecting at the point of the body, but rather by the mutual constitution of characteristics. If bodies are tied to mind and if bodies themselves are always sexually and racially distinct, then forms of subjectivity are specific and nongeneralizable as well, as are forms of knowledge. Since the body is the disavowed condition of knowledge, then all forms of knowledge must be reconceptualized so that the effects of specific corporealities are acknowledged. Such reconceptualization is required of knowledge of the body as much as any other area of knowledge.

> [T]he body is (not) in any sense natural or raw i.e., non- or presocial. Nor, on the contrary, can the body itself be regarded as *purely* a

social, cultural, and signifying effect lacking its own weighty materiality. . . . Instead, the interimplication of the natural and the social or cultural needs further investigation—the hole in nature that allows cultural seepage or production must provide something like a natural condition for cultural production; but in turn the cultural too must be seen in its limitations, as a kind of insufficiency that requires natural supplementation. Culture itself can only have meaning and value in terms of its own other(s): where its others are obliterated—as tends to occur within the problematic of social constructionism—culture in effect takes on all the immutable, fixed characteristics attributed to the natural order [p. 21].

Grosz tries to capture this interimplication with the metaphor of the Mobius strip, the inverted three-dimensional figure eight used by Lacan as an image for the body in which inside melts into outside and outside twists into inside without any break. The tracings of pedagogical, juridical, and economic texts which inscribe the "outside" surface of the body, carve out a decipherable social subject, capable of labor, while biological functioning, "using libido as its marker pen" (1994b, p. 117) marks the "interior" surfaces of the body. While restrictions on this intertextuation of bodies are set from both directions, that is, the materiality of the body on the one hand and the limits of representation on the other, ultimately body is psyche as well as culture, and culture is body as well as and psyche. They are continuous, indissociable transformations of each other and our experience of their integrity is artifactual. Furthermore, since it is the "outside" surface of the body which is the point of inscription, our experience of deep, essentially private, internal intrapsychic space is also artifactual.

In lieu of psychical mechanisms such as internalization being the means through which the social enters the subject's interior, in this corporeal model social values are etched upon the subject's body.

Whereas in earlier models desire, through its constitutive lack, induces the subject from within to accept the mediation of social regulations in its attempts to gain gratification, . . . whereas, in other words, there is something already inside the subject (need, desire) that impels it toward others and, through others, to the social, in the inscriptive model it is the social exterior, or at least its particular modes of inscription, that commands or induces certain kinds of behavior and practices. Punishment[s], . . . (like) socialization, . . . are forms of codification of the social onto the corporeal. . . .

[From this surface perspective we are best undersood as]: a series of surfaces, energies, and forces, a mode of linkage, a discontinuous series of processes, organs, flows and matter. The body does not hide or reveal an otherwise unrepresented latency or depth, but is a set of operational linkages and connections with other things, other bodies. The body is not simply a sign to be read, a symptom to be deciphered, but also a force to be reckoned with. The energetics, or rather the politics, of signification must here be recognized [p. 120].

Here Grosz is influenced by the work of Deleuze and Guattari (1983), who conceive of organisms as assemblages, nontotalized, machinelike groupings of heterogeneous elements and forces. The body is not an integrated, organic totality, capable of a "welling up of the subject's emotions, attitudes, beliefs or experiences, [but rather a grouping of] organs, processes, pleasures, passions, activities, behaviors linked by fine lines and unpredictable networks to other elements, segments and assemblages" (1994b, p. 120). In the tradition of Spinoza, the body is not conceived as an organically determined site of consciousness, but rather in terms of what it can do or perform, the linkages it establishes, the transformations and becomings it undergoes. Analysis of such a body consists of mapping the segments, their relations, their flows and intensities, speeds, and durations. It is concerned with the functioning or performance of the linkages within and between parts, with the proliferation of capacities, rather than with defining putative underlying "competence."

This formulation provides fertile ground for feminists because it sidesteps the inherent heterosexism of psychoanalysis and other theories that ground desire in lack and absence. Instead, this model codes desire as what produces or connects, as an affirmative, creative force.

Instead of aligning desire with fantasy and opposing it to the real, instead of seeing it as a yearning, desire is an actualization, a series of practices, bringing things together or separating them, making machines, making reality. Desire does not take for itself a particular object whose attainment it requires; rather, it aims at nothing above its own proliferation or self-expansion. It assembles things out of singularities and breaks things, assemblages, down into their singularities. It moves; it does. . . . But the surpassing of the model of lack does not, should not, return us to the affirmation of pure plenitude or presence. Presence and absence are coupled in and to the same framework. In place of plenitude, being, fullness or self-identity is not lack, absence, rupture, but rather becoming [p. 165].

For Grosz, herein lies the potential for a liberatory figuration of female subjectivity. Free from preconceptions of hierarchy, a machinic model stresses endless experimentation, transformation, and reassemblage. And free from notions of teleology, it envisions a desiring subject, or rather, a "desiring machine" (p. 168), which is fundamentally "nomadic . . . meandering, creative, non-repetitive, proliferative, unpredictable" (p. 168). The possibilities for nonlimiting, nonpatriarchal theory are rich.

Grosz demonstrates this by exploring, in the final section of the book, what a model of sexed bodies might look like.

[B]iology cannot be regarded as a form whose contents are historically provided, nor as a base on which cultural constructs are founded, nor indeed as a container for a mixture of culturally or individually specific ingredients. It is an open materiality, a set of (possibly infinite) tendencies and potentialities which may be developed, yet whose development will necessarily hinder or induce other developments and other trajectories. These are not individually or consciously chosen, nor are they amenable to will or intentionality; they are more like bodily styles, habits, practices, whose logic entails that one preference, one modality excludes or makes difficult other possibilities [p. 191].

Our styles of representing male and female physiologies illustrate these ideas. Although they can certainly be represented in a great variety of ways, highlighting different body parts or processes, women's bodies and their bodily fluids have been coded as polluting and contaminating. They are constructed not only as lack or absence of the phallus, but also as lacking self-containment, as leaking, uncontrollable seeping liquid, "a disorder that threatens all order" (p. 203).

Male bodies and their fluids, in contrast, have been characterized very differently. Based on a consideration of come shots in porno movies,

Grosz asserts that rather than representing seepage, semen is constructed primarily in terms of what it makes or achieves, as a causal agent, a thing, a solid. While she has much to say about these constructions, one idea Grosz presents is that a woman-centered subjectivity might be rooted in a metaphysics of flow and fluidity. "Fluids surge and move, and a metaphysic that thinks being as fluid would tend to privilege the living, moving, pulsing over the inert dead matter of the Cartesian world view. . . ." (Young, cited in Grosz, 1994b, p. 204).

Once concreteness is granted to the various embodiments of alterity, for example, race, sex, sexualities, ethnic and cultural specificities, we may identify the ways in which particular alterity conditions inform, as well as are a product of, the plasticity of bodies. This concreteness removes these groups from their current positioning as other, with all the negativity and lack that designation holds, and offers the opportunity for multiplicity and difference that current models prohibit. It is this project to which *Volatile Bodies* is devoted.

As one who was unfamiliar with the writings of Deleuze and Guattari prior to reading Grosz, I found these ideas quite fascinating. Although her conceptual framework is so different from that of psychoanalysis that I can't fully grasp its implications for therapeutic practice, I marveled at what a world might look like refashioned from such a new vantage point. Clinical thinking in the field has already been profoundly altered by some of these ideas. For instance, as I mentioned at the outset, our current intersubjective approach entails attention to surface over depth, two-person present over intrapsychic past. Part of this refocusing involves a dramatic refashioning of our concept of the unconscious, from a psyche that endlessly and inevitably repeats its conflicts regardless of the behavior of the analyst, to one that interacts with the real behavior of a real analyst, albeit at times with a selectivity based on past experience.

This model, in which patient-analyst encounters represent different currents of interaction on the part of both participants, echoes Grosz's idea of mutually interacting assemblages. I am very taken with the possibility in her formulation of tracking fluidity and multiplicity in ourselves and in our patients. Most of us are well aware that we are more attuned on certain days than on others as well as responsive in different ways to different types of material, from open and creatively present, to stuck, rigid, and blind. It might be useful to describe certain therapeutic impasses as moments in which both our own interactive patterns and those of our patients become stereotyped, embedded in our respective pasts, while our most creative moments are those in which dead, inert, stylized contacts take on new life, allowing fresh reassembly.

Further, I believe that Grosz's use of the Mobius strip metaphor is a provocative and useful one. Although psychoanalysis has long assumed that clear boundaries are possible, in our current cultural milieu inside/outside, private/public resist clear delineation. Psychoanalytic theorizing itself has been taught as though most of Freud's ideas (except for a few which were attributed to his Victorian setting) were the product of a brilliant and visionary mind thinking in a vacuum. Only recently have we recognized the inseparability of our work from the social context in which we live and the inevitable overlap of political beliefs and theory, power, and knowledge.

In addition, recognizing the continuity of psychoanalysis and politics may provide a necessary—although certainly not a sufficient—condition for the survival of our field. If we do not more fully consider the sociopolitical implications of our normalizing ideas, we will surely wither and die. A particular interest of mine is the erasure of race from psychoanalytic discourse (Schoenberg, 1999). Grosz's emphasis on the diversity of socially lived bodies and the consequent need for multiple systems of knowledge which take into account multiple racially, ethnically, and class specific experiences of life, offers us the opportunity to broaden our theorizing to accommodate a variety of voices heretofore silenced.

Although I found her (1994b) book stimulating, it seems to me that ultimately, despite Grosz's best efforts, body does become reduced to psychic meaning. I don't believe that my personal corporeal experience can accurately be described as uncontainable flow. Even menstruation, certainly a significant event for many if not most women, is not a singular experience. For example, one woman I know felt she was killing a baby every time she menstruated. Certainly many of us have quite different associations to this event. Where she saw death, others see a life-affirming opportunity for joy and still others see nothing more than an inconvenient occasion for discomfort. It is the meaning attributed to the corporeal experience rather than the physical experience itself that determines its place. I suppose that all women who have menstruated have something in common that distinguishes their experience from that of men. Certainly the fear of pregnancy for menstruating women who have sex with men may have commonality for many in a way quite different from the experience of the men they have sex with. Yet even that situation is quite variable.

Similarly, a patient of mine scheduled to undergo a mastectomy following her diagnosis with breast cancer was comforted sympathetically by a neighbor with the comment that this surgery was every woman's worst nightmare. My patient was quite surprised by this comment, since she herself was more concerned with the possibility of hair loss should chemotherapy be required. Although both women were middle-class and white, their relationship to their breasts as aspects of their sexuality differed markedly. Thus, it appears that precedence should be accorded to the meaning attributed to the corporeal qualities rather than to the qualities themselves. Of course, this may merely represent the prejudiced view of one who lives more in her head than in her body. If so, my disagreement would actually support Grosz's contention that knowledge is corporeally specific.

Grosz's view of desire as creative and self-affirming, as actualization, opens a new window on the topic of female subjectivity. What would our work look like stripped of its teleological premises?

> [How would we think if we believed that] the subject's psychical interior, or "soul," [is] nothing more than the self-inversion of the body's forces . . . [if] consciousness, soul, or subjectivity is nothing but the play of the body's forces that, with the help of metaphysics, has been congealed into a unity and endowed as an origin . . . [if] the body's forces, instincts, are not simply part of nature or essence . . . [but] entirely plastic, fluid, capable of taking any direction and any kind of becoming [p. 124].

Although she engages the question of whether bodies may be innately sexed, separate from culture, the body can never be fully understood separate from culture. However, our efforts to examine and interrogate both culture and the body as fully as possible has transformed, and will continue to transform our theory and practice. Despite differences in their visions of "the fleshy origins of subjectivity" (de Lauretis, 1994, p. 164), both de Lauretis and Grosz offer challenging and provocative avenues for us to explore. Interestingly, de Lauretis edits the series in which Grosz's book appeared. I await with pleasure the surprising, unexpected offspring of such cross-fertilization.

References

Bersani, L. (1995), *Homos.* Cambridge, MA: Harvard University Press.

Butler, J. (1990), *Gender Trouble.* New York: Routledge

Chodorow, N. (1989), *Feminism and Psychoanalysis.* New Haven, CT: Yale University Press.

de Lauretis, T. (1994), *The Practice of Love: Lesbian Sexuality and Perverse Desire.* Bloomington: Indiana University Press.

Deleuze, G., & Guattari, F. (1983), *Anti-Oedipus: Capitalism and Schizophrenia,* tr. R. Hurley, M. Seem, & H. R. Lane. Minneapolis: University of Minnesota Press.

Deutsch, H. (1932), On female homosexuality, tr. E. Jackson. *Psychoanal. Quart.,* 1:484–510.

Doane, M. A. (1989), Commentary: Post-utopian difference. In: *Coming to Terms: Feminism, Theory, Politics,* ed. E. Weed. New York: Routledge, pp. 70–78.

Foucault, M. (1980), *The History of Sexuality,* Vol. 1, tr. R. Hurley. New York: Random House.

Freud, S. (1905), Three Essays on the Theory of Sexuality. *Standard Edition,* 7:123–243. London: Hogarth Press, 1953.

Fuss, D. (1995), *Identification Papers.* New York: Routledge.

Grosz, E. (1994a), Refiguring lesbian desire. In: *The Lesbian Postmodern,* ed. L. Doan. New York: Columbia University Press, pp. 67–84.

——— (1994b), *Volatile Bodies: Toward a Corporeal Feminism.* Bloomington: Indiana University Press.

Hall, R. (1928), *The Well of Loneliness.* New York: Avalon Books, 1981.

Kristeva, J. (1987), *Tales of Love,* tr. L. S. Roudiez. New York: Columbia University Press.

Kuhn, T. (1996), *The Structure of Scientific Revolutions.* Chicago: University of Chicago Press.

Lacan, J. (1977), *Ecrits. A Collection,* trans. A. Sheridan. New York: W. W. Norton.

McLaughlin, S. (1987), Director. *She Must Be Seeing Things.* [film]

Merleau-Ponty, M. (1963), *The Primacy of Perception.* Evanston, IL: Northwestern University Press.

O'Connor, N., & Ryan, J. (1993), *Wild Desires and Mistaken Identities: Lesbianism and Psychoanalysis.* New York: Columbia University Press.

Schoenberg, E. (1999), Writing sex, erasing race: Rereading Freud's lesbian dream. In: *That Obscure Subject of Desire: Freud's Female Homosexual Revisited,* ed. R. Lesser & E. Schoenberg. New York: Routledge, pp. 215–230.

Sedgwick, E. (1990), *The Epistemology of the Closet.* Berkeley: University of California Press.

Siegel, E. (1988), *Female Homosexuality: Choice Without Volition.* Hillsdale, NJ: Analytic Press.

Spinoza, B. (1986), *The Ethics and On the Correction of the Understanding,* tr. A. Boyle. London: Dent.

Young, I. M. (1990), *Throwing Like a Girl and Other Essays in Feminist Philosophy and Social Theory.*Bloomington: Indiana University Press.

10

Straight Talk from Heinz Kohut: The De-Erotization of the Homosexual Subject

Virginia L. Blum

C ertainly self psychologists do not profess to cure homosexuality. Nevertheless, they have a propensity for "curing" not only male homosexual impulses but male homosexual identities. One might ask how they accomplish such "cures" in the face of both the DSM-III-R's (APA, 1986) elimination of homosexuality as a curable "perversion" and a political climate that would hardly favor such an agenda. (Nevertheless, when introducing the case history of a homosexual patient, Kohut prefaces it as one of "two frequently occurring instances of self pathology in men" [1977, p. 194].) Unlike many analysts who have been unabashedly committed to treating homosexuality as mental illness, self psychologists tend to closet the perceived relationship between homosexuality and disorders of the self.

Several years ago, a case history of a young man who entered analysis living an overtly homosexual identity was presented by a Kohutian analyst to a group of mental health professionals. Two years into the analysis, this man was cured of what the analyst described as his mirroring disorder of the self and, incidentally, "cured" of his homosexuality as well. The patient is now married with children. There was no attempt at a cure as such for his sexual "deviance." Rather, the analyst suggested that the homosexual behavior was merely a sexualization of nonsexual "disturbances of the self." I was reminded on this occasion of one of Heinz Kohut's case histories in which he offers the following in reference to the homosexual impulses of Mr. A: "Although he entered analysis with the complaint that he felt sexually stimulated by men, it soon became apparent that his homosexual preoccupations constituted only one of the several indications of an underlying broad personality defect" (1968, p. 90). Thus, lived homosexualities or homosexual fantasies are not to be taken either at face value or as a legitimate life choice. (What is most curious about this refusal to take literally the presented homosexual thoughts is its contrast to the standard Kohutian analytic methodology regarding dreams, which are almost always interpreted in terms of their manifest content.) If the *Diagnostic and Statistical Manual*, under duress, (Isay, 1985, p. 239; Greenberg, 1988, pp. 429–430), has dropped the category of homosexuality as mental illness, self psychology has reconfigured it as a corollary to a disorder of the self, one of the most common manifestations of a narcissistic personality disturbance.

Because the work of Heinz Kohut has gained increasing popularity among both psychoanalysts and psychotherapists, particularly his theorization of the role and effects of empathy ("vicarious introspection") in the analytic relationship, it is critical to explore the implications of his theories and their sequelae. Kohut is regarded by his followers as a revolutionary of sorts, and I will show, through the following discussion, that his work may well be the most repressively conservative trend to date in psychoanalysis—a trend that is profoundly antipsychoanalytic in its ultimate goal of curing the human subject of sexual desire.

The Defective Homosexual

Curing homosexuality is nothing new for psychoanalysts—nor are their putative "success stories." Nevertheless, as Richard Isay (1985) points out, often the patient is motivated to conform to social imperatives that the analyst is only too glad to uphold. Drawing on his experience with a highly conflicted patient, Richard Isay illustrates why patients enter analysis in the hope of changing their sexual orientation: "It became clear after several weeks . . . that A's wish to please his ambivalently viewed mother and his introjection of hostile social values inimical to his sexual feelings were motivating his request for change. It also became clear that these factors had produced a ready transference to which his previous therapist had responded, not by an attempt to understand the conflicts underlying the wish, but by complying with it" (1985, p. 242). For the distressed homosexual patient, the analyst offers the possibility of relief from familial and social ostracism. Indeed, the analyst stands for (transferentially) social norms. The danger is that the analyst's own countertransference (needing to impose her or his own heterosexual imperatives on the patient) might collude with the patient's defenses. As I show below, both the patient's idealization of the analyst as purveyor of normative values as well as the therapist's need to impress his or her own image on the patient, are at the root of self psychology's purported "cures."

While Kohut (1984) accused Freud and Melanie Klein of subscribing to, calcifying, and reproducing sexual norms, he claimed that he on the contrary was remarkably open to sexual diversity: "Although the attainment of genitality and the capacity for unambivalent object love have been features of many, perhaps most, satisfying and significant lives, there are many other good lives, including some of the greatest and most fulfilling lives recorded in history, that were not lived by individuals whose psychosexual organization was heterosexual-genital or whose major commitment was to unambivalent object-love" (p. 7). Although Kohut wrote this statement in 1982, it is important specifically that it was published in 1984, because American psychiatry was by then pretending to reject active attempts to cure perceived sexual deviance (Kohut was already dead by 1984). Thus, in offering such a disclaimer, Kohut positioned himself as a member of a contemporary "open" sexual–political community in contrast to those outmoded sexual conservatives, Freud and Klein.

Nevertheless, compared to what I will show is Kohut's deep-seated horror of the divisive effect of the drives on the imagined potential cohesiveness of the human subject, Freud and Klein were hardly normative. Although many of Freud's successors have actively sought to cure homosexual orientations, Freud himself held that such a cure was unlikely if not impossible. Indeed, Freud's letter to an American mother sounds remarkably similar to Kohut's disclaimer quoted above: "Homosexuality is assuredly no advantage, but it is nothing to be ashamed of, no vice, no degradation; it cannot be classified as an illness. . . . Many highly respectable individuals of ancient and modern times have been homosexuals, several of the greatest men among them" (1975, p. 423). Yet Kohut goes so far as to represent himself as the sexual liberal vis-a-vis these conservative precursors. For strategic reasons, he needs Freud and Klein to stand for sexual "straight"-jacketing, in part to sell his program as new and revolutionary, in part to deflect attention from his own normative agenda.

While Freud's analysands tended to accuse him of finding sexual themes in the superficially most innocent of parapraxes, dreams, and fantasies, the analysands of Kohut and his followers can escape their analytic sessions with all of their defenses intact. They are comforted by the knowledge that their worrisome sexual preoccupations are no more than sexualized symptoms of really rather tame psychical materials such as an understimulated self ensuing from distant and unempathic parental selfobjects. Indeed, in the face of the suggestion that sexual preoccupations are no longer in need of repression in our more "liberated" postmodernist society, we need only point to self psychology as the defense par excellence to illustrate that sexual shame is alive and well. In *The Restoration of the Self,* Kohut (1977) explains that:

[In Freud's late Victorian society] where children were formerly overstimulated by the emotional (including the erotic) life of their parents, they are now often understimulated . . . it is clear that children often undertake both solitary sexual activities and group activities of a sexual, near-sexual, or sexualized nature in the attempt to relieve the lethargy and depression resulting from the unavailability of a mirroring and of an idealizable self-object. These activities are the forerunners of the frantic sexual activities of some depressed adolescents and of adult perversions [pp. 271–272].

It is the narcissistic personality disorders that for Kohut constitute the large part of contemporary mental illness. Whereas an emphasis on oedipal-level issues might have been useful for Freud's overstimulated analysands, today's understimulated analytic subjects tend to be produced by emotionally desiccated caretakers. Kohut employs a deficit model of the human subject in contradistinction to the Freudian conflict model. Hence, where a Freudian treats neurosis as the result of conflict among psychical agencies, for example, an overbearing superego, Kohut's deficit model posits a profound structural lack; what the caretaker did not give her or his child is simply *not there*. As he writes: ''psychoanalysis cures by the laying down of psychological structure'' (1984, p. 98). It is central to his project that ''the defective self of the patient with a narcissistic personality disturbance will mobilize its striving to complete its development'' (1984, p. 4). Yet, as Homer Curtis maintains, bad parenting produces ''not a 'nothing' but a 'something' '' even if the ''something'' does not accord with Kohut's paradigm for a structurally healthy self (1985, p. 363). Frederic Levine (1985) argues that one will not simply find an empty space where the normative psychic structure should exist. Rather, the child will ''form some substitutive structure, but there will not simply be a gap in the mental apparatus'' (p. 225). Indeed, from the point of view of Freudian conflict theory, the perceived structural gap is generally the patient's fantasy, a way of defending against impulses that cannot be consciously acknowledged. In interpreting the dream of a young man suffering from castration anxiety, Freud noticed that the castration theme emerges in the very structure of the dream: ''My mother and sister were undressing—here are some gaps in the dream'' (1900, p. 368). Freud does not assume that what is missing is truly absent; rather the ''gaps'' asserted by the patient are very much *something*—a something denied by both the analyst and the patient in self psychological analysis. According to Freud, the impulses defended against were nearly always sexual in their nature. Yet here we find Kohut, conversely, elevating into theory a defense against intolerable impulses, as though to corroborate the patient's fantasy that they are by far too dreadful to exist; in their place is installed the ''nothing'' where the feared not-being (the castration) of the phallus ''lives.'' The fantasied loss oppressing the patient is transformed into a *real* loss that can be replaced—the sexual loss is translated into a self-deficit. What is being lost in all of this is the patient's sexuality, insofar as the sexual anxieties are replaced with an antisexual vocabulary of the self. ''Behind castration fear,'' Kohut tells us, ''is a fear of disintegration of the self'' (1984, p. 21). Such rhetoric underscores Kohut's literalization of the mental apparatus—an edifice seriously threatened with internal collapse because a brick or so is missing. Eagle (1984) says: ''[At times] Kohut and his followers write about *lack of self-cohesiveness, fragmented self,* and *self-defects* as if they were referring to actual 'cracks'; in a substantive structural entity, much like one would describe faults in a geological structure'' (1984, p. 66).

But what is missing is more than the phallus that cannot be taken if *there is nothing to take;*[1] the core absence is the sexuality the phallus represents. In this light, one is reminded of Ernest Jones's (1927) description of castration anxiety as *aphanisis,* the fear of losing one's sexual desire. Yet, it is this very gap in the self (sexuality) that the self psychologist invites with the desexualizing therapeutic discourse. This would constitute a reversal into its opposite of self psychology's avowed mission— the imagined gap in the subject they seek to fill is, on the contrary, a gap they install.

One self psychologist, E. R. Moberly (1986), traces a homosexual orientation to such developmental deficits. The absent or unloving father causes a deficit in same-sex attachments. The patient's chronic need to compensate for these deficits leads to homosexuality. Moberly goes on to postulate that "heterosexuality may become a realistic option when the same-sex developmental process has been fulfilled" (p. 206). Like Freud, the self psychologist articulates a normative ideal, heterosexual object love, as its goal, in relation to which homosexuality indicates a failure. Nevertheless, where Freud (1905) shows the extent to which all sexualities find their sources in infantile complexes[2] (Weeks, 1985, p. 131; Greenberg, 1988, p. 425), and that sexual preference is not biologically innate, the Kohutian program represents heterosexuality as virtually predetermined; the subject innately craves the completion of her or his developmental tasks, what Kohut describes as the "enduring wish to complete his development and thereby realize the nuclear program of his self" (1984, p. 148). Such completion necessitates a heterosexual orientation that naturally emerges from the repaired subject of Kohutian analysis. Levine rightly questions "how the individual would sense that there is a lack, and try to fill it" (1985, p. 225), but underlying self psychology is the conviction that the structurally deficient subject unconsciously recognizes such deficits and longs to "grow up" normally. Thus, Moberly's (1986) speculation on the cured subject who is now back on track developmentally, suggests that establishing these self-structures will lead to a mature and integrated heterosexuality. Freud too represented heterosexuality as "mature" in contrast to the developmentally fixated homosexuality. The difference between him and Kohut, however, is that

---

[1] I am reminded here of Freud's (1927) reading of the suspensory-belt fetishist. By covering his genitals, he can deny the potential loss.

[2] Indeed, in *Three Essays on the Theory of Sexuality* (1905), Freud claims that exclusive heterosexuality is a form of fixation as well.

he did not treat adult patients as though they were actually children who were never ready to "grow up."

The Coherence of Heterosexuality

The subject suffering from a narcissistic personality disturbance experiences what Kohut calls selfobject transferences rather than the libidinal transferences enumerated by Freud. The patient disturbed in the narcissistic arena has experienced as a child a deprivation in one or more sectors of its self-selfobject relationships. Either the maternal selfobject did not adequately mirror her child or the paternal selfobject could not be idealized (see Edward Jones [1985a] for his evaluation of the profound sexism underlying such models).

A third self-selfobject relationship is that of twinship, or the alter ego, the reconfirming experience of an essential alikeness with another human being. Kohut and Wolf describe a selfobject as "objects which we experience as part of our self; the expected control over them is, therefore, closer to the concept of the control which a grown-up expects to have over his own body and mind than to the concept of control which he expects to have over others" (1978, p. 414). The failure on the part of an archaic selfobject eventuates in fundamental structural defects in the subject; in self psychological analysis, the patient begins where she or he left off, pursuing developmental phases artificially via analytic transmutations. The therapist serves as the selfobject(s) required by the analytic subject to fulfill her or his developmental potential. It is useful, in this context, to compare Kohut's deficit model psychology to that of Jacques Lacan, who also employs a deficit model—with a rather significant difference. Whereas the Kohutian analyst offers to repair or fill up the deficit, Lacan argues that the analyst offers the patient what she or he does not have to give. For Lacan, a central part of the therapeutic success, the resolution of the transference, depends upon the analytic subject's recognition that the analyst does not have what the patient desires, that the deficit is unappeasable. Such, for Lacan, is the nature of desire. The Kohutian analyst, conversely, conspires with the patient's fantasy that some kind of structural wholeness is recuperable.

The increased sexual activities and especially the so-called sexualization of the transference encountered in the early phases of some

analyses of narcissistic personality disorders are usually manifestations of the intensification of the patient's need to fill in a structural
defect. These manifestations should not be understood as an eruption
of drives but as the expression of the patient's hope that the selfobject will now supply them with the needed psychological structure
[Kohut, 1977, p. 217].

Kohut transmogrifies the sexual desire of Freudian drive theory into
the desire for structural coherence. It is not the analyst's phallus that the
patient desires, a phallus that will plug up the empty space marked by
an inarticulable desire, but rather the analyst's structurally perfect self.
In this deficit model, desire is fulfilled and thus annihilated; with the
structural completion of the analytic subject, desire has no space in which
to emerge. Paul Hamburg maintains that "in contrast to Lacan's interpretations, which seek to place disharmony and division within a symbolic
structure, Kohut's seek to reconfirm wholeness. The valued goals of self
psychological treatment are wholeness, becoming embedded in a matrix
of sustaining relationships, and Cure" (1991, p. 352).

It follows that a homosexual orientation or homosexual impulses proceed from structural incompleteness. "If a child enters the oedipal
phase," Kohut writes, "with a firm, cohesive, continuous self, he will
then experience assertive-possessive, affectionate-sexual desires for the
heterogenital parent and assertive, self-confident, competitive feelings
vis-a-vis the parent of the same sex" (1977, p. 230). Elsewhere, he explains that as a result of parental pathology, "the [Oedipal] child's self
becomes fragmented, weakened, and disharmonious and his normal nonsexual affection and normal non-hostile assertiveness become grossly
sexual and hostile" (1984, p. 24). Following in the tradition of non-
Kleinian object-relations theory, Kohut diminishes dramatically the centrality of the Oedipus complex.[3] In healthy relations with empathic selfobjects who oversee with joy and pride the child's entrance into a gender
identity, the child should feel affectionate not sexual, assertive not hostile
and aggressive. If all goes well, the child should proceed smoothly and
nonconflictually into a heterosexual position. Implicitly, Kohut indicates
that the homosexual position is entered as a result of a self that is not
"firm, cohesive, and continuous." Indeed, the homosexual subject is

---

[3] I am importing here Toril Moi's (1989) distinction between the Kleinian school of object
relations and later trends found primarily in the work of Fairbairn, Winnicott, and Guntrip.

structurally incapacitated and homosexuality itself is marked (implicitly) as a tremulous sexualization of self-deficits erroneously experienced as desire.

It is no wonder, in light of his theorization of this ideal structurally continuous and cohesive subject, that Kohut needs to revile Freudian drive psychology. Drive psychology posits a subject sundered by intractable component drives that only coalesce under the tyranny of the genital, provisionally, as a subjection to the imperatives of civilization—not because, as Kohut would have it, the aim of the nuclear self is its own development, but because of social conditions that compel such concessions from the polymorphously perverse infant. The emergence of the drive, for Kohut, is a disintegration product, a fracture in the continuity-bound self that structurally is destined for coherence. Writes Kohut: "The primary psychological configurations in the child's experiential world are not drives . . . drive experiences occur as disintegration products when the self is unsupported" (1977, p. 171). The drives are explosive, unreliable, ever threatening to unravel the tightly coiled pretense of a unified human subject. Drives speak of alterity, a discontinuous subject reemerging repeatedly as different in and of itself. This is why self psychology is so committed to overthrowing the conflict model of drive theory. Where drive theory describes the tensions ensuing from the subjection of pleasure-driven subjects to the exigencies of social law, the self psychologists would have us believe that psychic necessity can harmoniously interfuse with the outside world.

The Empathic Guide

Of course, given Kohut's representation of ideal caretaking, the constant gratification of the child would necessarily bring the outside world more closely in line with the child's demands. Conflict would accordingly be minimized through preempting obstacles to satisfaction. The paradigm for childrearing is to be found in the empathic analyst's relationship with her or his patient. After illustrating the unusual level of soothing Kohut offers to one patient, Marshall Greene wonders "what would be unwarranted gratification? If the patient felt hurt because she was not kissed on her return to treatment, would that too be in order because of her special needs at the time? This interaction is only one of many which strongly suggest that 'optimal frustration' in self analysis really means the least frustration possible'' (1984, p. 52). Although self psychologists believe that these optimal frustrations are critical for both child and analysand in the process of individuation from the parent-analyst, it is difficult to understand, as Greene (1984) remarks, what self psychologists mean by frustration. Drives proceed from actual frustration and it is just this that Kohut needs to disavow as inevitable.

> It is the self of the child that, in consequence of the severely disturbed empathic responses of the parents, has not been securely established, and it is the enfeebled and fragmentation-prone self that (in the attempt to reassure itself that it is alive, even that it exists at all) turns defensively toward pleasure aims through the stimulation of erogenic zones, and that, secondarily, brings about the oral (and anal) drive orientation and the ego's enslavement to the drive aims correlated to the stimulated body zones [1977, p. 74].

Where Freud (1900, 1905, 1909) in many ways "normalized" the perversions enumerated by late nineteenth-century sexologists by showing how closely they parallel "normal" sexual fantasy and behavior, Kohut transforms what has been hitherto represented as normal psychosexual stages into perversion. Again, we have a sense of the radical reversals of psychoanalytic thinking being promoted by self psychology. Freud's commitment was to demystifying the perceived deviance of the individual by establishing the universality of socially transgressive fantasy. Kohut, on the other hand, resubmits fantasy to the status of guilt from which Freud tried to rescue it. Intriguingly, Kohut claims that he is substituting his own account of Tragic Man for Freud's Guilty Man—another odd projection (1977, p. 132). His strategy is to propose that we have nothing to feel guilty about—not by normalizing the guilt-inducing thoughts, but by negating them.

Although Kohut seems to celebrate the gratification of the instincts on the one hand by trying to minimize frustration, at the same time it is the instincts (or drives) that he defends against. What the child/patient wants *should* be offered, he tells us, but it would be a mistake to believe that any child wants to have sex with her or his parent or that any analysand really wants to have sex with a same-sex partner. Rather, they want to recapture a sense of aliveness. They want their self-esteem shored up by their selfobjects. It is easy to offer the child whatever it demands if one disavows the transgressive dimension of the demands. It is precisely self psychology's emphasis on the empathic attunement of the therapist-cum-caretaker that misleads many into believing that Kohut's program is the permissive answer to Freudian prohibition. But in fact Kohut's program is more essentially prohibitive to the extent that the self psychologist neutralizes the sexual demands. Although telling a patient that her or his sexual impulses are sexualizations of nonsexual materials may well shore up a patient's guilty defenses, at the same time, in dismissing the reality of such urges, the analyst acts in the service of repression.

In denying the formative centrality of the drives, Kohutian psychology represses *all* deviance, meaning in this sense both sexual deviance and deviation from the idealized route toward the completion of the self. Hence, the perverse analysand of self psychology is in the process of learning that deviance as such is to be shunned. No wonder then, that Kohut and his disciples ignore the legitimacy of a homosexual identity. The homosexual subject throughout the history of psychoanalysis has been associated with drives unassimilated to reproductive necessity. The homosexual subject, as Jeffrey Weeks (1985) has argued, is the marked sexual subject par excellence; sexuality that does not submit to civilized reproductive responsibilities. It is not that Freud did not discuss homosexuality as developmentally deviant as well. Assuredly, his developmental model is premised on a normative heterosexual passage through the defiles of the psychosexual stages. For Freud, in contrast, heterosexuality is no more innate than homosexuality; it is arrived at and generationally reproduced through a particular configuration of the family. For Kohut, part of the essential nature of the self is its heterosexual developmental project, not that it is aiming toward heterosexuality per se; it is just that if the self is in fact healthy and intact, somehow it will assume a heterosexual orientation. Again, we are plagued with indirection, a refusal to interrogate a suppressed agenda which symptomatically presents as turning perverse sexual behavior into normal, not because homosexuality is wrong but rather because if the self is healthy it will not be, could not possibly be, homosexual. Such miraculous and inadvertent "cures" point to the latent task of the self psychologist, which is to cure altogether the human subject of its sexuality. It is important to explore the connection between the homosexual cure and this desexualizing proclivity as well as how it happens that homosexuality is in fact cured.

Curing the Homosexual Subject

In each instance of homosexual behavior or impulses on the part of the analytic subject, the self psychologist refuses the sexuality of the lived experience. Mr. I, who suffered from "compulsive promiscuity," experienced unwanted homosexual urges. His transference to the analyst was marked by homosexual fantasies. "What would I do," he wondered, "if I had an erection right here on the couch?" (Goldberg, 1978, p. 23).[4] The analyst writes that "he recalled that in some of his dreams he had intercourse with his sister and in some others he had a homosexual relationship with the analyst. He knew these were his ways of 'achieving repair' [of establishing a relationship to a mirroring self-object] and preventing further painful regression" (Goldberg, 1978, p. 48). Thus, for the patient, the frightening eruption of homosexual desire is transmuted by the analyst into the facile and obfuscating discourse of self-reparation. It is not the analyst's phallus by which Mr. I longs to be penetrated; rather, it is the calming insinuation of a mirroring selfobject into his structural deficit—not his bodily orifice. My point is not that it would be preferable for this patient to come to terms with his latent homosexuality and openly assume a gay gender identity. Instead, I want to know why his sexual fantasies are being labeled nonsexual. What concerns me about saying, as the analyst does, that these homosexual impulses are not really homosexual is that it seems to be subserving a heterosexist position that such feelings *are* deviant. Never fear, the analyst is urging, these impulses you have are not at all derived from that alien sexual territory, the hellish deviance of the real homosexual. To say that these sexual fantasies are a sexualization of nonsexual issues entails a suppression of the body and its desires which is precisely what Freudian psychoanalysis tried to liberate. When Mr. I has a fantasy of swallowing the analyst's penis, the analyst interprets this as an identification with the values of the analyst—an absolute reversal of the Freudian model which finds sexuality in ostensibly neutral statements.

Certainly, a crucial issue in psychoanalytic theory is whether intrapsychic configurations are premised on the body or the body is mapped according to an innate psychical geography. Thus, I am not suggesting that it is altogether inappropriate for the analyst to metaphorize in the way he does the analysand's sexual fantasy. It is important, however, to

---

[4]This casebook was a group project; the identities of the individual analysts are concealed.

avoid privileging either sector. To eliminate the body from the analytic scene is to be complicit with a fantasy that the patient already has—that she or he is not a victim of potentially uncontrollable drives, the psychical derivatives of the body's impulses. The resolution of Mr. I's analysis was that he married happily, and overcame his homosexual impulses as well as his promiscuous heterosexual activity (another form of socially menacing deviance).

Mr. Z was engaged in a homosexual relationship with an older teacher between the ages of 11 and 13. Kohut (1979) explains that for Mr. Z this man functioned as the idealized selfobject he lacked in his own father. The analyst writes: "Mr. M himself had frequent sexual dreams about young boys, and he had occasionally felt that older men, including his father, were sexually attracted to him. He did not think of himself, however, as someone who had reason to worry about homosexuality" (Goldberg, 1978, p. 126). "The analyst interpreted Mr. M's first reference to the possibility that his father may have been sexually attracted to him as a child's wish for closeness with the father" (Goldberg, 1978, p. 136). The analyst determines that "Mr. M used the erotization of painful affects as a way of mastering them" (Goldberg, 1978, p. 136). Mr. M developed a close relationship with a young boy. "[H]e was relieved that his love for the boy was devoid of sensual or erotic affects ('I love John, but I don't want to make love to him; I would rather do that with my girl friends')" (Goldberg, 1978, p. 147). The analyst takes this statement at face value. The possibility of negation is overlooked. Mr. E was an understimulated personality who resorted to peeping at men's penises in public restrooms. The analyst explains that "Mr. E's perversion was an attempt to reintegrate a crumbling sense of self" (Goldberg, 1978, p. 293). Interestingly, the case of Mr. E, who was cured of his perversion, offers us a clue as to the efficacy of the Kohutian homosexual cure. One weekend, Mr. E painted a picture of his analyst. Kohut writes:

> The key to the understanding of this artistic production lay in the fact that in it the analyst had neither eyes nor nose—the place of these sensory organs was taken by the analysand. On the basis of this evidence and of additional corroborative material, the conclusion could be reached that a decisive support of the maintenance of the patient's narcissistically cathected self image was supplied by the analyst's perception of him. The patient felt whole when he thought that he was acceptingly looked at by an object that substituted for

an insufficiently developed endopsychic function ... [1968, pp. 99–100].

First, the patient is fantasying a merger with the all-powerful analyst (a fantasy, by the way, that remains undiminished in Kohutian analysis) through whose own mind the patient's senses are informed. Second, the patient is dependent on the analyst's perception of him, which has been introjected as the patient's self-perception. In fact, Mr. E's cure proceeds directly from this merger with the analyst, an analyst whose perspective is incorporated by the patient as the truth. This leads us to the instrumental role played by the selfobject transferences in self psychology in founding an unambivalent heterosexual subject in place of a sexually "protean" subject (to use Kohut's own description of Mr. E). Whereas the conflict analyst (ideally) tries to lead the analysand out of idealizing and mirroring transferences, the self psychologist welcomes these transferences as the beginning and the end of the curative process. The goal is for the selfobject imago of the analyst to be, as Kohut observes, "transmuted into smoothly functioning psychic structures" in the analysand (1984, p. 155). Kohut elaborates: "Should an ill-disposed critic again claim gleefully that he has caught me red-handed, that once more I have openly admitted that ... we are indeed providing 'corrective emotional experiences' for our patients, I could only reply once more with 'So be it!' " (1984, p. 153).

Shapiro treats the homosexuality of his patient as a "perversion" and works to restore an interest in his heterosexual marriage. From the outset, his homosexuality is accounted for as fantasies and experiences that can "protect him from the fear and pain associated with aloneness" (1985, p. 166). "The homosexual erotic experience served to stabilize his fragmenting sense of self" (1985, p. 171). Homosexuality is a strategy for defending against emotional experiences, whereas, somehow, heterosexual activity would not be. For example, upon his grandmother's death, the patient experienced "soothing feelings . . . when he fondled the testicles of his lover"—while we are expected to understand that heterosexual behavior, conversely, would *not* be compensatory (1985, p. 168). Let us consider in this light Freud's statement on the relative "health" of homosexual versus heterosexual object-choices:

Psycho-analysis considers that a choice of an object independently of its sex—freedom to range equally over male and female objects—as it is found in childhood, in primitive states of society and early periods of history, is the original basis from which, as a result of restriction in one direction or the other, both the normal and the inverted types develop. Thus from the point of view of psycho-analysis the exclusive sexual interest felt by men for women is also a problem that needs elucidating and is not a self-evident fact based upon an attraction that is ultimately of a chemical nature [1905, pp. 11–12n].

In short, heterosexuality as well is a brand of fixation that "needs elucidating"; indeed, Freud asserts that it cannot be held up as simply the psychically healthy model in contrast to which homosexual behavior is neurotic and ultimately unsatisfactory. Sexualities and sexual behaviors, Freud repeatedly maintains, are always drive derivatives which are *always* to some degree in conflict. Because sexuality is the locus where drive activity is most visible, it has become imperative for self psychology to invent an uninterrogated ideal of sexual practice—a "safe" place for the sexual subject, a place immune to the destabilizing fallout of the drives. Thus, whereas Freud wants to know where *both* heterosexuality *and* homosexuality come from, the Kohutians only ask about homosexuality (or "compulsive" heterosexuality), thereby shoring up heterosexuality as the reliable ground from which any deviation reveals psychopathology.

Arnold Goldberg (1993) is quite sensitive to the difficulty of distinguishing between sexualizations of fundamentally nonsexual issues and "normal sexual activity." In fact, he asserts that it is important to recognize that much homosexuality is not a sexualization, hence not pathological. Nevertheless, his clinical example of a case of sexualization involves a patient who recently decided to "come out of the closet as a homosexual" (p. 390). This patient, who had constant homosexual fantasies, was advised by Goldberg that "he had problems that seemed not to have much to do with sex, either homosexual or heterosexual" (p. 390). By the end of the treatment, although Goldberg's patient no longer "sexualizes" his problems, it remains unclear whether he will pursue a homosexual or heterosexual lifestyle. Notwithstanding Goldberg's recognition of homosexuality as often a "manifestation of a choice of a sexual object which is satisfying and fulfilling," he promises future work on "the particulars of some homosexual behavior as a form of compensatory structure" (p. 396), precisely Moberly's (1986) explanation. This version of homosexuality is presented in contrast to sexualized homosexuality.

Thus, despite Goldberg's initial emphasis on therapeutic openness to diverse sexual preferences, we are left with two possible aetiologies of homosexuality—both neurotic. Further, given the imperatives of self psychology, that is committed to changing the self through rebuilding its structure, one can see where the theory of compensatory structure might lead. Certainly, Moberly's theory of the rebuilt self that now progresses toward heterosexuality shows us the dangers of Goldberg's position.

Selling Normative Values

The nature of the transferences elicited by the self psychological enterprise invites the patient to identify with the values of the analytic selfobject imago. It does not matter in fact what the analyst's own sexual orientation is because a Kohutian analyst (by the very therapeutic methodology) is destined to form a countertransferential need to be idealized by the patient, hence provoking the analyst to represent (even unwittingly) normative goals and values. Donald Spence worries about an overinvestment in the therapeutic alliance: "The therapeutic alliance has come to describe the analyst's need to see himself in the patient. He wants to turn the patient into a mirror of his hopes and fears. To strengthen the alliance, therefore, he has projected onto the patient his own needs and tries to behave in such a way that the patient will begin to act like him" (1982, 207). Further, given the emphasis on this mythical construction of a coherent, continuous, smoothly functioning self scoured clean of any potentially disruptive lacunae in a perverse enactment of a kind of psychical housecleaning, the analytic endeavor necessarily invokes general cultural norms of sameness, adherence to the status quo, and a flight from alterity.

Ernest Wolf's description of the alter ego transference shows how the analysand is encouraged to incorporate the analyst-imago's own normative value-system, including her or his prescriptive representation of sexuality. "It manifests as a need, in general, to be like the analyst in appearance, manner, outlook, and opinion" (1988, p. 125). Indeed, in recounting one case history, Kohut mentions the gratification he experienced when the patient began to imitate his voice. The transference was underway. Wolf defines the mirror transference as "the reestablishment of an early need for acceptance and confirmation of the self by the selfobject. It manifests as demands on the analyst (or defenses against such demands) to confirm the patient's self by recognizing, admiring, or praising the patient'' (1988, p. 125). Hence, we have a patient desperate to be praised, confirmed by the analyst as valuable. It only stands to reason that the patient would want to do what it takes to become the object of the analyst-imago's approbation. Again, I am not referring to the actual analyst but to the analyst who, for the patient treated according to a self psychological model, represents cultural homogeneity as well as generally received standards of sexual behavior. The idealizing transference constitutes the ''re-establishment of the need for an experience of merging with a calm, strong, wise, and good selfobject. It may manifest as the more or less disguised admiration of the analyst'' (1988, p. 126). In each transferential instance, we have the problem of the analytic subject's desperation to please the analyst (even if disguised); and, more to the point, we have an analyst who *invites* the patient to engage in just such gross distortions. It is worth considering in this context Lacan's injunction against the strategy of Fairbairnian object-relations treatment, about which he writes: ''any theorisation of analysis organised around the object relation amounts in the end to advocating the recomposition of the subject's imaginary world according to the norm of the analyst's ego. The original introjection of the rejecting object, which has poisoned the exciting function of the said object, is corrected by the introjection of a correct ego, that of the analyst'' (1988, p. 254). This strategy of non-Kleinian object-relations theory, which proposes reconfiguring the psychic structure of the patient, is self-consciously modeled along the lines of idealized parenting.[5] As discussed earlier, implicit in Kohutian theory as well is that the analyst is the exemplary parent. This is a psychoanalytic practice that ultimately idealizes the analyst as the one who knows what the patient needs. Ernest Wolf offers an analogy that unintentionally highlights the invidiousness of such an approach: ''The essence of a certain kind of salesmanship (or advertising) is exactly the salesman's empathic 'in tuneness' with the customer's needs and wishes, and the

---

[5]''As a defensive maneuver against just this possible objection to his program, Kohut writes: Although it should be obvious, it may need to be said that I am not speaking about gross identifications with the analyst's personality. Whereas these do occur and have a legitimate place as a temporary phase of the working through that ultimately leads to transmuting internalizations, their persistence clearly indicates that the analysis is not complete, that the patient's self has been supplanted by a foreign self and has not been rehabilitated'' (1977, p. 263). What is so especially worrisome about this disclaimer is Kohut's inability to see how ''rehabilitation'' happens as a result of just such ''gross identifications'' with the social values of external objects.

ability to sell on the basis of making the customer feel that his needs and desires are understood, regardless of whether the sold product is really needed or in fact harmful'' (1988, p. 132n).

Of course, Kohut is basically stripping the heterosexual subject as well of his or her sexuality—and here, it is worth considering Jeffrey Weeks's point that the heterosexual subject really emerged in many ways as a result of the classification of homosexuality (1985, p. 69). Hence, when Kohut suggests that someone can live an active and creative life *"even in the absence of pleasure"* (1977, p. 285) he is implying that sexuality itself, by which he seems to mean the body and its excitations, is secondary to the human subject, which is fundamentally a bodyless self. Thus, he can talk about the joyful approach to death befitting a healthy and wise old age. Why should someone care about the end of the life of the body when death marks the culmination of an incorporeal and developmentally bound self—that jubilantly surges forth to ever more perfect phases of its own revelation?

Homosexuality is the ''sex'' versus sexually unmarked heterosexuality (Wittig, 1980). It is sex for its own sake, which utterly repudiates the social fantasy of sexuality in the service of the species, a fantasy that ultimately transforms the drives into the factotums of a progressive evolutionary project. As a result, it is crucial for self psychology to eliminate homosexuality, the very sex it stakes its claim on denying, at the same time that it undervalues the power of sexuality; otherwise, sex would obtrude into the inviolate terrain where the self and its selfobjects cheerfully interfuse. Subtending Kohut's project is the necessity for ridding the world (at least the psychoanalytic world) of homosexuality as a lived space of the body and its desires—because self psychology is bent on a disembodying mission. The overemphasis on psychic structure occurs as a result of trying to deflect attention from the corporeal body of the pleasure-driven subject. If the homosexual body is neutered into a fragile vessel of faulty selfobjects, if a patient's homosexual fantasies are mere perversions (note the mere, it is always crucial to this project to minimize the horrific threat) of the self's fundamentally healthy trajectory toward merger with an idealized selfobject, then all drives crumble forthwith into no more than the detritus of failed selfobject relationships. If the ultimate sexual body, the homosexual body, is demystified, then we are thoroughly rid of the body and its dangerous potential to disrupt the fantasy of the continuous self once and for all.

It is important to note that it is generally male homosexuality that is cured, not female. One reason might be the neutralization of female sexuality *as* sexuality. Female sexuality would necessarily represent less of a threat to self psychologists inasmuch as it is not taken seriously as sexuality per se. We need only look at the historical reception of lesbianism to see how unimaginable sexuality is in the absence of the penis. Lillian Faderman (1981) gives the example of a famous nineteenth-century trial in England where two schoolmistresses were accused by one of their students of lesbian practice. The court concluded the impossibility of sex between two women; how could there be sex, the judge asked, when there was no penis involved? Self psychology persists in the nineteenth-century fantasy of the desexualized woman. One woman patient who entered treatment because of her difficult relationships with men seemed to her therapist to be cured when she renounced interest in dating: " 'Once she could see clearly what she had been doing, the patient lost interest in men as suitors. Her work preoccupied her, and she was reluctant to invest the time and effort required to play the dating game . . . ' '' (Basch, 1980, cited in Curtis, 1985, p. 354). Curtis accuses the therapist in this instance of colluding with the patient's sexual anxieties. ''In so doing, he was indeed enacting the role of the powerful parent forcing her, in collusion with her own resistance to her sexual urges, to renounce sexuality and, like a good latency child, 'single-mindedly' attend to her studies'' (1985, p. 355). Seen in the light of a fundamental disavowal of female sexuality, one might add that this therapist's objective was to cure his patient of her original therapeutic agenda. The ''normal'' romantic life she wanted is transformed into pathology; the cure entails submitting her to a permanent latency that confirms the ''father's'' wish that his ''daughter'' is not a sexual subject.

Oddly, the twinship relationship with the analyst, that essential feeling of alikeness, is considered unacceptable when it is with a same-sex partner. Indeed, twinship relationships are fostered in one arena and discouraged in the other. This world without difference that is the core agenda of self psychology gets lived out in analysis as the compliant swallowing of the analyst's values—like Mr. I whose fantasy of swallowing the analyst's penis suggests the degree to which *something* of the analyst's is being passively ingested—or forced down his throat (Shapiro's patient has an identical fantasy [1985]). In another related case, Mr. A's fellatio fantasy is interpreted as eating the strength of idealized males (1977, p.

125). Sanford Shapiro's patient "reported a dream in which he was sucking a man's penis and swallowed the semen. 'It was a lot to swallow,' he said. Associations led to the interpretation that if he swallowed what I told him I would be in control" (1985, p. 168). Thus, we are led back to the central fantasy of the narcissistic personality—that everyone else is a mirror image of oneself. Yet here we find the theory in the position of the narcissist, casting itself as the model for imitation—by patients, by other analytic doctrines. Christopher Bollas (1986) notes Kohut's excessive and rather querulous concern with being understood by his readers in his book *How Does Analysis Cure?* Bollas wonders if this is the treatment one must endure at the hands of Kohut when one rejects the dutiful position of selfobject. Thus, imitation and alikeness are correct if they imitate the analyst (the bearer of self psychology); alikeness is wrong if it is homosexual because such deviant behavior would not adequately mirror the theory's normative heterosexist values.

Once again we encounter a fundamental contradiction between the theory's expressed commitment to a heightened understanding of the patient's needs (the privileged status of empathy) and an underlying investment in imposing a given set of values. Although self psychologists frequently are accused of failing to go beyond the manifest content of the patient's speech (including dream reports), in the case of the patient described above, it is precisely her avowed wish that is overlooked by the analyst in favor of an antisexual narrative (the good student) that more effectively sustains the *analyst's* defenses. It is in the elaboration of the theory of selfobjects that we find a clue to both the pernicious role of empathy and the ultimate self-mirroring strategy of Kohutian theory and practice. As Morris N. Eagle (1984) observes about the concept of "healthy narcissism," all relationships are narcissistic in the Kohutian economy. This concept, he writes, "implies a rejection of this reciprocity principle [that Freud "posited between narcissistic and object libidinal investments"] insofar as the former permits the concurrent operation of both object involvement and narcissistic motives" (p. 56). The differentiation between self and object accomplished by the child upon transcending the state of primary narcissism—collapses back into the same. In the world of selfobjects, all alterity is finally obliterated; like the infant's intolerance of needs that compete with its own, the Kohutian subject denies difference through the incorporation of the object world. But where the therapist pretends to be offering her- or himself as a selfobject to the patient, it is in fact the patient who is ingested into the *therapist's* personality. Again, we return to the problem of alikeness, invited in therapy and reviled when it emerges as a homosexual orientation. Thus, the reason homosexuality is disavowed by self psychology as a serious sexual orientation is because it literalizes for Kohutians a prevailing fantasy that remains otherwise repressed; homosexuality comes to stand for a world without difference—which is the ultimate objective of self psychology. The repudiation of homosexuality constitutes a defense against the theory's unstated and uninterrogated aim. Homosexuality then comes to stand for (and in for) the fantasy of alikeness that cannot be spoken. To deny homosexuality as a lived sexual orientation is in effect to deny the repressed fantasy motivating self psychological theory.

References

Bollas, C. (1986), Who does self psychology cure? *Psychoanal. Inqu.,* 6:429–435.

Curtis, H. (1985), Clinical perspectives on self psychology. *Psychoanal. Quart.,* 54:339–378.

Eagle, M. N. (1984), *Recent Developments in Psychoanalysis: A Crtical Evaluation.* New York: McGraw-Hill.

Faderman, L. (1981), *Surpassing the Love of Men: Romantic Friendship and Love between Women from the Renaissance to the Present.* New York: Morrow.

Freud, S. (1900), The Interpretation of Dreams. *Standard Edition,* 4. London: Hogarth Press, 1953.

——— (1905), Three Essays on the Theory of Sexuality. *Standard Edition,* 7:123–243. London: Hogarth Press, 1953.

——— (1909), Analysis of a phobia in a five-year-old boy. *Standard Edition,* 10:1–147. London: Hogarth Press, 1955.

——— (1927), Fetishism. *Standard Edition,* 21:147–157. London: Hogarth Press, 1961.

——— (1975), *The Letters of Sigmund Freud,* ed. E. L. Freud; tr. T. & J. Stern. New York: Basic Books.

Goldberg, A., Ed., with the collaboration of Kohut, H. (1978), *The Psychology of the Self: A Casebook.* New York: International Universities Press.

——— (1993), *The Problem of Perversion: The View from Self Psychology.* New Haven, CT: Yale University Press.

Greenberg, D. F. (1988), *The Construction of Homosexuality.* Chicago: University of Chicago Press.

Greene, M. (1984), The self psychology of Heinz Kohut: A synopsis and critique. *Bull. Menninger Clin.*, 48:37–53.

Hamburg, P. (1991), Interpretation and empathy: Reading Lacan with Kohut. *Internat. J. Psycho-Anal.*, 72:347–361.

Isay, R. A. (1985), On the analytic therapy of homosexual men. *The Psychoanalytic Study of the Child*, 40:235–254. New Haven, CT: Yale University Press.

Jones, Edward (1982), Critique of empathic science II: Sexism and the hidden society. *Psychol. & Soc. Theory*, 3:53–68.

Jones, Ernest (1927), The early development of female sexuality. *Internat. J. Psycho-Anal.*, 8:459–472.

Kohut, H. (1968), The psychoanalytic treatment of narcissistic personality disorders: Outline of a systematic approach. *The Psychoanalytic Study of the Child*, 23:86–113. New York: International Universities Press.

——— (1977), *The Restoration of the Self.* New York: International Universities Press.

——— (1979), The two analyses of Mr. Z. *Internat. J. Psycho-Anal.*, 60:3–27.

——— (1984), *How Does Analysis Cure?* ed. A. Goldberg with P. Stepansky. Chicago: University of Chicago Press.

——— Wolf, E. S. (1978), Disorders of the self and their treatment: An outline. *Internat. J. Psycho-Anal.*, 59:413–425.

Lacan, J. (1988), *The Seminar of Jacques Lacan*, Book 2, ed. A. Miller; tr. S. Tomaselli. New York: W. W. Norton.

Levine, F. J. (1985), Self-psychology and the new narcissism in psychoanalysis. *Clin. Psychol. Rev.*, 5:215–229.

Moberly, E. R. (1986), Attachment and separation: The implications for gender identity and for the structuralization of the self: A theoretical model for transsexualism, and homosexuality. *Psychiatric J. Univ. Ottawa*, 11:205–209.

Moi, T. (1989), Patriarchal thought and the drive for knowledge. In: *Between Feminism and Psychoanalysis*, ed. T. Brennan. New York: Routledge, pp. 189–205.

Shapiro, S. (1985), Archaic selfobject transferences in the analysis of a case of male homosexuality. *Prog. in Self Psychol.*, 1:164–177.

Spence, D. P. (1982), *Narrative Truth and Historical Truth: Meaning and Interpretation in Psychoanalysis.* New York: W. W. Norton.

Treurniet, N. (1983), Psychoanalysis and self psychology: A metapsychological essay with a clinical illustration. *J. Amer. Psychoanal. Assn.*, 31:59–100.

Weeks, J. (1985), *Sexuality and Its Discontents: Meanings, Myths, and Modern Sexualities.* London: Routledge.

Wittig, M. (1980), The straight mind. *Feminist Iss.*, 1:103–111.

Wolf, E. (1988), *Treating the Self: Elements of Clinical Self Psychology.* New York: Guilford Press.

Part III

The Impact of Culture

11

Postmodern Ideas about Gender and Sexuality: The Lesbian Woman Redundancy

Ann D'Ercole

W hat are the roles of gender and sexuality in lesbian identities? Does a lesbian consider herself a woman? Or, as Freud (1920) and much of the world has implied, is she but a man in drag; not a real woman and only a copy of a man? How helpful is psychoanalytic theory in addressing these questions? For me, psychoanalytic theory and practice are both helpful and insidious in regard to questions of gender and sexuality. Beginning with Freud's Darwinian psychoanalysis (Dimen, 1995), a trap was set that both captured and set free the feelings and fears prevalent at that time about human behavior; namely, that human sexuality is extremely plastic and nonspecific with regard to sexual objects. Whether or not these feelings are catalogued as such and organized into open behavior and lifelong identities is dependent on a variety

Portions of this paper were presented at the Annual Conference of the Institute for Human Identity, New York, 1995.

of social and cultural dynamics (Menaker, 1995). In Freud's psychoanalysis, the drive to reproduce was formulated as the essential element in human development, ultimately creating our identities. In contrast, nascent postmodern scholarship has criticized these biological and morality based assumptions about sex and gender and their dualistic imprisonment (e.g., male-female, feminine-masculine, heterosexual-homosexual). Rather, it reveals these dichotomized notions as scientifically unfounded, noncoherent, and as unstable socially and politically biased formulations. As a result, for those of us of the social constructivist persuasion in psychoanalysis, sexuality has been freed from its singular procreative purpose. Finally, we are without gender as the quintessential path to understanding sexuality. Viewed through this new postmodern lens, the fluid constructs of gender and sexuality are expanded into a variable wardrobe of postures and poses worn and discarded as the fashion and context change.

By way of illustration, recall a scene from a play by Terrence McNally, *Love! Valour! Compassion.* By using this example, I do not mean to equate lesbian existence with the existence of gay men for there are clear political ramifications of gender that must be acknowledged. Nonetheless, I think this portrayal is something we can all relate to. In the play, two characters are seen on stage, one of the men is trimming the hair growing inside the other man's ears. During this delicate, intimate task, the character doing the trimming says to the other, "I'm such a queen!" He takes it back immediately saying, "No, I'm a butch!" He explains, though it's not clear if it's to himself, his partner, or the audience, "I know how to throw a ball, I've always been good at sports, but I can't fix a flat tire." In exasperation as he realizes he doesn't do either gender well, he declares, "I'm not even a good gay man, I hate the opera!" This dialogue gets right to the central dilemmas presented by the theoretical linking of gender and sexuality; the formed choice between male-female, butch-queen, gay-straight, and the lack of language to express how ill-fitting these categories can be.

A traditional psychoanalytic look at the McNally character's predicament might imply that he suffers from gender identity confusion; that his internal object relation organization and his phases of erogenous zone primacy, an idea which began with Freud, are disordered. Using a postmodern paradigm permits us to hear the character speak to the difficult experience of trying to squeeze himself into social categories where criteria for inclusion change with time and context. In this way, we can see how feelings and behavior have had to match a predetermined model or else be condemned to exclusion or annihilation. As therapists, we are familiar with this struggle to conform by minimizing self-expression.

Thinking of gender and sexuality as aspects of social relationships, rather than as traits derived from fixed developmental stages, moves them into the interpersonal interactive arena where relational acts are performed in contexts, and connected to subjective experience more than objective reality. Return for a moment to our character from the McNally play. Why does he make the declaration, "I'm such a queen"? Does he feel like a "queen" when he cuts the hair in his lover's ears? We, the audience, suspect that he does not feel like a "queen" all the time but rather the act of ear hair trimming brings about the feeling. What about the act leads to this feeling? As I think about this activity, it seems to me that cutting the hair in someone's ears requires a steady, gentle hand. It is a nurturing act, stereotypically, one might say, a female one. As a spectator, I wonder if my presence creates the character's discomfort or permits self-expression. I also wonder if the character in this play feels a different gendered self at that moment, or if he does gender, rendering him a man doing woman. Does the fact that he is engaged in this delicate, intimate act of cutting the hair of another man arouse his feelings about his sexuality? Do gay men cut the hair of their lovers' ears? Or, said another way, what does a gay man do to solidify his inclusion in the identity category gay man?

Identities and Clinical Practice

Solidifying inclusion in the identity category lesbian presents a similar dilemma. In psychoanalytic practice some patients can be seen rigidly clinging to labels like lesbian, gay, or straight as a way to hold their identities together. This rigid clinging is understandable in a world that neither recognizes nor tolerates difference. Other patients may abandon labels altogether, feeling themselves more or less than the label signifies. Finding the words to explain this elusive experience is difficult; *density* and *performance* may be ways to think of this confluence of subjectivity and experience.

Consider a patient, I'll call her Amy, who relies on a rigid set of identity categories to regulate her anxiety and make sense of the world. Amy seemed obsessed with thoughts about a former lover. She would comment on her experience as "weird," and "stupid," saying, "I know we aren't lovers anymore, but I can't stop myself from thinking about her." She described how she hated living alone, and how much she wanted to be "married." Her obsessive ruminations seemed to be attempts to defend against the despair of isolation. Amy had used marijuana daily since adolescence and had used alcohol heavily on and off since even earlier in her life. One late Friday afternoon session, she told me how she spent the prior weekend with a friend, drinking a bottle of wine and smoking marijuana until she felt she would pass out. Then she got in her car and drove home. Immediately I heard myself saying that if she was going to indulge in that kind of self-destructive behavior, I would not be able to work with her. She was as stunned at my response as I was, and she asked me, "What was self-destructive about that?" While it is not unusual for me to take this strong a position, the strength of my feelings, and the urgency with which I felt them, were quite a surprise. I really felt she could hurt herself. She tried to assure me she knew what she was doing, emphasizing how she had done it many times before. I wasn't convinced and became more resolute. I said, "Driving while drinking or stoned is just not a contract I can work with." Like all countertransference moments this one happened before I realized how frightened I had become. I asked her about suicidal thoughts and found that she was unaware of any thoughts of killing herself. I discovered that what she was most aware of was that she didn't think it would make any difference to anyone whether she was dead or alive, that she didn't matter.

This session was clearly marked by an urgency, threat, and concern that had not appeared in our work before, and it set the stage for a dream which she reported in the following session. Before Amy related the dream, she announced proudly that she had not used marijuana in the week since our last session, and was resigned to not using it again. She described being upset following our last session, and astonished that no one had ever worried about her safety before. Then she told me a dream: "I had a dream," she said, "It's weird, I'm embarrassed to tell you. I dreamt I was having sex with Ed. I can't believe I dreamt it; it's weird, I don't think of him that way." "Sexually?" I asked. "Yeah," she said, and grew silent. "How did it go?" I asked. "I'm embarrassed to tell you. It was good! We communicated very well. He wasn't just interested in himself. He was caring. He was a good partner. We were having oral sex." Then Amy laughed and said, "That's what I like anyway." She then paused for what seemed like a long time and I commented on how it seemed she was having a hard time talking to me about this. She agreed saying again that it felt embarrassing and weird. The enactment in the dream of our previous session did not escape me. I offered an interpretation which I thought might put her at ease. I said, "He was pleasing you, and you were pleasing him." Amy and I wondered together about her feeling embarrassed and weird. She explained that one aspect of her embarrassment had to do with his feeling like a brother. "We are pals," she said. After a long silence, and in a very low voice, accenting a kind of secrecy, she told me, "I've never had a dream about having sex with a man. It's too weird." "Weird! Why weird?" "I'm a woman. I like women," she said. Silence. I said to her. "You really believe in these categories woman and man." She said, "Yeah, don't you?" "No," I admitted, "not so much," and shared with her my shortened version of gendering. I said that I think people move back and forth, being one now then another. For example, I said, "I wonder if the man in the dream is me. Perhaps I'm behaving like a man by telling you what to do and you feel cared for." Amy said, "I did feel like you cared about me. Nobody has ever told me not to drive because I might get hurt. Nobody cared."

My point in describing this material is to emphasize how the rules of gender and sexuality permeate psychoanalytic practice, and second, how interaction is the substratum of all aspects of psychoanalytic practice. Amy had heard my concern for her in my statements in the previous session and further seemed able to use the self-protectiveness of my comments for herself. She described how she liked to take care of her girl friend. She laughed as she said, "I feel like I'm the husband. I want to take care of her but I also want her to take care of me." She went on to describe how they would divide up roles around the house with Amy responsible for the work outdoors and her partner cooking and taking care of the inside, domestic work. Despite the obvious gendered roles, there was a mutuality that Amy seemed to value. However, there was also a dissatisfaction and uneasiness which was captured in her lamenting, "Sometimes I think I would be much happier if I could be the boy; I can 'do boy' better." Amy's "boy," is very traditional, stereotypic in fact.

Identities and Performance

It was important for Amy to define herself categorically. To be open, free, and ambiguous created tremendous anxiety. She was aware of the performance aspect of her self. As she clearly states, she "does boy"; Amy does not feel herself to be a boy, nor does she want to be a boy. Instead, what she wanted was to feel more comfortable, less "weird" and "stupid." Her discomfort and awkwardness seemed to come from squeezing herself into the traditional feminine mold. On the surface she talked about not knowing how to cook and feeling uncomfortable nurturing herself and others. At times she seemed identified with her younger brother who was her constant companion and playmate as a child. They had shared their thoughts, toys, and even clothes. Their coupling formed a buffer between them and their angry, unhappy parents. As an adolescent, Amy surpassed her brother in athletic prowess; as he became interested in girls, she did too, although her interest was secret and guilt-ridden. Throughout her development, she received atypical gender messages from her mother which were heavily mixed with very conventional gender prescriptions from her father. She organized her discrepant familial experiences in a way that allowed her to feel competent. She could "do boy." Her doing boy in various ways in her life permitted her to erotically desire a woman. Amy explained that she was most at ease with herself and others when she was on a field playing ball. She seemed to experience a denseness of interpersonal configurations that coalesced in her doing boy. Her destabilized "gendering" promoted an agency that allowed for achievements and satisfactions, but at the same time, she was left feeling socially isolated with only words like *weird* and *stupid* to explain herself to herself and others. For her, sexuality and gender were so entwined in her mind that what became most important in the treatment was the untying of this knot, and the exploration of each strand of experience and underlying assumptions. It was true that Amy's difficulties extended beyond issues of gender and sexuality. Her rigidity limited her relationships as well as career achievements. In the initial stages of our work, however, we focused on her views of gender. We often would move back and forth between the categories of man and woman; how she felt like a daughter, a son; how she experienced herself as a man, a woman. Sometimes these experiences seemed dense; thick and close as if she had brought all her interpersonal experiences into one moment. Other times these experiences were thin and hardly recognizable to her or to me. As we moved back and forth in our discussions we generated an openness and freedom in place of fixed positions. This way of working was experienced by Amy as helpful. But let me be clear, I am not saying that everything was up for grabs at every moment; for example, my position regarding her use of drugs and alcohol while driving remained very fixed and she abided by those limits.

There is so much more to say about this material, and of course many ways to hear the dream she reported, but for the moment consider the dream as a commentary on our relationship. In this way, Amy's commentary reveals something about her experience of being in treatment with me. It's not just about understanding, it's a relational act that has an impact. In our discussions of gender and sexuality, we unfolded social conditions, institutions, forms of belief and perception revealing the way we each organized our experiences. This opened up a way to talk of other feelings in action between us, those of concern, protection, impatience, and frustration; her fear of being judged, and not being cared for. We were each involved in this therapy and it brought a vitality to the adventure of coming to know one another. This way of working is light years beyond clarification and insight; it involves interaction that leads to expansion and creation. Thinking of the connection between therapist and patient as one that involves action reflects the shift going on throughout psycho-analytic practice (Wolstein, 1977; Ghent, 1995). Within this model, subjectivity is never fixed, it is constantly in process within competing discourses influencing identity.

Identities and Labels

Amy experienced herself as a woman while including behaviors and feelings usually off-limits to women. She remains fully a woman and a lesbian. For me, this attests to how these categories are not exclusive but redundant. They are fluid and expanded identities composed of multiple constituent parts which are continually configured and reconfigured. For Amy, being a lesbian means having the option of *doing boy* without giving up her experience of *woman.* This way of thinking recasts the patterns of gender and sexuality into political categories while allowing us to discover their psychological implications. It also problematizes the redundancy of the identity category *lesbian* and *woman.* Amy finds herself outside of language as she puzzles over her self-experiences. She is not alone in this dilemma, for language in a positivist world has seriously confused and misled us, in some cases foreclosing expression and imposing silence (Derrida, 1978). Daring to speak outside of what has been called *phallogocentric* language, requires new words or, in some cases, new definitions (Wittig, 1993).

Lesbians have always been outside of psychoanalytic language, represented clinically as "female homosexuals." As O'Connor and Ryan (1993) have pointed out, no lesbian would use this term to describe herself. Instead, protesting absence from language, the terms *dyke, queer, femme,* and *butch* are sometimes used as self-proclaimed inventions of an identity continually denied by culture. These self representations envelop sexuality and gender, partly in parody, partly in play, and in resistance. These self representations are discernible throughout today's culture, and in our clinical practices. Unfortunately, for some therapists and patients, these self representations are misheard as organizing elements of identity, rather than as fluid concepts composed of various interpersonal and cultural configurations.

Toward a Conception of Density

I think it important to understand that these fluid self representations vary in quantity and quality depending on the setting. For example, sometimes these self representations are thick, as if all the different parts of experience are packed into a moment of experience. Other times self representations seem thin and shallow as if only fragments of subjective experience are brought to the moment. For me, the concept of *density* is helpful in describing the closeness of these constituent parts of subjective experience. It draws attention to how variable experience can be and how dependent it is on context and rules of acceptance. Related to the idea of identities is *performance,* the act of doing, of putting these identities into play. Take for example, the action involved when a patient questions a therapist about an identity category, for example, Are you married? Are you a parent? Jewish? Catholic? For me, the question of whether or not I am gay often arises. When asked, knowing this question has meanings unique to each patient, I usually respond by saying, "Why do you ask?" But as I think of my reactions to this question I am most aware of becoming aware. I don't think any of us consider ourselves in categorical terms unless there is a reason to do so. Generally, when I am asked this question, I am more likely to be thinking of myself as a therapist, not a woman, not a sexual woman. What follows this question during a session usually includes: "What does it mean if I am; what does it mean if I'm not?" But there is the moment of categorizing myself. The "density" of my feelings is dependent on my relationship with the patient, including the sensations, intensities, bodily excitations that are happening at the moment with the patient. In this way, I think of the different densities of my sexed being; of my gendered self-consciousness; and at times, of sexual desire. For me, density is always dependent on context and includes a sense of how much of any category is appropriate for me in a particular context; appropriate to my style of doing a category. This is not a fixed gender or sexuality but rather a dynamic relationship one has with oneself and with others in one's world. This concept of gender or sexual density provides room for new levels of awareness. Density of gender and sexuality is experienced according to what we know about the rules of each and according to how much anxiety we are able or willing to tolerate in deviating from the rules. This deviation is of course not limited to gender and sexuality. Density can be applied to other socially constructed concepts like race, ethnicity, and class. To illustrate, a patient recounted how upset she became when a friend told her she "danced like a white girl." Her style of dancing, while consistent with her identity or "black consciousness," was inconsistent with her friend's. Not everyone enacts race in the same way. Imbedded in the friend's accusation was the idea that my patient was masquerading as a white woman by not performing according to the demands of a particular context.

How does one do what one is? Butler (1993a) offers an answer to the question of how this performance of self is set into motion. She summarizes her ideas in her comments to friends prior to speaking at a conference on homosexuality. "I found myself telling my friends beforehand that I was off to Yale to be a lesbian, which of course didn't mean that I wasn't one before, but that somehow I, as I spoke in that context, I was one in some more thorough and totalizing way, at least for the time being." Her sense of a "more thorough and totalizing way" of being corresponds with my idea of density; that all the various parts of herself come together in a conscious moment. She continues, wondering, how she can be one, and yet endeavor to be one at the same time.

When and where does my being like a lesbian, come into play, when and where does this playing a lesbian constitute something like what I am? To say that I "play" at being one is not to say that I am one, "really"; rather, how and where I play at being one is the way in which that "being" gets established, instituted, circulated and confirmed. This is not a performance from which I can take radical distance, for this is deep seated play, psychically entrenched play and this "I" does not play its lesbianism as a role [p. 311].

Our character from the McNally play does not have to be a "queen" to feel like a "queen." He can do "queen"; and if he does "queen" he does not have to be aware of doing it; just as the patient Amy does not have to be a boy to do boy. She knows what is required of boys and feels she is able to meet those requirements, at least to a large degree. I think Joan Riviere (1929) had a glimpse of these postmodern notions. For example, she suggested womanliness could be assumed and worn as a mask, both to hide the possession of masculinity and to avert expected reprisals if she was found to possess it. This masquerade allows a form of "passing" and passing becomes a complex sociological deception that allows a rebellious identity to survive although compromised and silent.

Butler uses object relational notions in her own unique way when she locates the destabilization of the categories that make up gender and sexual identity as a melancholic incorporation of an "other." This incorporation renders gender a kind of imitation for which "there is no original, and performance [is] the way we enact symbols and words that comprise and structure experience." Amy's "doing boy" is an act of imposture, a kind of momentary participation in an illusion reminiscent of Riviere's masquerade. She can do boy and she can do girl with varying levels of confidence and density.

The Contributions of Post-Freudian Psychoanalysts

While Freud's developmental ideas resulted in fixed identity categories, other psychoanalysts have been less wedded to the fixed notion of identity categories. For example, Winnicott (1971), in a more subjective object relations model, describes a flexible vision of gender and sexuality. He reports in *Playing and Reality* on a phase of work with a patient briefly sketched by him as a middle-aged, successful, married man with a family.

The patient came and reported much as usual. The thing that struck me on this Friday was that the patient was talking about penis envy. I use this term advisedly and I must invite acceptance of the fact that this term was appropriate here in view of the material and of its presentation. Obviously this term penis envy, is not usually applied in the description of a man. . . . On this particular occasion I said to him: I am listening to a girl. I know perfectly well that you are a man, but I am listening to a girl and I am talking to a girl. I am telling this girl; "You are talking about penis envy" [p. 73].

He goes on to say, "I wish to emphasize that this has nothing to do with homosexuality." (Winnicott seems to acknowledge that sexuality and gender are separate categories.) While speaking of the dissociative process affecting male and female split-off elements, Winnicott and his patient focused on seeing and hearing a girl talking, holding constant the man on the couch. Winnicott saw, indeed felt, that the patient wanted to speak "girl" and that the patient wanted the therapist to recognize that part of him was "girl." He recognizes the constantly changing configurations of inner experience involving fantasies, identifications, memories, wishes and feeling all tied to a *repertoire* of inner characters. For Winnicott these characters are derived from past and present relationships both actual and imagined. His conception of gender appears fluid, and suggests increased possibilities, but he stays confined to a system of psychic structures; of object relationships, where behavior is thought to be the expression of these unconscious objects. This system, while introducing the environment, limits agency to experience and experience to unquestioned cultural assumptions.

Sullivan (1953), on the other hand, was perhaps the first to take up this issue of how we create the categories of our world and experience the world in terms of those categories. He rejected classical drive theory as inadequate and emphasized the social–cultural context of human development and behavior. Sullivan has yet to receive the credit he is due for bringing psychoanalysis to the edge of the postmodern world, pointing out as he did so the futility and meaninglessness of social categories and the continual interaction involved in all aspects of human relating. Unfortunately for us and probably also for Sullivan, he never dared to cross the line fully into the postmodern.

In contrast, the classically minded McDougall (1985) understands that our inner selves may move about as freely as characters on a stage, but while she uses the theater metaphor to more accurately capture the way people experience themselves, she doesn't deal with the stage or the context in which one moves about. For McDougall, psychoanalytic systems are confined by unexplored prescriptive assumptions ultimately placing limits on change.

Definition as Limitation

For some therapists and patients these self representations are misheard as organizing elements of identity rather than as fluid concepts. Trop and Stolorow (1992) is a good example of how a therapist's wish to pigeonhole the patient, whether conscious or unconscious, obviates growth. They present the case material of a man who sought treatment "because he felt deeply depressed about himself and did not know whether he was homosexual or heterosexual. His sexual experiences with women were few, and his primary sexual activities were infrequent, isolated homosexual experiences with different partners." The authors describe "the patient's defensive retreats from heterosexual involvement" and how they became a central focus of the analysis. Trop and Stolorow (1992) fall into the tar pit of identity categories, seeing them as real productions of a developmental matrix, rather than as fantasy constructions of a sociopolitical moment. Entrapped in their belief in universal elements of human development they fail to see how their beliefs may influence what they say and do. Isay (1985) has noted how most psychoanalysts assume that homosexuality is an unfavorable and unconscious solution to developmental conflicts. And so go Trop and Stolorow (1992); they describe the patient's primary developmental yearning in the transference as a longing for the guidance of a strong father who would help him face the dangers of being close to women. This "deep developmental longing for a strong father to help him face the extreme dangers that were preventing him from enjoying a sexual involvement with a woman" was seen as pivotal to the analysis. Trop and Stolorow (1992) seem embedded in a positivist notion of development, one that assumes a universal basic truth about development. Cushman (1991) has critiqued these obscured ideologies that hide and mystify the impact of political forces on individual lives. He has taken Daniel Stern's (1985) concept of the development of self and demonstrated the unexplored assumptions and the dangers inherent in our collective blind romance with developmental theories.

Returning to the idea of performance again, for the moment, think of the story as told by "the patient" through Trop and Stolorow (1992) as a performative act. Alan presents himself to his therapist as "deeply depressed and confused as to whether he is 'homosexual or heterosexual.' " Each analyst would focus on a different part of this complaint because each would hear and see different parts of this presentation. For example, one could focus on the "deeply depressed" aspect. Is he saying, "Don't expect to find things on the surface, for me the action is deep?" How does he perform "deep"? Does this patient live his life in terms of surface and depth? Does he split his sexuality too? Is he homosexual or heterosexual? Is one on the surface and one deep? Which sexuality is performed down deep and depressed? Which is performed on the surface? My personally associative questioning wonders how this man puts his world together. I might say to him, "So what's the difference for you if you are homosexual or heterosexual?" What is a life lived as a homosexual like? What is life lived as a heterosexual like? These questions do not come from a tolerance of difference. They are drenched in my personal value system, which does not view sexuality as what one is but rather what one does with one's desires. There are no certainties here, only questions. I ask them from my perspective and I hear the answers through my position. The patient's perspective and mine may agree or disagree. It is our mutual ability to tolerate, and one hopes, come to know each other that is at the center of whether we will change and grow emotionally. Trop and Stolorow do not question identity categories but rather accept and get caught up in them, in the way their patient accepts them and becomes entangled. This could be seen as empathic or it could be seen as a resolution to the patient's crisis by ordering an adaptive identity. In contrast, Wolstein (1974) has warned that, "We cannot resolve crises in individuality with adapted identities." His warning is not one that Trop and Stolorow heed, thus, they never push the patient to resolve his crisis in identity with expanded self-expressions. Instead, the sociopolitical challenges of this case stay locked by the way the problem is framed: Am I heterosexual or homosexual? The patient's unique expressions of self are never revealed to him or shared with his analyst. The success of this analysis seems to rest on what is agreed, approved, and expected as adaptive in relatedness and communication.

The Unlinking of Gender and Sexual Desire

Postmodern conceptions of self offer exciting changes in the way we think about identity categories. Fueled by the writings of psychoanalytic gender revisionists (Dimen, 1991; Goldner, 1991; Harris, 1991), and queer theorists (Butler, 1993b, 1995; Wittig, 1993), sexuality in psycho-analysis is being redefined and expanded (O'Connor and Ryan, 1993; Domenici and Lesser, 1995; Glassgold and Iasenza, 1995). These writers bring us beyond the view of sexuality as a defensive structure, compro-mise formation, or symptom (Chodorow, 1992). Instead we move past theories of psychopathology "so that the psychodynamic contributions to the varieties of sexual orientation, sexual behavior and sexual longings can be explored and appreciated" (Mitchell, 1978, p. 263).

I have been arguing for the position that as analysts, we do better to understand both sexuality and gender as performative acts rather than as fixed, stable categories resulting from some normative developmental sequence. We have yet to generate a theory solid enough to allow us to take for granted the circumstances that define affection, tenderness, and erotic excitement for anyone. If as analysts we believe inner experience involves constantly changing configurations of fantasies, identifications, memories, wishes and feelings derived from past and present relation-ships both actual and imagined then there is even a question as to who is having sex. For example, Aron's (1995) reconceptualization of the primal scene explores sexuality in this new way. He provides a picture of a "primary threesome" infusing the notion of a "primal scene" with an exchange of body parts and places. He situates these body parts and places in the mutual performance of sexual gratification, and postulates that this leads to creativity.

While deconstructive positions are elegant ways to stretch and chal-lenge our outworn rhetoric of metaphysical truth and embrace a potential for reshaping existence, it doesn't always preclude "personally essential-ist" positions which can later undergo deconstruction. Existence can then meet the standard of "a satisfied, secured and fulfilled sense of individuality" knowing that "the tension of psyche and culture is never resolved by ignoring either in the name of the other" (Wolstein, 1974).

For me, gender and sexuality have become something that we *do* rather than something we *are*. This shift has an impact on issues broader than gender and sexuality in psychoanalysis. It displaces the focus of current analytic models that depend on structure to explain the enduring effects of the past, to a focus on process where past experience is understood as part of the present. This change could have a major impact on how we hear our patients' struggles in their lives. Ultimately this shift may unlink gender from sexuality in a way that informs both theory and praxis. This way of thinking raises many questions. How are gender and sexuality regarded, preserved, and performed in each individual's life? Do gender and sexuality performances, or acts, include elements of chance, desire, and choice? Are they forms of sexual theater for the audience of sexual partners and/or spectators? Is masquerade a critical part of the performance of sex and gender? Who scripts the performance or is it merely unanalyzably existential? (These questions were first posited by Wolstein in a personal communication.)

In conclusion, I suggest we question all social constructions of identity, and ask, do they inhibit or promote an individual's life? We have been warned that we cannot ask our patients to abandon identities that are already fragile and inconsistent and embark on what may be a deconstructive journey to nihilism (Flax, 1993). Nonetheless, it is in the abandonment of identities that are fragile, rigid, and confining that a space is provided for the formulation of better and expanded possibilities. This is where postmodern and psychoanalytic paradigms extend each other. Rather than being distinctly different, viewed as a continuum they can stretch and reshape our theories and practices.

References

Aron, L. (1995), The internalized primal scene. *Psychoanal. Dial.,* 5:195–237.

Butler, J. (1993a), Imitation and gender insubordination. In: *The Lesbian and Gay Studies Reader,* ed. H. Abelove, M. Barale, & D. Halperin. New York: Routledge.

——— (1993b), *Bodies That Matter: On the Discursive Limits of Sex.* New York: Routledge.

——— (1995), Melancholy gender—refused identification. *Psychoanal. Dial.,* 5:165–180.

Chodorow, N. (1992), Heterosexuality as a compromise formation: Reflections on the psychoanalytic theory of sexual development. *Psychoanal. & Contemp. Thought,* 15:267–304.

Cushman, P. (1991), Ideology obscured: Political uses of the self. *Amer. Psychologist,* 46:206–219.

Derrida, J. (1978), *Writing and Difference.* Chicago: University of Chicago Press.

Dimen, M. (1991), Deconstructing difference: Gender, splitting, and transitional space. *Psychoanal. Dial.,* 1:335–352.

——— (1995), On "our nature": Prolegomenon to a relational theory of sexuality. In: *Disorienting Sexuality: Psychoanalytic Reappraisals of Sexual Identities,* ed. J. Domenici & R. Lesser. New York: Routledge.

Domenici, T., & Lesser, R., Eds. (1995), *Disorienting Sexuality: Psychoanalytic Reappraisals of Sexual Identities.* New York: Routledge.

Flax, J. (1993), *Disputed Subjects: Essays on Psychoanalysis, Politics and Philosophy.* New York & London: Routledge.

Freud, S. (1920), The psychogenesis of a case of homosexuality in a woman. *Standard Edition,* 18:145–172. London: Hogarth Press, 1955.

Ghent, M. (1995), Interaction in the psychoanalytic situation. *Psychoanal. Dial.,* 5:479–491.

Glassgold, J., & Iasenza, S., Eds. (1995), *Lesbians and Psychoanalysis: Revolutions in Theory and Practice.* New York: Free Press.

Goldner, V. (1991), Toward a critical relational theory of gender. *Psychoanal. Dial.,* 1:249–272.

Harris, A. (1991), Gender as contradiction. *Psychoanal. Dial.,* 1:197–224.

Isay, R. (1985), On the analytic therapy of homosexual men. *The Psychoanalytic Study of the Child,* 40:235–254. New Haven, CT: Yale University Press.

McDougall, J. (1985), *Theaters of the Mind: Illusion and Truth on the Psychoanalytic Stage.* New York: Basic Books.

McNally, T. (1995), *Love! Valour! Compassion.* New York: Plume/Penguire.

Menaker, E. (1995), *The Freedom to Inquire: Self Psychological Perspectives on Women's Issues, Masochism, and the Therapeutic Relationship.* Northvale, NJ: Jason Aronson.

Mitchell, S. (1978), Psychodynamics, homosexuality, and the question of pathology. *Psychiatry,* 41:255–263.

O'Connor, N., & Ryan, J. (1993), *Wild Desires and Mistaken Identities: Lesbianism and Psychoanalysis.* New York: Columbia University Press.

Riviere, J. (1929), Womanliness as a masquerade. *Internat. J. Psycho-Anal.,* 10:303–313.

Stern, D. (1985), *The Interpersonal World of the Infant.* New York: Basic Books.

Sullivan, H. (1953), *The Interpersonal Theory of Psychiatry.* New York: W. W. Norton.

Trop, J., & Stolorow, R. (1992), Defense analysis in self psychology: A developmental view. *Psychoanal. Dial.,* 2:427–442.

Winnicott, D. W. (1971), *Playing and Reality.* London: Tavistock.

Wittig, M. (1993), One is not born a woman. In: *The Lesbian and Gay Studies Reader,* ed. H. Abelove, M. Barale, & D. Halperin. New York: Routledge.

Wolstein, B. (1974), Individuality and identity. *Contemp. Psychoanal.,* 10:1–14.

———— (1977), Psychology, metapsychology, and the evolving American school of interpersonal psychoanalysis. *Contemp. Psychoanal.,* 13:128–154.

12

Talking About Lesbians: Minnie Bruce Pratt and Her Poetic Journey

Arlene Kramer Richards

During the negative oedipal phase a little girl wants to be her mother's lover. What she wants is to be loved exclusively and sexually by her mother. She wants to sleep in mother's bed, spend all of her time with mother, and share secrets, games, and toys. She wants all the men out of her mother's life. This phase, Freud thought, is normal and transitory. For some girls and some women the phase continues in the sense that they love and long for the love of a woman for all or most of their lives. Such women are called lesbians. This definition does not focus on genital sex because lesbian self-definitions do not do so. It centers on the work of relating, the pleasures of interaction, and the human contact all lovers, heterosexual or homosexual, seek. This definition includes women who see themselves as "butch" or "femme," women who are neither, women who alternate between those poles, women who knew their sexual orientation very early in life, and women who lived part of their lives as heterosexual.

In *Three Essays on the Theory of Sexuality* (1905) Freud referred to homosexuality as *inversion*. He used that term to differentiate it from what he called *perversion*. Homosexuality was not a perversion, but a variant object choice, equally valid as heterosexual object choice. Throughout his life, Freud continued to assert that homosexuality was not an illness, not a deviant form of sexuality, and not to be cured, although he also continued to express the opposite view (Young-Breuhl, 1990). Late in his life, he treated the bisexual woman poet H. D. (1956). He helped her to accept her longings for love with women and her lifelong liaison with a woman partner with whom she raised a child, and also to believe that she was best off sublimating her sexual wishes. Here Freud gave H. D. the same advice he gave his own daughter, Anna, and it was also the course he himself wished to pursue.

Freud's relatively open and benign attitude toward what he called "object choice" was contradicted by the later psychoanalysts who believed that same-sex object choice necessarily implied psychopathology (Bak, 1953; Socarides, 1963), arrested development (Blank and Blank, 1979), or both (Gillespie, 1964). Waelder (1960) believed that homosexual object choice was like a neurotic symptom, analyzable so as to remove it from what was seen as normal: the path to heterosexual fulfillment.

McDougall (1970) addressed the issue of lesbian development by asking: "If, as suggested here, homosexual libido in women is normally absorbed in object relations of a sublimated kind, in the narcissistic self-image, and in sublimated activities, what then, is the situation with regard to the overt homosexual?" (p. 173).

What is an overt homosexual? A person who chooses a lover of the same sex. Analytic thinkers have separated object choice from gender and from sex. The distinctions are several. Sex is the name given to the physical evidence of male and female; that is, genetic code, primary sexual organs at birth, and secondary characteristics developing at puberty. Gender identity is the name given to the child's awareness that she is a girl. This awareness has been shown to be demonstrable at about 18 months of age when a toddler will correctly and reliably reply to the question, "Are you a girl?" Gender role refers to the behaviors considered appropriate for the person of a specific gender. Object choice refers to the selection of a lover based on an image, the "object" formed from traits derived from experiences with childhood caregivers. It does not imply that the person making the choice is free to change or to make another type of choice (Siegel, 1988). It does restrict the idea of homosexuality, freeing it from implications of lack of gender identity and from biological sex. An advantage of this concept is that it allows gender role to be defined separately, thus avoiding the mistake of ascribing masculine traits to all lesbians, as has been the case in the United States and Europe since the nineteenth century (Greenberg, 1988).

Sex is biological, gender identity is psychological and cognitive, and object choice is psychological and largely determined by affective considerations. Sex is in the genetic code from conception, gender identity is relatively immutable after the third year of life, and object choice is thought to be stable by the close of adolescence (Tyson and Tyson, 1990). Complicating this already complex schema is gender role, a concept that encompasses what may be considered socially as appropriate to gender; for example, girls giggle, or real women don't tell jokes.

This schema attributes the ambiguities and changes in the course of a person's life to a gradual uncovering of what was already present but hidden in the person's psychological makeup. Some future homosexuals already had longings for same-sex lovers early in childhood. Freud attributed his homosexual woman patient's (1920) same-sex object choice to her experience of having her mother give birth to a son when the patient was an adolescent. Deutsch (1932) asserted that lesbian object choice always has infantile roots, but is probably decided in adolescence.

Some women seem to lead heterosexual lives while they are adolescents and young adults and become lesbians later. Saghir and Robbins (1980) see this pattern as homosexual behavior in a heterosexual person. Wolff (1971) sees it as belated discovery of a homosexual self. In her essay on lesbian motherhood and poetry, Adrienne Rich (1993) introduces the work of Minnie Bruce Pratt, a poet who had lived a heterosexual life, married, and had two children before falling in love with a woman. Rich describes and analyzes the importance of motherhood to a lesbian, using excerpts from Pratt's poetry. Rich's essay is enriched by her own experience as the mother of two sons who then became a lesbian when she was already middle aged.

Of particular interest in the work of these poets is their attitude toward men and masculinity. An important part of the social and particularly of the male attitude toward female sexuality is fear of the too aggressive woman. The work of these poets addresses that fear. Do lesbians really hate men? Exploring her own feelings toward the husband she has recently left, Pratt describes a complex ambivalence. In *Love Poem to an Ex-Husband*, Pratt says: "You were always the one/I asked to kill things . . . until one day you refused/ . . . You had not acted like a man/ and I never loved you better . . ." (pp. 27–28).

The story of this poem is simple. A wife tells her husband to kill the wounded animals she cannot save. He accepts the role of killer. When one day he refuses, she puts the tortoise out of its misery. It seems to me that she is not talking only about the tortoise, but also about her marriage. Both were shattered, both had to be ended. The love in this poem is the most surprising part. The poet does not hate men or the particular man who was closest to her, her husband. Pratt sees the connection between her illegitimate use of her husband to express her own aggression and her need to separate from him. The poem implies that she had, like many women, safeguarded her sense of innocence and goodness by attributing her own aggression to men. Forced to do her own killing, she must take responsibility for her own aggression. In this sense, it is a poem of psychic development. No longer able to project her own feelings onto another, she becomes more of a responsible person. No longer clinging to the vision of herself as someone without aggression, she expresses her aggression openly and accepts a new vision of herself in relation to other people in the world.

But the aggression in the poem is aggression in the service of love. The killing she has asked her husband to do is a mercy killing, needing to be done for the ultimate good of the victim. This aspect further complicates the poet's relation to her husband. If the thing she is asking him to kill is their marriage, his refusal to let her go becomes an ultimate cruelty. Like other women who kept house for their families at the cost of sacrificing their own careers, Pratt was likely to be too valuable for him to let easily. Her husband's refusal to let go of the marriage thus required her to assert her own needs and to be the killer of the doomed sufferer.

Pratt published that love poem to her husband in a book of poetry that she called *The Sound of One Fork*. In ''My Mother Loves Women'' (1981b), Pratt examines the roots of her love for women. An excerpt from that poem says:

My mother loves women.
She sent me gold and silver earrings for Valentine's.
She sent a dozen red roses to Ruby Lemley
when she was sick and took her eight quarts
of purplehull beans, shelled and ready to cook.
She walks every evening down our hill and around
with Margaret Hullman. They pick up loose hubcaps and talk
about hysterectomies and cataracts.

At the slippery spots they go arm in arm. . . .

I don't think she's known a man except this brother
and my father who for the last twenty years has been waiting
for death in his rocking chair in front of the TV set.

During that time my mother was seeing women
every day at work in her office. She knit them
intricate afghans and told me proudly
that Anne Fenton could not go to sleep without hers.

My mother loves women but she's afraid
to ask me about my life. She thinks
that I might love women too [p. 29].

In this poem Pratt shows love for other women as natural, familial, homely. Expressed through gifts "for Valentine's," flowers and food when the loved one is sick, through the loving evening walks, the frequency of contacts and confidences, her mother's love for women is warm and unexceptionable. But Pratt includes conflict over the erotic aspect, her mother and her friend talk, on their evening walks, of hysterectomies and cataracts; hysterectomies for the removal of female reproductive parts and removal of cataracts that obscure vision, and untreated end in blindness. The poet asks the reader to see how her mother's love for women can blindly include a sexuality she cannot bear to see. In the image of the afghan her mother has constructed for her friend without which her friend cannot go to sleep, she evokes lovers entangled before sleep. Why is it that her mother cannot accept her daughter's love for women? Because she is afraid to recognize her own love for women. Pratt's idea seems to be that homophobia is a defense against homophilia, that love for women precedes love for men and may be the unrecognized mainstream of love in a woman's life. It is especially poignant that she begins the poem with a reminder that her mother sent her a love gift, "gold and silver earrings for Valentine's." She reminds her mother that loving her is loving a woman, that the primary love relation in a woman's life is always that with the mother, another woman. The image of her passive and unrelated father provides contrast. Who could love him?

The title poem of The Sound of One Fork, its importance underscored by its use as the title of the book, describes what she left her husband and children for: solitude. The poet is aware that she is too easily subsumed in the lives of others, too easily gives up her own aggression and her own desires. She describes herself in the poem as a neighbor woman, and as a blue heron. She tells us that she prefers loneliness to life with the people she loves. This hard choice is inevitable for someone who cannot experience herself as herself when in the presence of others. Like the heron, she cannot bear too much light, too much activity. When with other people, she is exquisitely sensitive to their needs and desires. She experiences herself as completely responsive, not active at all. Her only way out of the state of not being is the painful but preferable state of loneliness. The price of a sense of living on her own is to reject others, to be like the heron and the neighbor, alone. Competent to do for herself, she has no need for the borrowed aggression she rejected in the love poem to her ex-husband.

Part of ''The Sound of One Fork'' goes this way:

. . . I can hear the random click of one fork
against a plate. The woman next door is eating supper
alone. She is sixty, perhaps, and for many years
has eaten by herself the tomatoes, the corn
and okra she grows in her backyard garden.
Her small metallic sound persists, as quiet almost
as the windless silence, persists like the steady
random click of a redbird cracking a few
more seeds before the sun gets too low.
She does not hurry, she does not linger.

Her younger neighbors think that she is lonely,
that only death keeps her company at meals.
But I know what sufficiency she may possess.
I know what can be gathered from year to year,
gathered from what is near to hand, as I do
elderberries that bend in damp thickets by the road,
gathered and preserved, jars and jars shining
in rows of claret red. . . ,
In the morning and the evening we are by ourselves,
the woman next door and I. Sometimes we are afraid
of the death in solitude and want someone
else to live our lives. Still we persist.

I open the drawer to get out the silverware.
She goes to her garden to pull weeds and pick
the crookneck squash that turns yellow with late summer.
I walk down to the pond in the morning to watch
and wait for the blue heron who comes at first light
to feed on minnows that swim through her shadow in the water.
She stays until the day grows so bright
that she cannot endure it and leaves with her hunger unsatisfied.
She bows her wings and slowly lifts into flight,
grey and slate blue against a paler sky.
I know she will come back . . . [p. 12].

Here the poet examines her own feelings about her wish to live alone.
She understands herself to be like the woman next door. The image is a
homely one and an ironic contrast to the "girl next door." While the
girl next door is the one boys fall in love with, the woman is the antithesis
of the male construction of what is desirable and romantic. A woman of
60. Not young, not glamorous, capable of eating, not luscious, not "good
enough to eat." Pitied rather than envied by her neighbors, she eats in
such profound aloneness, such silence, that the sound of her fork on her
plate is the loudest sound in the universe of the poem. The poet understands that the woman needs to be alone to enjoy the claret red memories
stored up with friends and lovers. Why does she need to leave the family
and lovers she misses? Because she needs to persist, to follow her own
flight plan like the heron, to respond to her own impulses, to protect
herself from an intensity of heat and light which is unbearable to her.
Like the heron she needs to retreat from the world in order to have the
light under the curve of her wings. This is a story of the artist's experience
and the artist's need for solitude in order to work over that experience,
assimilate it by preserving it, and taste it in solitude, in her own time,
and the safety of her own space.

What is especially lesbian in this experience? Pratt tells us in "Southern Gothic." The final portion of that poem reads this way:

. . . I see myself stand on the steps, the bearded lady,
my hairy legs ready to run wild over the road,
living like wisteria, gnarled and twisted,
trailing with a lover down the steps
like purple meteors of wisteria bloom

while to themselves the neighbors murmur
how peculiar, how queer [p. 36].

In this poem Pratt completes the outline of her journey of revelation.
Her move from leaving her husband to living alone to find her voice to
living entwined with a female lover is complete. By the end of the poem
she accepts herself as an outlaw, a purple twisted wisteria, a person about
whom the neighbors whisper *"how peculiar, how queer."* In this she
separates herself from her social surround; to become an outlaw is to
separate from the people who knew her as a child and young woman. To
become an outlaw is to define a new universe which has many disadvan-
tages and much pain but is her only possibility of connection. Because
it is chosen by her and not for her it allows her to be herself in a context
that will not overwhelm her. Like the heron she can and will come back,
but now she comes back into a universe defined by the arch of her wing,
a universe where she is the measure of all things. In her later poetry there
are many echoes of the fear of being overwhelmed by closeness to a
lover. Her old need for solitude and fears of intimacy repeat in many
contexts. For example in a later poem she calls herself *"Daughter of the
Earth* who walled herself against/love and tenderness that menace the
freedom of women"* (1985, p. 63), but she still seems to be able to
maintain herself and herself in relation to others as long as she remains
in the self-selected world.

From this point, she will become more and more entwined in a lesbian
life, a social system and a community which, for her, is outlawed, romantic, tragic and nurturant.

I believe that the ego psychologists were correct in saying that lesbian
psychology is much concerned with nurture. For this reason, it is much
concerned with mother–daughter relationships, but not simply with regression to the infantile state of needing nurture. Being the mother can
motivate some lesbians as having a mother does others. In her poem, *All
the Women Caught in Flaring Light* (1990a), Pratt says:

... Say we walked around to 8th or 11th Street
to drop in on a roomful of women, smiling, intense,
playing pool, the green baize like moss. One
lights another's cigarette, oblique glance.
Others dance by twos under twirling silver moons
that rain light down in glittering drops.

If I said in your ear through metallic guitars,
These women are mothers, you wouldn't believe me,
would you? Not really, not even if you had come
to be one of the women in that room. You'd say:
Well, maybe, one or two, a few. It's what we say.

Here, we hardly call our children's names out loud.
We've lost them once, or fear we may. We're careful
what we say. In the clanging silence, pain falls
on our hearts, year in and out, like water cutting
a groove in stone, seeking a channel, a way out,
pain running like water through the glittering room.
. . . But things have been done to us that can never be
undone. The woman in the corner smiling at friends,
the one with black hair glinting white, remembers
the brown baby girl's weight relaxed into her lap,
the bottle in her right hand, cigarette in her left,
the older blond girl pressed tense at her shoulder,
the waves slap on the rowboat, the way she squinted
as the other woman, her lover, took some snapshots,
the baby sucking and grunting rhythmic as the water.

The brown eyed baby who flirted before she talked,
taken and sent away twenty years ago, no recourse,
to a tidy man-and-wife to serve as daughter.
If she stood in the door, the woman would not know her,
and the child would have no memory of the woman,
not of lying on her knees nor at her breast, leaving
a hidden mark, pain grooved and etched on the heart.

The woman's told her friends about the baby. They
keep forgetting. Her story drifts away like smoke,
like vague words in a song, a paper scrap in the water.
When they talk about mothers, they never think of her.

No easy ending to this pain. At midnight we go home
to silent houses, or perhaps to clamorous rooms full
of those who are now our family. Perhaps we sit alone,
heavy with the past, and there are tears running bitter

and steady as rain in the night. Mostly we just go on [1990a, pp. 29–34].

Being a mother whose children are taken away from her is an important part of Pratt's experience. In other poems she expresses the loss when her husband forced her to choose between being a lesbian and keeping her children, the loss when her mother refused to let her live with her children in her parental home and forced her to choose between staying with her husband and giving up her children. By the time she writes this poem, she already knows many other mothers who have lost their children in just the same way. She expresses her own pain through theirs and their pain is filtered through hers. The empathic connection intensifies the poet's feeling.

Pratt is the mother of two sons. This makes her attitude toward men especially poignant. She is faced with the conflict: how can she hate men and love her sons? Her way of dealing with the problem is to write it into a poem.

"Talking to Charlie"

The cafeteria. Women, and alone, an eighteen year old
boy eating breakfast, diffident mouth, scant food. School.

I do not have to sit with him, not my child, but I do,
and eat my flat fried egg: cynical eye, yellow crocus
in the snow outside, speaking mouth. He opens
his mouth. The words will be: Hate men, don't you?
Last night I'd read a poem aloud: men, rape, the screw-
driver, the woman's eyes.

   His face convulses red,
muscles of his mouth struggle to push words fleshed
out, a new thing, onto the table between us. I gave
him something. He is giving me back a bloody live
making of his own.
   He says: *The righteous anger of*
women, the times I hate myself as a man. Not
to be. I get lonely.

His face. My sons' look at me.

The three of us, faces bright as early suns, grinning
reflected in the creek's surface, summer. We wade in,

swim until four shadow men arrive in the slipping light,
gage with eyes how close we are until night, nod politely.

We leave. I rage. My oldest says: *If you hate
them-men-you hate us.* My voice answers: *Rape,
history, the grasp of danger.* My voice splits, frantic
in the tiny car, classroom. Their faces blank.

At the table Charlie waits for me to answer. No shadow
faces float in the dull formica. *I get lonely* I say.
What will you say to the other men? And to my sons? [1990b, pp.
22–85].

Here the poet ostensibly tries to explain herself to a young man who
is not her son, to convey to him why she is a lesbian as if she owes him
heterosexuality. She speaks to him as she would to her sons, using him
as a bridge to them. When he reacts to her reading rape poems by saying
"The righteous anger of women. The times I hate myself as a man. Not
to be. I get lonely," she evokes the "four shadow men" who menaced
her and her sons. She is afraid of aggressive men, men who can rape.
She explains her love of women simply by echoing his words: "I get
lonely," she says. Her love comes out of longing just as his does. Then
she challenges the reader to understand: "What will you say to the other
men? And to my sons?"

In her nonfiction essays, collected in *Rebellion* (1991b), Pratt explores
her evolution in a less personal way. There she attributes her turn toward
a woman lover as the outcome of joining a consciousness-raising group.
She describes her gradual evolution into a person who identifies with
and attempts to comfort the underdog, the victim of oppression and greed,
as she herself is deprived of the privileges won for her by her white
Southern ancestors. She sees those ancestors as having taken the land
they owned from the Indians whom they killed or ousted. She identifies
with her mother who was a welfare worker, and turns away from her
father, a man who was a professional security guard and a full-time

alcoholic. She understands herself as a person who could do no other than she did for a complex set of intrapsychic and interpersonal as well as political reasons. She presents herself as a daughter of privilege, but also as a woman raised with a social conscience. She describes the complicated compromises necessary for the people she grew up among and the dilemmas she was faced with when she began to question the gulf between what she was taught and what she experienced. "All men are brothers," contrasted with "Black people don't come in our house except as servants." "All God's children," contrasted with, "Miners live in the hollow, masters live on the hill." These essays may serve as another kind of context for understanding the poet and her love life. They are like the case history we take before starting analytic work. They provide the particulars of the person's life as she is aware of it before treatment.

Yet the question may be asked with regard to her later poems: Has she returned to a mode of thinking and of defense that characterized her before she wrote *Love Poem to an Ex-Husband?* Has her journey led her back to ascribing her own aggression to men? Has male violence become the cover and the metaphor for her own rage? Has her courage in abjuring projection gotten lost? In *S/HE* Pratt (1995) describes what heterosexuality means to her in more general and in specifically sexual terms. In a short essay or prose poem called *Pillow Talk,* she recalls Doris Day and her competent, perky image. Now, as a grown woman, Pratt knows that Day had submitted to male violence. Day's "husband had beaten her, kicked her in the stomach when she was pregnant. I said to myself: *There is her weakness, like mine.* I told myself to be strong, to be ready to fight back, the films were fantasy, male fantasy" (p. 130).

In *S/HE* Pratt takes lesbian experience to what seems another level of being in opposition. She exults in her butch lover's dildo, in what looks like an imitation of a heterosexual coupling. She gives up egalitarian sexuality in favor of a relationship where she is penetrated. Now, however, she experiences this as her own desire, not as a forceful entry into the privacy of her body. What can she answer to those who reject her for loving a woman, and what can she say to those who reject her for loving someone who masquerades as a man? "I wonder what judgements are being made of me, as lesbian, as femme, leaning at the edge of the room, at the edge of almost everybody's limits, the ones who think I need a real woman, and the ones who think I just need a real man" (p. 133). The point she insists on is that her desire is her own, she must find for herself what she needs, she must define herself through her desire.

Confronting her own conflict, she must find her own compromise. She ends with this:

Years later, in this crowded room, I have another answer for her: *Desire is like a poem. The knife can mean life and death, but whose hand holds it? The rose can mean petals and canker in the bud, but whose hand spreads it? With each criss-crossing gesture the meaning of* lust *will shift. If we dare claim our bodies as our own, we must read all the poems we write with our bodies* [p. 134].

Discussion

Many paths may lead to lesbian object choice. The particular path articulated by Minnie Bruce Pratt may not be generalizable. But I believe that if we know this path, it may be easier to compare and contrast other reports. For Pratt, the start is the poet's willingness to abjure attributing her aggression to her husband. This change can be seen as giving up defensive projection of her own aggression onto men. While the poem about her mother loving women can be seen as normalizing her object choice, it also asserts identification with her. Pratt's need for solitude to contain, recall, and work over her feelings is seen in the poem *The Sound of One Fork.* Her need for her mother's love and her conflict over that need are most important in the poem in which she describes the lesbian mothers in a barroom. Her need to *be* a mother, to *give* nurturance underlines the importance of that need to her. Finally, her wish to explain herself to her sons and to the man who stands as surrogate for them, circles back to her love poem to her husband.

Pratt tells stories of male violence and female fear of violent men, especially of rape. The stories reflect internal images confirmed by direct experience of violence or, as Pratt asserts, derived vicariously from the experiences of women lovers. In this she is like the homosexual woman McDougall describes. McDougall differentiates two types of lesbians, roughly corresponding to "butch" and "femme." She describes the latter type as fearful of male violence. Pratt regards herself as "femme." According to McDougall both types of lesbians' "difficulties are determined in part by a common failure to identify with a genital mother." Further, she believes that, "None of the limited number of articles on homosexuality stresses the fact that the girl, in making a homosexual attachment, is making a bid for freedom from the real mother as an external obstacle'' (p. 206). However, this bid inevitably fails, and the girl discovers that the object she is attempting to flee is actually internal. McDougall ends:

> In conclusion we might sum up the psychic economy of female homo-sexuality as follows: an attempt to maintain a narcissistic equilibrium in face of a constant need to escape the dangerous symbiotic relation-ship claimed by the mother imago, through conserving an uncon-scious identification with the father, the latter factor being an essential element in a fragile structure [pp. 211–212].

McDougall believes this to be neither neurotic nor psychotic, but per-verse. The perverse aspect is the acting out of an internal drama in the external world. Such a formulation might fit the internal world of a woman who sees her father as ineffectual and her mother as powerful and demanding. This is not so far from the world Pratt shows us. But it does not differentiate lesbians from any other women. The need to pre-serve one's narcissistic equilibrium is universal, as are the dread of sym-biosis and the fragility of identification with an opposite-sex object.

Gillespie (1964) considered the underlying fantasy in all lesbian rela-tionships is that of a needy baby and a cruel, denying mother. Eisenbud (1982) described a pattern of exclusion from either nurturance or protec-tion by the mother and a consequent erotic wooing of her by the little girl as one path to lesbian choice. She thought that another pattern was the little girl's reversal of dependency in reaction to a coercive mother. Quinodoz (1989) asserts that the lesbian may either identify with the penis or with the baby. The latter identification is the one he believes results in the woman becoming a partner to a more aggressive male-identified lesbian. He believes that the latter type of patient is the less analyzable, more regressed, and less differentiated. He thinks that more than one analysis may be necessary for such a patient to become able to form a sufficient positive transference to overcome ''the patient's ten-dency to project onto the analyst the part of the ego containing the depres-sion . . .'' (p. 61). He, like McDougall, thinks that the root of lesbian development is hatred and spite toward the parents. This is a view in Proust's (1928) novel. Mlle. Vinteuil has been brought up by an overly solicitous father who wants her to be a dainty feminine child instead of the sturdy boyish one she feels herself to be. Her lesbian lovemaking features spitting on his picture. This expression of aggression frees her to experience pleasure as her own.

An alternative view holds that object choice is closely bound up with gender identity and that both may be determined biologically. Stoller (1964) stated: "In addition to the anatomy of the external genitalia and the infant–parent relationships—the more easily observable components in the production of gender identity—there is a third, usually silent component: a congenital, perhaps inherited biological force" (p. 225). Yet not all women choosing a lesbian lifestyle seem to have been homosexual all their lives. Those women who, like Pratt, choose a female lover for some part of their adult lives, even though they have been heterosexual before making that choice, are not simply living out a biological program. Saghir and Robbins (1980) do not consider such women homosexual because they do not have a lifelong pattern of lesbian choice. Wolff (1971) saw that situation as a belated discovery of oneself rather than as a new choice.

Some evidence for the importance of permission for anger toward the parents is available in Pratt's work. Her gratitude to her husband for forcing her to act on and recognize her own aggression echoes Proust's scene of the lover giving permission to Mlle. Vinteuil to spit on the portrait of her father. The wish seems to be acceptable even when you are enraged.

Pratt's attitude toward male violence appeared already in her very first poem to her husband. There it was with the awareness that he had been violent in response to her requests, not on his own. Her wish to be loved by a man and her love for men may have been clouded by her love for her alcoholic father. If so, her wish for her sons to be strong and effective people clashes with her need to love those who are weak and are victims rather than those who are strong and aggressive. The last poem in the sequence therefore seems to wrap back to the first and illuminate the conflict between her need for the love of someone vulnerable and her nurturant wish to make the children she loves strong. Altogether, the sequence of poems seems to me to show the poet wrestling with the conflicts between positive and negative oedipal wishes, with complex ambivalences of love and hate. She constructs compromises (Brenner, 1983). In this she is like every person, heterosexual or homosexual. How little we know about how lesbian object choice is made. De Lauretis (1994) reminds us of how little we know about heterosexual object choice. Pratt used poetry to express affect and prose to express rational connections; poetry for the private, internal, intrapsychic, and prose for the public, external, extrapsychic. It is to her poetry that one can look for motives and conflicts at the level to which analytic concepts are appropriate. I believe that by doing so we can enrich the store of analytic ideas with which we attempt to understand our patients in their gallant attempts to cope with the complex and multiple ways in which sexual object choice interacts with other aspects of personality.

Coming back to the initial questions, lesbian object choice seems to have been determined for Pratt in much the same way that heterosexual object choice is for other women. Erotic feelings for the mother are universal (Wrye and Welles, 1994). Aspects of the personalities of each of her parents interacted with aspects of her own endowment and temperament to make her select the particular "femme" lesbian attitude in love relationships that she explores in her last book *S/HE* (1995). In that book she tells of prejudices and exclusions within the lesbian world as restrictive and as exclusionary as those within the straight world. She finds the same aggressivity, the same intensity of feeling about sexual preferences as she sees in the straight world. She finds, as analysts find, that compromise formations are no respecters of political correctness or incorrectness. She shows her readers a world which is completely familiar internally even as it is unfamiliar externally. It is not a picture of perversion in which the particular partner is less important than the scenario. It is a world in which lesbians (Schuker, 1996) are doing the best they can with the fantasies they bring to their realities. It is a world in which each person lives by the code of her own desire.

References

Bak, R. (1953), Fetishism. *J. Amer. Psychoanal. Assn.,* 1:285–298.

Blank, T., & Blank, R. (1979), *Ego Psychology,* Vol. 2. New York: Columbia University Press.

Brenner, C. (1983), *The Mind in Conflict.* New York: International Universities Press.

de Lauretis, T. (1994), *The Practice of Love.* Bloomington: Indiana University Press.

Deutsch, H. (1932), On female homosexuality. *Psychiatric Quart.,* 1:484–510.

Eisenbud, R. (1982), Early and later determinants of lesbian choice. *Psychoanal. Rev.,* 69:85–109.

Freud, S. (1905), Three Essays on the Theory of Sexuality. *Standard Edition,* 7:123–243. London: Hogarth Press, 1953.

——— (1920), The psychogenesis of a case of homosexuality in a woman. *Standard Edition,* 18:145–172. London: Hogarth Press, 1955.

Gillespie, W. (1964), Symposium on homosexuality. *Internat. J. Psycho-Anal.,* 45:199–202.

Greenberg, D. (1988), *The Construction of Homosexuality.* Chicago: University of Chicago Press.

H. D. (1956), *Tribute to Freud.* New York: New Directions, 1984.

McDougall, J. (1970), Homosexuality in women. In: *Female Sexuality,* ed. J. Chasseguet-Smirgel. Ann Arbor: University of Michigan Press, pp. 171–212.

Pratt, M. (1981a), "Love Poem to an Ex-Husband." In: *The Sound of One Fork.* Washington, DC: Night Heron Press.

——— (1981b), "My Mother Loves Women." In: *The Sound of One Fork.* Washington, D.C.: Night Heron Press.

——— (1981c), "The Sound of One Fork." In: *The Sound of One Fork.* Washington, DC: Night Heron Press.

——— (1981d), "Southern Gothic." In: *The Sound of One Fork.* Washington, DC: Night Heron Press.

——— (1985), "I Admit the Need." In: *We Say We Love Each Other.* Ithaca, NY: Firebrand Books.

——— (1990a), "All the Women Caught in Flaring Light." In: *Crime Against Nature.* Ithaca, NY: Firebrand Books.

——— (1990b), "Talking to Charlie." In: *Crime Against Nature.* Ithaca, NY: Firebrand Books.

——— (1991a), "Pillow Talk." In: *Rebellion.* Ithaca, NY: Firebrand Books.

——— (1991b), *Rebellion.* Ithaca, NY: Firebrand Books.

——— (1995), *S/HE.* Ithaca, NY: Firebrand Books.

Proust, M. (1928), *Remembrance of Things Past.* New York: Random House.

Quinodoz, J. (1989), Female homosexual patients in psychoanalysis. *Internat. J. Psycho-Anal.,* 70:55–63.

Rich, A. (1993), The transgressor mother. In: *What Is Found There.* New York: W. W. Norton pp. 145–163.

Saghir, M., & Robbins, E. (1980), Clinical aspects of female homosexuality. In: *Homosexual Behavior,* ed. J. Marmor. New York: Basic Books, pp. 280–295.

Schuker, E. (1996), Toward further analytic understanding of lesbian patients. *J. Amer. Psychoanal. Assn.* (Suppl.), 44:485–508.

Siegel, E. (1988), *Female Homosexuality.* Hillsdale, NJ: Analytic Press.

Socarides, C. (1963), Historical development of concepts of overt female homosexuality. *J. Amer. Psychoanal. Assn.,* 11:386–414.

Stoller, R. (1964), The study of gender identity. *Internat. J. Psycho-Anal.*, 45:220–226.

Tyson, P., & Tyson, R. (1990), *Psychoanalytic Theories of Development*. New Haven, CT: Yale University Press.

Waelder, R. (1960), *Basic Theory of Psychoanalysis*. New York: International Universities Press.

Wrye, H., & Welles, J. (1994), *The Narration of Desire*. Hillsdale, NJ: Analytic Press.

Wolff, C., Ed. (1971), *Love between Women*. New York: Harper & Row.

Young-Breuhl, E. (1990), *Freud on Women*. New York: W. W. Norton.

13

It's a Queer Universe: Some Notes Erotic and Otherwise

Adria E. Schwartz

> I have always wanted to be both man and woman, to incorporate the strongest and richest parts of my mother and father within/into me—to share valleys and mountains upon my body the way the earth does in hills and peaks.
>
> I would like to enter a woman the way any man can, and to be entered—to leave to be left—to be hot and hard and soft all at the same time in the cause of our loving. I would like to drive forward and at other times to rest or be driven [Prologue to *Zami*, Audre Lorde, 1982]

How do we understand Audre Lorde in the prologue to *Zami* (1982), a "biomythographical" tale of her struggle as a West Indian girl growing up in New York City, finding her way as a black woman and a lesbian. She draws from the wellspring of her masculine and feminine identifications to enjoy a sexual subjectivity which is both active and receptive, penetrating, embracing, and desirous of being "driven."

According to McDougall (1986), "Homosexual desires in children of both sexes always have a double aim. One is the desire to possess, in the most concrete fashion, the parent of the same sex, and the second is the desire to be the opposite sex and to possess all the privileges and prerogatives with which the opposite-sex parent is felt to be endowed" (p. 219). Yet, Lorde eschews that basic binary model, embedded as it is within a heterosexual matrix, by celebrating her womanhood. She continues. "When I sit and play in the waters of my bath I love to feel the deep inside parts of me, sliding and folded and tender and deep. Other times I like to fantasize the core of it, my pearl, a protruding part of me, hard and sensitive and vulnerable in a different way. . . . Woman forever . . ." (p. 7).

We are unused to the clitoral imagery, and are apt to mistake it for phallic (Kulish, 1991). Lorde, however, reflects an internal bodily representation which holds a facet of lesbian eroticism, the essence of which is that it transcends what psychoanalytic theory has sought to label an infantile notion of undifferentiated bisexual completeness. It has been difficult for psychoanalytic theory to transcend a binary gendered world in order to don the lens necessary to recognize the underpinnings of the lesbian imaginary.

Fast (1984), in a critique of Freud's theory, presents a developmental model of gender identity acquisition based on differentiation and the falling away of infantile notions of omnipotence, of limitless possibility.

In her theory Fast proposed an undifferentiated and overinclusive early matrix of gender representations where no attribute, physical or psychological, is excluded because it is gender inappropriate. Girls may imagine that they have a penis just as boys may wish or imagine that they have the procreative capacities that girls do. Having a penis, for a girl, does not negate her ability to nurture, nor alter her representations and identifications with mother and other things traditionally thought of as feminine. Fast takes issue with Freud's premise that girls, before acknowledging the anatomical distinction between the sexes, are "little men" (Freud, 1925). The clitoris is not a "masculine organ." For Fast, however, the normative process of differentiation does involve coming to terms with the limits of one's biological sex ("penis or reproductive organs . . . breasts seem to be absent") and the array of attributes culturally assigned to one gender or the other.

Thus, Audre's pearl is recognized for the female organ that it is, but her expressed wish for bisexual completeness would be viewed by Fast as an indication of unresolved issues with childhood omnipotence. Fast finds residues of this early childhood overinclusive and undifferentiated matrix of representations in bisexual myths and primitive art (p. 17). Although Fast discusses the necessity of coming to terms with both features of biological sex and gender attributes, she deals with the former (i.e., male wishes to have babies, female phallic strivings) quite specifically and only vaguely with the latter. The "girl must give up the possibility of having a penis and gender-inappropriate self representations." What those gender inappropriate self representations are, and their relation to sexuality, is never delineated by Fast. How one is to be a woman, and how that womanliness is related to one's sexual aims is the heart of the matter for Zami, and the voiceless young woman, in Freud's infamous "case of female homosexuality" (Freud, 1920; Harris, 1991).

Clinically and experientially we know that bodily self representations are vitally linked to sexuality and eroticism. Need they be linked to gender?

For Fast, identification with mother's generativity seems to be the key both to her female identification and the shift in her libidinal affections from mother to father. The wish for a baby from the father is not only an attempt at compensation for the girl's lack of a penis, but also a manifestation of her identification with mother in her child-bearing capacity (p. 22). Where Freud emphasized penis envy as the touchstone of female heterosexuality, Fast sees identification with biological reproductivity. But, what of desire? Fast ignores, as Freud did not (1931), the "problematic" issue of the girl's continuing erotic tie to her mother. In Freud's model there is a constant pull toward the female homoerotic but it is fraught with the baggage of "masculine identification." Fast rejects the phallocentricity of viewing the clitoris as a penile analogue, and with that rejection comes the rejection of the biological basis of Freud's theory of bisexuality for women. "In Freud's view the girl's central struggle is to overcome her masculinity; in the differentiation framework it is to overcome her narcissism," that is, her sense of unlimited possibility (p. 32).

It becomes the developmental task in this process of gender differentiation to work one's way out of the earlier state of infantile overinclusiveness and narcissistic omnipotence. And with this, according to Fast, comes an inevitable heterosexual path for desire. Fast's theory does not account for adult homosexual object choice in women.

Audre Lorde speaks to the tension between identity and desire. It is a tension which runs throughout (though in no way defines) lesbian eroticism, and is not adequately explained either by Freud's phallocentrically based theory of innate bisexuality (which encompasses the gender linked psychosexual attributes of activity and passivity), nor Fast's critique based on an essentialist model of gender differentiation (Freud, 1905, 1937).

In her way, Lorde remains encapsulated in the "bi-ness": bigendered, bisexuality, of our language. French feminists have attempted to write in or write about the necessity of formulating new language which speaks to the specificity of the female body and female eroticism (Irigary, 1985; Cixous, 1986). Wittig attempted, through fiction, to invent a language in which to speak exclusively about women's pleasure in loving women (Wittig, 1975). Although they speak from very different intellectual camps (Irigary coming from an essentialist position and Wittig from feminist/marxist materialism), each struggles with the inadequacy of language to express female (Irigary's 1985), and specifically lesbian (Wittig, 1975) eroticism.

The Lesbian Subject

The problem of language is inextricably tied to subjectivity. According to Case (1989) the task of feminist theory in the 1980s was the deconstruction of a subject position marked historically by masculinist function and the simultaneous construction of a female subject position. Now, in the next decade, as postmodernism has gained sway in crucial feminist and psychoanalytic circles, it is not the existence of a female subject which is at issue, but the possibility of the female subject standing outside of her own locatedness so that she might be an agent of change, which comes into question. For de Lauretis (1987) it is the feminist subject "who is inside and outside of [an] ideology of gender and conscious of being so, conscious of that pull, that division, that double vision" (p. 10), who offers the possibility of a transcendent subject.

Moving beyond de Lauretis, Case (1989) suggests that it is the butch–femme couple who meet the requirements for the ideal, quintessential feminist subject; a radical claim given the general approbation of the feminist community toward butch-femme as a mark of continued heterosexist oppression within lesbian ranks.

Case refers to Riviere's paper (1929) to support her argument. In Riviere's now almost classic case, a successful woman lecturer would follow each acclaimed public appearance by compulsive coquetry and approval seeking from the older men in attendance. This was understood as an unconscious attempt at reassurance that this obviously bright and assertive woman who had laid claim to the public arena, was in fact a woman (she had no penis) and furthermore, served as a denial of her wishes to castrate the phallically privileged father-figures in her midst (Schwartz, 1999). According to Case, and it seems true, that within butch–femme scenarios, especially as they were constituted before the second wave of feminism and in their current retrorenaissance, women play on the phallic economy rather than to it. The lesbian roles are underscored as two optional functions for women in the phallocracy, while as demonstrated by Riviere, the heterosexual woman's role collapses them into one compensatory charade (p. 292). The agentic heterosexual woman adopts the masquerade of conventional nonagentic femininity so as to allay her own and others' fears lest she appropriate phallic privilege. With tongue in cheek, as it were, the butch in phallic regalia plays to the masquerading femme, each in disguise, reveling in the not knowing of what each other so clearly knows. As Case envisions the eroticism of this ideal lesbian subject, "the female body, the male gaze, and the structures of realism are only sex toys for the butch–femme couple" (p. 297).

The theoretical debate continues as to whether butch–femme occupies a unique place outside the ideology of gender, as Case would maintain, or whether it represents a toxic residue of patriarchal oppression and sex roles with its tops and bottoms, stone butches and feeling-caring femmes. Rubin (1992) suggests that traditional stereotypes in the lesbian butch–femme community no longer hold, that it is not true that butches always desire femmes and must always "top" (that is, orchestrate the sexual encounters). There are femmes who maintain control, butches who seek out sexually dominant femmes or sexually aggressive butches; there are butch tops and butch bottoms, femme-femme partners and butch couples (p. 471). The role-play is intrinsic to the eroticism, it would seem, but, Rubin maintains, the issue is one of desire rather than fixed gender identifications.

For Roof (1991):

Butch/Femme seems to be a resolution of the "inconceivability" of lesbian sexuality in a phallocentric system, recuperating that inconceivability by superimposing a male/female model on lesbian relations. . . .

Butch/Femme, however, is internally self-contradictory from the beginning: inconceivability is nonetheless conceivable; a woman is nonetheless a man. What is important in the case of Butch/Femme is that the two processes—inconceivability and recuperation—and their internal contradictions coexist in a tension that never quite resolves itself, producing a systemic challenge to the necessary connection between gender and sexuality while appearing to reaffirm heterosexuality and forcing a consciousness to the artificiality and constructedness of gender positions [p. 245].

Hence desire ripples off multiple identifications and object aims forcing us to surrender notions of "femmunculus-like" monolithic internal objects, and shift to notions of internalized object relations, with the freedom to assume various identifications and seek after complex objects in a multigendered internal arena.

In an interesting autobiographical essay Jeanne Cordova (1992), a former nun and editor of one of California's first lesbian feminist newspapers, traces her struggle to affirm her life as a "butch" within what she labels as the growing discrimination against this form of lesbian by feminist and lesbian-feminist theory. The second wave of feminism had broadened the acceptable boundaries of "real" womanhood with one exception: "I could be anything I wanted to be, except butch" (p. 290).

Cordova sees being butch as being about resistance. Or as she would put it, being "ornery." As a 5-year-old she was "ornery" and continued throughout her life to fight sex role definitions and prescriptions. She defines butch-femme as the ornery spirit self that refuses definition, the core of a woman who transcends gender (p. 291). Cordova rejects the blind identification of gender role with biological sex and seeks to create a multiplicity of genders that more accurately signal sexual desire, and temperament.

"To me, a butch is a recombinant mixture of yin and yang energy. Like recombinant DNA, a butch is an elusive, ever-synthesizing energy field, a lesbian laser that knits the universes of male and female. Some have said feminist butch is an oxymoron. I say it's a paradox. A feminist butch is a dyke who has survived the Cuisinart blades of feminist rhetoric.

To survive being butch you have to have been born with an ornery spirit'' (p. 273).

When the illusion of being her father's "son" crumbled at puberty, Jeanne realized that as a daughter she was "superfluous in the scheme of family power" and that only men had what she wanted—power and money and women.

"I would eventually become a political activist, because my ornery spirit knew, long before my mind could explain, that our gay place in the world had been fundamentally misdefined. If men and women weren't divided and had it been gender were accepted as fluid, I wouldn't be perceived as deviating from a non existent norm. And neither would the other one or two billion queers like me" (p. 280).

Grahn (1984), another "butch" writing in the time of the feminist sex wars, puts it this way, "Our point was not to be men; our point was to be butch and get away with it. We always kept something back: a high-pitched voice, a slant of the head, or a limpness of hand gestures, something that was clearly labeled female. I believe our statement was 'Here was another way of being a woman' not 'Here is a woman trying to be taken for a man' " (p. 31).

Of these complementary gender performances "butch" is obviously the most transgressive in that it decenters phallic privilege; whereas the "femme" parodies, but nonetheless operates within the realm of more traditional womanhood. The femme doesn't challenge traditional gender role ascriptions. Her transgression is that she desires another woman.

Clearly, Case's position, that the butch–femme couple is the ideal feminist–lesbian subject, is both radical and regressive. Butch-femme does call into question the implicit connection of biology, gender, and sexuality (Roof, 1991). However, proposing the butch–femme couple as the ideal lesbian subject both obfuscates the wide range of actual lesbian sexual practice and plays with, but ultimately does not transcend, the confines of the heterosexually based gender binary.

If The Shoe Fits . . .

This brief discussion of butch-femme, brought to mind the countless clinical hours that have been spent in work with lesbians on shoes, and the difficulty that many lesbians have in choosing, wearing, and feeling good about their fit. Three instances come to mind:

One analysand, who painfully and ambivalently strained at the confines of traditional gender role expectations, remembers that as a young girl she kept "losing her shoes" much to the dismay of her mother, and her classmates awaiting her on the school bus. Interpreted as a passive–aggressive attempt to avoid school by her mother, the loss of her shoes, and most often one shoe, more accurately expressed both the analysand's sense of castrated helplessness in the face of a simultaneously intrusive and neglectful mother, and her rebellion at being forced into a type of femininity which did not fit. As an adolescent and young adult, she wanted to wear "flip flops," rubber thong-like sandals which are unisexual and hence gender indistinguishable. Other shoes just weren't comfortable. Dreams were filled with images of casting off her shoes and running barefoot, free of having to fill both familial and gender expectations.

In another case, a lesbian who often complained of not feeling "like a real girl" claimed that she was only truly comfortable when wearing sneakers. The structure of her feet rebelled against the tightly fitting shoes common in women's fashion, she reported. She wouldn't be caught dead in high heels which were designed to keep woman walking slowly, with an unsteady gait, appealing to but never competing with men. Her search to join a law firm (and implicitly what kind of work she would do) was partly determined by which office or larger work environment would allow her to wear her Reeboks. Terry maintained that she could never work anywhere where they required traditional women's dress. Her feet just wouldn't fit "girls' shoes."

Yolinda, who into her third year of analysis talked about how she had never before purchased a pair of women's shoes, expressed her ambivalence and her wide ranging sense of gender dysphoria most directly. A big-boned, somewhat large woman she had, since adolescence, bought all of her shoes in the men's department. She had assumed that they would be more comfortable. Although this in itself never seemed problematic to her, she often complained about feeling ugly. On vacation with a new lover, and while the subject of her womanhood was in the forefront in her analysis, she had "somehow decided" to enter the women's shoe department and found to her surprise that they had comfortable shoes to fit her as well. Modeling pumps, she took a new look at her legs. She liked their shape. They were woman's legs, she surmised with surprise and obvious pleasure. Then, Yolinda began to sob.

"I don't want to be a woman. If you're a woman you have to wait around 'til someone fucks you. You have to wait until someone desires you."

For differing reasons, none of these lesbians wanted to be in a woman's shoes. It was not a place of agency for them.

Polymorphous Diversity

Literary anecdotal evidence and clinical data suggest that lesbian eroticism lives on a continuum of the polymorphously diverse which extends through more traditional variants of lesbian couplings, sadomasochistic practice, butch–femme enactments in and out of the bedroom, to the new Boston marriage, where committed partners have little or no genital sex. The use of the word *continuum* here makes obvious reference to, but should not be confused with, Adrienne Rich's original and somewhat idiosyncratic use of the phrase (Rich, 1981).

> [A] range—through each woman's life and throughout history—of woman-identified experience, not simply the fact that a woman has had or consciously desired genital sexual experience with another woman. If we expand it to embrace many more forms of primary intensity between and among women, including the sharing of a rich inner life, the bonding against male tyranny, the giving and receiving of practical and political support . . . marriage resistance . . . we begin to grasp breadths of female history and psychology which have lain out of reach as a consequence of limited, mostly clinical, definitions of lesbianism [p. 239].

Daring as this conception was in the early 1980s, liberating women from the confines of heterosexually based genital sexuality while introducing the more agentic concept of resistance to a patriarchal limiting of the erotic for women, critics of the 1990s fear that such a definition "evacuates" lesbianism of any sexual content (Rubin and Butler, 1994).

Roof's (1991) coinage of the phrase *polymorphous diversity* more accurately describes the reality of lesbian sexuality. It not only differs among individuals, and within race, culture, and class, but also is represented differently as history permits. Roof makes the point that lesbian sexuality exists as a coherent category only in contrast to heterosexuality and male homosexuality.

"Lesbian sexuality exists more at the interstices of multiple differences rather than necessarily constituting a core identity strong enough to completely fix an individual. Such an essential identity tends to come from outside—from phallocentric culture, for whom the category lesbian is sufficient" (p. 251).

From an intrapsychic perspective, one might say that lesbians retain women as primary objects of gratification though not necessarily, identification. This does not exclude erotic connection to men, nor does it necessarily imply masculine identifications. Psychoanalytic theory has been based on the confluence of gender identification and object choice. Lesbian eroticism as theorized or practiced does not appear to be.

Resistance to Identity

If one were to look at *Bar Girls,* a mainstream film distributed in the Spring of 1995, what would one find? We are introduced to the characters in a women's bar in Los Angeles, supposedly representative of the culture there, a potpourri of lesbians, replete with pool tables, lesbians in "recovery," some brawling, and most seeking love.

There's Annie: a jock (athlete) who has been in a relationship with the same woman for eight years. They are celibate, however, allegedly because Annie's partner claims to be "straight." As the film progresses, Annie and her partner decide to have a more "open relationship" and the audience sees Annie with a variety of women as she seductively makes the rounds of the available sisters.

At the film's beginning, Victoria is also heterosexual, but she quickly becomes interested in women. She's very "femme" and picks out the "butch" from South Carolina who comes adorned with a black leather vest and Harley-Davidson motorcycle. Throughout the film, they appear to be the most compatible and most committed.

Loretta is desperate for declarations of love. Nonetheless, she is constantly being left by her partners. For her, love is sacred and she requires its declaration before she can have sex. There's Rachel who is married to a man but claims to be a lesbian. And JR, a "macho" police cadet who thrives on romantic conquest and the provocation of domestic disharmonies.

In true soap fashion (seduction through the evocation of jealousy), Rachel flirts with Loretta, has sex with JR. The triangulation forces a heated separation between Rachel and Loretta, which is ultimately healed and understood as a defense against closeness. Loretta also sleeps with JR in retaliation for what she experiences as Rachel's fear of closeness. Rachel and Loretta reconcile and become committed lovers themselves.

Men play no significant part in this movie.

Bar Girls seems to reflect the culture's splitting of love and sex. It is never quite clear whether the emphasis on seduction and conquest is a mask for the need for affirmation and love or whether the constant search for "love" is a way to make an aggressive sexuality legitimate in a culture where women are not to claim it for themselves, nor desire it in another woman.

Most clearly, *Bar Girls* could be seen as a movie about resistance, the refusal to be locked into culturally constructed categories of gender role or sexual preference.

Jacqueline Rose (1986) has argued for recognition of the resistance to identity which lies at the heart of psychic life. She uses the concept to help define bisexuality as a sort of "anti-identity," an unconscious refusal to be limited to one object of desire or one form of loving. Daumer (1992), in an essay on bisexuality, speaks to the possible embodiment of that resistance to identity when she speaks about women choosing to recreate their sexuality with options, which loosen them from the bonds of lesbian/straight, hetero/homo sexualities.

"Because bisexuality occupies an ambiguous position between identities, it is able to shed light on the gaps and contradictions of all identity, on what we might call the differences within identity" (p. 98). For Daumer, bisexuality also allows us to problematize heterosexuality in ways that distinguish compulsory heterosexuality and efforts to resist heterosexualism within and without heterosexual relationships.

Identity, for Rose or Daumer, has little to do with gender, and everything to do with the choice of sexual object and identification with a group by means of sexual preference. In writing about lesbians, it is nearly impossible to escape the confluence of gender and desire.

Yet , Daumer (1992) introduces an interesting perspective. For her, the construction of sexuality vouchsafes entrance into the "queer universe—in which the fluctuations and mutabilities of sexuality, the multitude of different, changing, and at times conflicting ways in which we experience our sexual, affectional, and erotic proclivities, fantasies, and practices can be articulated and acknowledged. In the queer universe, to be queer implies that not everybody is queer in the same way. It implies a willingness to enable others to articulate their own particular queerness'' (p. 100).

Bisexuality

It can be argued that part of Freud's radical genius lay in the manner in which he both theorized and clinically recognized the queer universe. Freud, following on the inspiration of his beloved nemesis Wilhelm Fliess, maintained a position of universal bisexuality, although the developmental foundation of that position changed as Freud's work matured from a biological to a psychic one, from a kind of infantile unisex containing both male and female aspects and erotically attracted to both, to a more mature lack of fixity in both identity and object choice (Garber, 1995).

Freud (1937) wrote:

> It is well known that at all periods, there have been as there still are, people who can take as their sexual objects members of their own sex as well as the opposite one, without the one trend interfering with the other. We call such people bisexuals, and we accept their existence without feeling much surprise about it. We have come to learn, however, that every human being is bisexual in this sense, and that his libido is distributed either in a manifest or a latent fashion, over objects of both sexes [pp. 243–244].

Notice that Freud's views here are in the spirit of Helene Cixous (1986), the French feminist analyst, who, some fifty years later, defined bisexuality as ''the location within oneself of the presence of both sexes, that gives permission to multiple desires...'' (pp. 84–85). Suleiman (1986) points out that Cixous' bisexuality is one of the ''multiple subjects who is not afraid to recognize in him or herself the presence of both sexes, not afraid to open him or herself up to the presence of the other, to the circulation of multiple drives and desires'' (p. 16).

Ultimately, the difficulty in theorizing bisexual practice is that it assumes that the ''object'' in object choice has to have a one-to-one mimetic relationship to the sex-gender binary. It might be said, though transgendered folks among others might disagree (Feinberg, 1993), that in everyday experience, which is our most common referent, one desires or has sex with either men, women, or both. Our conscious experiences seem to support reliance on the simple categories of homo/hetero sexual (implying exclusivity in practice if not in fantasy) or bisexual, implying an inclusiveness or lack of exclusivity.

But this simplistic conflation of gender and sexual orientation assumes a stable, continuous, and unigendered identity and a mimetic relationship of sex and gender which do not exist (Butler, 1990a,b; Harris, 1991; Zita, 1992). As our deconstructive efforts have amply demonstrated, internalized objects vary coterminously depending on what relation is being called upon for identification within object love. Male-masculine identifications and female-feminine identifications coexist internally within all of us, and these identifications are called upon differently within various erotic and nonerotic situations depending on what is at stake psychically.

Bisexuality, as it has been understood in the psychoanalytic community, has been implicitly pathologized. Despite Freud's (1937) later views, which encompassed a universal psychic bisexuality as the foundation of psychosexual development, bisexual practice remains suspect, undermining as it does the premise of heterosexuality as normative. For those with a pathologizing bent, bisexuality seems to suggest a defensive denial of difference, a failure to resolve infantile fantasies of omnipotence in Fast's (1984) sense, an inability to commit oneself to the reality of gender limits and hence object choice. "In the world of dreams we are all magical, bisexual, and immortal!" (McDougall, 1986, p. 215).

Psychoanalytic revisionists, on the other hand, critique the very binaries on which the concepts of masculine-feminine, active-passive rest, thus throwing into question the very foundation of the "bi"-ness of "bi"-sexuality (Goldner, 1991). The disputes in theorizing bisexuality parallel the disputes in the butch–femme discourse. Are the categories involved ultimately a reaffirmation of the essentialist dichotomies or a postmodern disruption of locatedness?

On the Privileging of Genital Sex

Within the continuum of lesbian relationships is a romantic but essentially asexual relationship between women which in this country has often been referred to as the Boston marriage.

Originating in the late nineteenth century, the Boston marriage of-fered middle-class career women companionship, nurturance, a commu-nion of kindred spirits, romance, and undoubtedly in some but not all relationships, sex, without the stigma of perversion. According to Fader-man, who has done the most extensive research in the area, a Boston marriage in the late nineteenth century offered all the advantages of having a significant other without the burdens of heterosexuality (Fader-man, 1981, 1993). But this was at a time essentially before there were lesbians. "Lesbianism" as a circumscribed category of sexuality (as con-trasted with the real existence of romantic physical relationships between and among women) was a creation of sexologists writing in the 1870s and whose work initially was not widely read. Hence women could live together and be "above suspicion." By the 1920s, however, paradigms of sexuality for women had changed; romantic friendships were no longer seen as innocent, and thus no longer condoned (Faderman, 1993). More-over, women themselves were forced to question and defend the presence or absence of their sexuality, in a way that might once have been un-thinkable.

Even today, many long-term lesbian relationships are not particularly genital; others are asexual or barely sexual. The term *Boston marriage,* describing a socially condoned relation amongst a particular class of women within a particular culture in a particular moment in history, is also an attempt to create language where there is none, for a continuing reality of lesbian life. Faderman suggests that "perhaps the sine qua non of a lesbian relationship is not genital sexuality" (p. 40). She, among others, questions the phallocentrically based prescription of sexuality which exists in our particular historiocultural era, and asks us to broaden our concept of the meanings and structures of committed love between women (Rich, 1981; Frye, 1990; Hall, 1993; Rothblum and Brehony, 1993). How is it that genital touching becomes the primary signifier of intimacy, they ask?

Marilyn Frye (1990) in a more radical position challenges the very category of sex as male and heterosexist. She objects to the privileging of penile-vaginal intercourse culminating in orgasm ("doing it"), as de-fining the discourse and hence leaving sensual touching, her sexual do-main, outside the realm of legitimate sexuality.

According to Frye, the rhythms of lesbian love and passion cannot be mapped on "eight minute" male definitions of sex. She maintains that lesbian sexuality is not encoded by this discourse. There is no linguistic matrix for the experiences of bodily play, tactile communication, the ebb and flow of intense excitement, arousal, tension, release, comfort, discomfort, pain and pleasure (p. 312). Ultimately, Frye argues, heterosexual intercourse is not synchronous with the ontology of the lesbian body.

Lesbian Bed Death

Yet, on a parallel but somehow paradoxical plane of the lesbian continuum we find the phenomenon of "lesbian bed death," one of the most common complaints heard in the consulting room vis-a-vis lesbian sexuality. In or out of the consulting room, in common parlance, "lesbian bed death" refers to the ongoing or impending cessation of genital sexuality as well as other forms of passionate or lustful sexual touching. Lesbian couples often separate or triangulate over what appear to be irreconcilable differences in the expression of sexual desire. Unlike Faderman's (1981) Boston marriage, or the New Boston Marriage described by Rothblum and Brehony (1993), women in relationships complaining of "lesbian bed death" mourn the loss of their mutually expressed desire. How does this come to pass?

Not speaking to the issue of "lesbian bed death" per se, but concerned about the lack of ongoing sexuality in mature lesbian relationships, Nichols (1987) suggests that lesbians, like many of their heterosexual sisters, are sexually repressed. She is not using the term in the classical psychoanalytical sense (Freud, 1916–1917, pp. 286–302), but rather to mean inhibited, constricted, suppressed or somehow rendered silent and inactive. She enumerates reasons for the falling off of sexuality: the inhibition of anger, internalized homophobia whereby eliminating genital sex demonstrates that one is not really a lesbian, the failure of each of the women to feel comfortable as sexual initiator or aggressor. It is primarily this last inhibition, the reluctance to initiate a sexual encounter, that lesbians share with their heterosexual female counterparts.

What Nichols approaches but does not fully apprehend, is that to be a subject of desire rather than its object, and to act agentically in accordance with that subjectivity, stands at odds with one's internalized gender role as a woman. Heterosexual women look to men to release them from this conflict, either by assuming the role of initiator, or by bestowing legitimacy on their feminine desirability. For two women, the conflict between agency and internalized gender role can become more paralyzing, especially if it is unknown or unacknowledged.

Issues of sexuality are often conflated with issues of true self (Bollas, 1989; Schwartz, 1996). It is perhaps not surprising, then, that lesbians complain of the disappearance of desire, either their own or as a presence in their relationship.

It has been my clinical experience, however, that what contributes most often to the falling away of passion within lesbian relationships, and by this I am not privileging genital sex as the signifier of said passion, is an avoidance of intense desire and sexual passion out of a fear of ruthlessness on the part of oneself or one's lover.

Bollas (1989) speaks to the issue in presumably heterosexual couples.

[I]n lovemaking, foreplay begins as an act of relating. Lovers attend to mutual erotic interests. As the economic factor increases, this element of lovemaking will recede somewhat (though not disappear) as the lovers surrender to that ruthlessness inherent in erotic excitement. This ruthlessness has something to do with a joint loss of consciousness, a thoughtlessness which is incremental to erotic intensity. It is a necessary ruthlessness as both lovers destroy the relationship in order to plunge into a reciprocal orgasmic use. Indeed, the destruction of relationship is itself pleasurable and the conversion of relating to using transforms ego libido into increased erotic drive. If a couple cannot assume this essential destructiveness, erotic intensity may not give in to mutual orgasms. Instead, reparation may be the fundamental exchange between such couples with partners entering into prolonged mother–child scenarios, of cuddling, holding, or soothing. This may be because such persons have not been able to experience a good destruction of the object, and reparative work is activated during the arrival of instinctual urges. When this happens, sexual uses of the object may be enacted as dissociated activities. Instead lovers may masturbate each other, with one partner relating to the other's sexual needs and mothering them through it, or at an extreme, in the perverse act, the couple may wear interesting garments and introduce curious acts to entirely split off the destructive side of erotic life in a kind of performance act [pp. 26–27].

I would take issue with Bollas in the universalizing of his theory. The absence of genital sex, mutual and/or singular orgasms in the presence of sensual and erotic touching, does not always signal a problem of desire/ true self. Similarly, I would argue that gender performance is intrinsic to many forms of sexuality rather than prima facie evidence of its dissoci- ation. Only a lesbian couple can make a diagnosis of their "bed death" with the pathology thus implied. It is the falling away of their sexuality, whatever its form. With the decentering of the phallocentrically derived privileging of genital sex, lesbians reconstruct their sexuality to include a spectrum of relationships and expressions of desire.

However, it is interesting to note that Bollas's discussion of ruth and the place of ruthlessness in lovemaking, comes in the context of a larger discussion of true self and object usage. Although theoretically, Winni- cott's (1971) distinction between object relating and object usage has a developmental tilt (with the former preceding the latter), I would suggest that within lesbian couples, the difficulty with ruthlessness is not so much a function of a basic fault, so to speak, but with a fear-avoidance of the emergence of the wanton and capacious I. A seeming requirement of ruthlessness, the consequent negation of the Other, even temporarily, is associated with a male-aggressive subjectivity so consciously eschewed in segments of lesbian culture. Lesbian couples who seek therapeutic help often seem to have difficulty incorporating healthy competition and aggression into their ongoing relationship (Lindenbaum, 1985). This sup- pression of aggression, avoidance of ruthlessness, manifests as a diminu- tion or deadening of the couple's libido. If acted out, a triangulation might occur both as an expression of one partner's anger and unconscious wish to resuscitate the passion by means of jealousy, possessiveness, and a legitimization by way of a hurtful retaliation.

To Conclude

Psychoanalytic theory has been based on the ultimate confluence of gen- der identification and object choice. Lesbian sexuality as theorized or practiced does not appear to be. Erotically, being and desiring a woman do not stand in a relationship of synedoche. Lesbian eroticism is more aptly a confluence of multiple identifications and positions of desire.

Notions of overinclusive matrices of gender identifications-represen- tations (Fast, 1984; Bassin, 1996) depathologized can help us understand the incorporation of phallic imagery within some expressions of lesbian sexuality without it signifying exclusive male identifications or signs of "masculine protest."

Lesbian eroticism as read by intention, unconscious fantasy, and practice calls into question the presumed essentialist connections of biology, gender, and sexuality. Lesbian sexuality and bisexuality can be read as resistance to fixed identities of gender role and object choice. Once positions of identification and desire are disrupted, once heterosexuality is removed as the underpinning of gender identification (Butler, 1995), then we are jettisoned from a classic psychoanalytic space into a queer universe of polymorphous diversity. Lesbian sexuality questions the privileging of genital sex, and the equation of "appropriate gender attribution" with mature sexuality. Lesbian sexuality as theorized and practiced suggests an eroticism which allows for multiple identifications, multiple positions of desire, and objects to reflect a polymorphously diverse sexuality.

Finally, lesbian eroticism is about gender performance (Butler, 1990a, b), the performative creation of a multiplicity of genders that more accurately signal individual sexual desire and temperament.

Clinical psychoanalysis is uniquely situated to traverse a universe of mature sexualities that is responsive to and desirous of a variety of sexual objects having differing but not necessarily contradictory resonances with a melange of early object relations.

Clinical psychoanalysis, then, is uniquely situated to traverse the queer universe.

References

Bassin, D. (1996), Beyond the he and she: Toward the reconciliation of masculinity and feminity in the post oedipal female mind. *J. Amer. Psychoanal. Assn.* (Spec. Suppl.), 4:157–190.

Bollas, C. (1989), *Forces of Destiny: Psychoanalysis and Human Idiom.* Deepvale, NJ: Jason Aronson.

Butler, J. (1990a), *Gender Trouble and the Subversion of Identity.* New York: Routledge.

———— (1990b), Gender trouble, feminist theory, and psychoanalytic discourse. In: *Feminism/Postmodernism,* ed. L. J. Nicholson. New York: Routledge.

———— (1995), Melancholy gender—Refused identifications. *Psychoanal. Dial.,* 5:165–180.

Case, S. (1989), Toward a butch-femme aesthetic. In: *The Lesbian and Gay Studies Reader,* ed. H. Abelove, M. Barale, & D. Halpern. New York: Routledge, 1993.

Cixous, H. (1986), "Sorties." In: *The Newly Born Woman,* by H. Cixous & C. Clement, tr. B. Wing. Minneapolis: University of Minnesota Press.

Cordova, J. (1992), Butch, lesbians and feminism. In: *The Persistent Desire: A Femme-Butch Reader,* ed. J. Nestle. Boston: Alyson, pp. 272–294.

Daumer, E. (1992), Queer ethics, or the challenge of bisexuality to lesbian ethics. *Hypatia,* 7:91–106.

de Lauretis, T. (1987), *Technologies of Gender.* Bloomington: Indiana University Press.

Faderman, L. (1981), *Surpassing the Love of Men.* New York: Morrow.

————— (1993), Nineteenth-century Boston marriage as a possible lesson for today. In: *Boston Marriages: Romantic but Asexual Relationships among Contemporary Lesbians,* ed. E. D. Rothblum & K. A. Brehony. Amherst: University of Massachusetts Press, pp. 29–42.

Fast, I. (1984), *Gender Identity.* Hillsdale, NJ: Analytic Press.

Feinberg, L. (1993), *Stone Butch Blues.* Ithaca, NY: Firebrand Books.

Freud, S. (1905), Three Essays on the Theory of Sexuality. *Standard Edition,* 7:123–243. London: Hogarth Press, 1955.

————— (1916–1917), Introductory Lectures on Psychoanalysis. *Standard Edition,* 16. London: Hogarth Press, 1961.

————— (1920), The psychogenesis of a case of homosexuality in a woman. *Standard Edition,* 18:145–172. London: Hogarth Press, 1955.

————— (1925), Some psychical consequences of the anatomical distinction between the sexes. *Standard Edition,* 19:241–258. London: Hogarth Press, 1961.

————— (1931), Female sexuality. *Standard Edition,* 21:221–243. London: Hogarth Press, 1961.

————— (1937), Analysis terminable and interminable. *Standard Edition,* 23:209–253. London: Hogarth Press, 1966.

Frye, M. (1990), Lesbian "sex." In: *Lesbian Philosophies and Cultures,* ed. J. Allen. Albany: State University of New York Press.

Garber, M. (1991), *Vested Interests: Cross-Dressing and Cultural Anxiety.* New York: Routledge.

————— (1995), *Vice-Versa: Bisecting and the Eroticism of Everyday Life.* New York: Simon & Schuster.

Goldner, V. (1991), Towards a critical relational theory of gender. *Psychoanal. Dial.,* 3:249–272.

Grahn, J. (1984), *Another Mother Tongue.* Boston: Beacon Press.

Hall, M. (1993), "Why limit me to ecstasy?" Toward a positive model of genital incidentalism among friends and other lovers. In: *Boston Marriages: Romantic but Asexual Relationships among Contemporary Lesbians,* ed. E.

D. Rothblum & R. Brehony. Amherst: University of Massachusetts Press, pp. 43–62.

Harris, A. (1991), Gender as contradiction. *Psychoanal. Dial.,* 1:197–224.

Irigary, L. (1985), *Speculum of the Other Woman,* tr. G. C. Gill. Ithaca, NY: Cornell University Press.

Kulish, N. M. (1991), Representations of the clitoris. *Psychoanal. Inq.,* 11:511–536.

Lindenbaum, J. (1985), The shattering of illusions: The problem of competition in lesbian relationships. *Feminist Studies,* 11:64–73.

Lorde, A. (1982), Zami: A new spelling of my name. In: *Zami, Sister, Outsider, Undersong.* New York: Quality Paperback Book Club, 1993.

McDougall, J. (1986), Eve's reflection: On the homosexual components of female sexuality. In: *Between Analyst and Patient: Dimensions in Countertransference and Transference,* ed. H. Meyers. Hillsdale, NJ: Analytic Press.

Nichols, M. (1987), Doing sex therapy with lesbians: Bending a heterosexual paradigm to fit a gay life-style. In: *Lesbian Psychologies: Explorations and Challenges,* ed. The Boston Lesbian Psychologies Collective. Urbana: University of Illinois Press, pp. 242–260.

Rich, A. (1981), Compulsory heterosexuality and lesbian existence. In: *The Lesbian and Gay Studies Reader,* ed. H. Abelove, M. Barale, & D. Halpern. New York: Routledge, 1993.

Riviere, J. (1929), Womanliness as a masquerade. *Internat. J. Psycho-Anal.,* 10:303–313.

Roof, J. (1991), *A Lure of Knowledge.* New York: Columbia University Press.

Rose, J. (1986), *Sexuality in the Field of Vision.* London: Verso.

Rothblum, E. D., & Brehony, K. A. (1993), *Boston Marriages: Romantic but Asexual Relationships among Contemporary Lesbians.* Amherst: University of Massachusetts Press.

Rubin, G. (1992), Of catamites and kings: Reflections on butch, gender and boundaries. In: *The Persistent Desire: A Femme-Butch Reader,* ed. J. Nestle. Boston: Alyson, pp. 466–482.

——— with Butler, J. (1994), Sexual traffic. *Differences* 6(2&3):62–99.

Schwartz, A. (1996), Coming out/being heard. A paper presented at the Annual Spring Meeting of the American Psychological Association, Division of Psychoanalysis.

——— (1999), Postmodern masquerade: Re-visiting Riviere. Commentary on Joan Riviere's "Womanliness as a masquerade." In: *Female Sexuality: Contemporary Engagements,* ed. D. Bassin. Northvale, NJ: Jason Aronson, pp. 115–125.

Suleiman, S. (1986), (Re) writing the body: The politics and poetics of female eroticism. In: *The Female Body in Western Culture,* ed. S. Suleiman. Cambridge, MA: Harvard University Press, pp. 7–29.

Winnicott, D. W. (1971), The use of an object and relating through identifica-
    tions. In: *Playing and Reality*. New York: Basic Books, pp. 86–94.
Wittig, M. (1975), *The Lesbian Body*. New York: William Morrow.
Zita, J. N. (1992), The male lesbian and the postmodernist body. *Hypatia*,
    7:106–127.

14

Daring Desire: Lesbian Sexuality in Popular Music

Shara Sand

This chapter will examine lesbian sexuality in popular music and the expressions of gender and desire that lay bare the multiple, often seemingly contradictory identifications that occur among lesbians. I will attempt to dislodge lesbian desire from the heterosexual, phallocentric paradigm often used to understand sexual expression between two women. To do so, I will use deconstructivist theories of gender and identification as well as theories of audience studies to ground my examination of two lesbian performers highly visible in the landscape of popular music, Melissa Etheridge and k.d. lang.

I have specifically chosen music as my vehicle, as its beauty and power lie in its ability to affect both mind and body, often moving the body in a manner beyond the control of the rational mind. Music creates a transitional space and allows for a fluidity of self-experience that fosters multiple meanings, associations, and identifications. It is these shifts in self states that reveal the multiply configured qualities of gender and desire. The performances of Etheridge and lang provide a unique forum in which aspects of lesbian sexuality are expressed, particularly the ability

Portions of this paper were published previously in *Psychoanalysis and Contemporary Thought* (1999), 22(3).

to play with gender and enact a multiplicity of positions vis-a-vis their partner.

Identification, Performativity, and Performance

The deconstructivist theory of identification rests on the premise of gender as accounted for by multiple identifications. Gender is viewed as a complexly constructed position reflecting numerous identifications and representations which may shift in continuous or discontinuous patterns. This does not necessarily imply abandoning the notion of identity, but rather, holding both identity and multiplicity together as a dialectical interplay (Aron, 1995). According to Butler (1995), these multiple identifications can constitute a nonhierarchical configuration of shifting and overlapping identifications. This no longer restricts us to the rather limited notions of fixed masculine or feminine identifications, but frees us to explore different combinations of them. She also theorizes that gender has no inner core but is only signified through its enactment. Thus gender is performed, expressing both acknowledged as well as repudiated and disavowed identifications.

Theories in audience studies illuminate the importance of identification in relation to gender, sexuality, and the musical performance. Citron (1994) writes of the literal embodiment of the process of musical communication and she places the gender of the performer in a position of particular importance regarding identificatory ties with another woman. This is apparent when one considers the popularity of Etheridge and lang, not only among lesbians, but heterosexual women as well. Dolan (1993) notes the performance does not necessarily simply mimic cultural stereotypes and perpetuate gender roles, rather, it creates many avenues through which a spectator can identify with the multiple, often seemingly contradictory stances taken by the performer. This position allows for a process of identifications and disidentifications to occur along a continuum, from those which are known and acceptable to the self, to those that represent the disavowed, subversive aspects of the self.

In examining gender identification and desire, the terms *masculine* and *feminine* are used out of linguistic necessity. It is not the intention of this chapter to reinforce the essentialist and limiting roles of masculinity and femininity, but rather to examine lesbian desire and its many complex manifestations. I will take the position that for many lesbians, masculine identifications are not disavowed, but are often rather accessible. There is the general agreement among lesbians that they do not feel bound to specific, socially derived gender roles. This allows for a freedom in constructing modes of sexual expression in their relationships that may be less available to many heterosexual women. However, the presence of masculine identifications does not mean an absence or negation of feminine identifications, as many theorists have posited. I propose that lesbians have greater access to multiply gendered identifications and that the expression of such is neither pathological nor the misplaced longing of the "I wish I were a man" syndrome.

There is often a tendency to refer to lesbian identifications and sexuality in regard to butch–femme roles that were very rigid and taken quite seriously in the culture of the 1950s and 1960s. In the 1990s, butch-femme came to represent a playful way of gender bending in which traditional aspects of masculinity and femininity become more flexible. Case (1989) argues that the performance of these roles does not reinforce heterosexual models of gender, but rather, subverts them for specifically lesbian purposes, thereby creating new meanings and identifications particular to lesbians. This allows lesbians to move fluidly between gendered positions while performing multiple desires (Weston, 1996; Esterberg, 1997). I believe it is the multiply gendered expressions of sexuality and desire exhibited by Melissa Etheridge and k.d. lang that have resulted in their enormous popularity among lesbians as well as heterosexual fans. Before looking at their performances, it is important to understand music's long, conflictual relationship to gender and sexuality.

Music, Gender, and Sexuality

Music, while thought of primarily as an aural experience, is also a visual experience. The recording industry is barely one-hundred years old, and until its existence, the live performance was the only way to experience music. The visual component of music invites the listener to gaze upon the performer and the combined sensations of sight and sound help create music's sensual power. It is in this way that the musical gaze becomes charged with sexuality, linked to the body and associated with the arousal and channeling of desire (Leppert, 1993). It is music's relationship to the body that is problematic, for it this link that raises questions regarding gender identity, desire, and sexuality.

Philosophical and cultural prescriptions have long located the body in the feminine and the mind in the masculine, thus music's association to the body situates it in the realm of the feminine. Paradoxically, it is also considered the most abstract and cerebral of the arts, which places it squarely in the masculine "mind." Nonetheless, music's emotional impact and its influence on the body has always put the male performer in a position perilously close to the feminine. To counter the fear of feminization and secure music's masculine status, particularly as a potent, virile form of sexual expression, women were excluded from the composition or performance of music for centuries (Leppert, 1993). Conversely, the horror of women treading dangerously close to masculine sexuality via the musical performance resulted in the restriction of women's participation, in instrumental music to instruments considered of a "feminine" nature (e.g., guitar, keyboard, harp). These required no alteration in facial or physical demeanor and their performance was limited to domestic settings. A woman was frowned upon for making her music too sexual, or taking it too seriously (McClary, 1991; Post, 1994).

Thus historically, music has served as an artistic reflection of gender, its social restrictions on women's performance can be interpreted as a societal fear of the expression of passion and desire by women. If we apply Butler's (1995) theory, perhaps this fear is related to the expression of disavowed masculine identifications. Similarly, the appropriation of music as a masculine province can also be seen as a fear of disavowed feminine identifications. Music is "something we do . . . as a way of explaining, replicating and reinforcing our relationships to the world or our imagined notions of what possible relationships might exist" (Cusick, 1994, p. 73). Thus, music and its performance is an enactment of the multiplicity of identity. It is through an exploration of these multiple identifications that I will examine the experience and construction of lesbian sexuality.

Lesbian Sexuality in Popular Music

Both Melissa Etheridge and k.d. lang seem to glide between positions of gender identification and shift in their expressions of desire in all aspects of their performance. Melissa Etheridge has five albums, numerous Grammys, and has often been cited as the heir apparent to Bruce Springsteen and the more masculine identified bastion of "stadium rock." She is known for exuding a passionate intensity in her lyrics and performance. Her voice, low and smooth in expressive ballads, can rise to a roar as she belts out hard-driving rock n' roll. If performativity can be interpreted as a performance of gender and sexuality, then Etheridge truly embodies this. She "does" her gender, performs her desire, exhibiting a mix of masculine and feminine identifications: long, blond hair, jewelry, black leather pants, t-shirt and boots, she seduces and wants to be seduced, she penetrates and wants to be penetrated.

Etheridge's music itself is an amalgam of cross-gender identifications. Melodic structures that unfold smoothly, rising and falling on a tide of emotions, are often combined with a vigorous bass, powerful drums, and incisive guitars. She utilizes dynamics and grabs the listener's attention as songs disappear into a whisper only to reemerge with a power and drive that are startling. A pulsating, insistent beat accompanies her lyrics and desire is transformed into a mixture of soft and hard, flowing and thrusting, surrendering and seducing.

Turning to her lyrics, what is noticeable is how desire is painted with sensual, sensory references and images such as

> The smell, the touch, the taste is so brand new
> The thrill of the eyes that capture this forbidden view [Etheridge,
>   1995, track 4].

The richness of her sexual desire is revealed when she sings "And when I awoke I tasted the sweat of desire on my mouth" (Etheridge, 1988, track 5). The sensuality of the imagery is more feminine, and captures the sensory, often nongenital aspects of lesbian sexuality, while the lyrics articulate a more active masculine desire. Etheridge interweaves themes of masculine and feminine imagery throughout her songs. Her lyrics are often nongendered and her abundant use of the pronouns *I* and *You,* allows for the opportunity to employ multiple identifications. Lines such as

> Am I the snake inside your garden
> the sugar in your tea
> the knock upon your back door

the twist that turns your key [Etheridge, 1989, track 7]

combine both penetrating and receptive desires, reflective of the capacity
for lesbians to explore both active and passive roles in the expression of
their sexuality.

Etheridge's songs often convey a swaggering bravado in which
women are confident, penetrating seducers who thrill, inject, and persist.
The following lyric is a wonderful example of a woman as an active
desiring subject, a role often off-limits to heterosexual women.

Tell me does she love you like the way I love you
Does she stimulate you attract and captivate you
Like the way I do
Tell me does she want you infatuate and haunt you
Does she know just how to shock and electrify and
    rock you
Does she inject you seduce you and affect you
Like the way I do [Etheridge, 1988, track 3].

With her agency she embraces disavowed masculine identifications acknowledging her power to seduce and enthrall. However, this agency
does not preclude expressions of the more "feminine" desires to be
seduced and penetrated. Lines such as

Spread these wings I'm on for the ride
Cruise these streets where my innocence hides
[Etheridge, 1992, track 1]

articulate a surrendering passion and once again allow for the possibility
of multiple identifications.

In performance, she turns an extended musical interlude into an erotic
encounter, conveying a very different sexual stance and relatedness from
most performers. Etheridge creates an atmosphere of mutual desire and
satisfaction. She is seductive and enticing, but not in a passive manner
and not as an imitator of male symbols. Her music and performance play
with the continuum of masculine and feminine identifications and to be
in the audience is to feel her presence and sexuality as a powerful woman.
As a lesbian, Etheridge does not refuse homosexual love and as such her
masculine identifications may be as available to her as her feminine ones.

She is a woman who juxtaposes active and passive representations, allowing subject and object to shift and express the wish to play multiple roles.

k.d. lang has also released five albums and won several Grammies in popular and country music. Both her appearance and performance style are drastically different from Etheridge's, but she too performs her gender, while lang presents with an androgynous, boyish look, that belies a voluptuous shape. Her vocal style is far from hard-driving rock n' roll, rather she is a crooning balladeer with a love of the torch song and roots in country music. She brings more than a touch of camp to her performance and her delight in gender bending is apparent. lang can be coyly mischievous, yet passionate as her voice, smooth as silk, radiates a lush feminine sensuality, while her visual countenance suggests the more masculine stance of a teasing rogue.

lang sustains this multiply gendered position through her vocal style and choice of music. Her voice can feel like velvet, offering the gentlest of caresses, or she can bend, slide, growl, and rip her way through notes in the most erotic, suggestive, and sometimes even lewd ways. She writes much of her own material, and like Etheridge, her lyrics are strikingly nongendered in her almost exclusive use of an *I-you* form of address. This fosters the potential to employ multiple identifications in the manifestation of desire. lang also performs and records the songs of others, often identifying with the masculine position of the composer. However, she does so with the satiric edge of a woman who has her own subversive intentions, creating bold, new interpretations of well-worn songs (Mockus, 1994).

lang uses the musical performance to play with gender, striking many apparently contradictory poses. It is her embodiment of "masculine" bravado and "feminine" wiles, which reflects the complex nature of lesbian desire, that makes her so appealing. On her album, *Drag,* a tongue-in-cheek tribute to smoking, one need only see lang wearing a pinstripe suit, lying on a fake fur rug, with a come hither look reminiscent of the pinups of the 1940s and 1950s, to feel the erotic tension of her sexual contradictions.

lang plays with these contradictions in her rendition of Wynn Stewart's *Big Big Love*, which has the following verse:

Can't you feel my love a-growin'
Can't you see it, ain't it showin'

Oh you must be knowin'
I got a big big love [lang, 1989, track 9].

She revels in the sexual innuendo and double entendres offered by these lines. What meaning do we construct from such phallically erect images when they are sung by a woman? They articulate the symbolic portrayal of a woman's love as big and powerful, and more literally, are representations of erectile sensations experienced by the hardening of the nipples and clitoris. Thus, lang's delight is not in the literal possession of the phallus, but in the agency and self-determination she asserts in the expression of her sexual desire.

Conversely, she is just as comfortable playing the more typically passive "feminine" role. She gives herself over to her lover when she sings

I can exist being caught by your kiss
Willingly
Or grant you control
Of my body and soul
Ask it and so it should be [lang, 1992, track 5].

Like Etheridge, lang uses sensual, sensory imagery to express the rich patina of sexual delights reflective of lesbian desire. Lines such as,

You swim
Swim through my veins [lang, 1992, track 4]

and

Drink from my spell
Quench
Love's drying well [lang, 1992, track 4]

speak to a sexuality that precludes a primary focus on genital intercourse.

lang has an awareness, as does Etheridge, of her own masculine identifications which allows her to mischievously and joyfully juxtapose them alongside more conventional feminine positions. In her rendition of Tom Jones's *What's New Pussycat?*, she is raucous and almost lewd. Her style softens in when she sings Steve Miller's song *The Joker*; however, her subjective agency is conveyed through the lyrics which she delivers in a soft, smooth, seductive manner. lang can maintain this same style as she has demonstrated by flirting playfully with Tony Bennet in many a concert.

Discussion

Both Etheridge and lang exhibit a range of gender and sexual identifications in all aspects of their performance. They show us a continuum of gendered experience that is individually constructed from combinations of masculine and feminine identifications that exist sequentially and simultaneously within all of us. They are women who possess a powerful, subjective, sexual agency. They do not simply emulate phallic symbols, but rather, use their bodies and words to represent themselves as both desired and desiring, seduced and seducing, lover and beloved. Etheridge and lang both express aspects of disavowed gender identifications that clearly resonate with the lesbian community. However, it is important to note that their popularity also extends to the vast heterosexual majority. This speaks to the more universal aspects of female sexuality they express, particularly regarding the multiple identifications which comprise gender and desire.

It is quite evident from examining these women's performances that there is no simple "lesbian" desire. Rather in decentering the notion of gender, there is the recognition that "masculine" and "feminine" behaviors can be enacted in an inclusive way by women, without necessitating a rejection of femininity as is often assumed. Rather, the wish to be male and the wish to be female, to have both and be both, is represented. Thus, desire is exposed for its complex, discontinuous, and often ambiguous qualities that may be the expression of unconscious and disavowed aspects of self. It is in the acknowledgment of the complex identifications that construct desire that we can begin to understand the subjective experience of sexuality between two women. This becomes clinically relevant as we strive to understand and to help our patients understand the meaning of the many contradictory feelings and identifications they experience regarding their gender, sexuality, and desire.

References

Aron, L. (1995), The internalized primal scene. *Psychoanal. Dial.,* 5:165–181.

Butler, J. (1995), Melancholy gender—Refused identification. *Psychoanal. Dial.,* 5:165–180.

Case (1989), Toward a butch-femme aesthetic. *Discourse: Journal for Theoretical Studies in Media and Culture,* 11:55–73.

Citron, M. (1994), Feminist approaches to musicology. In: *Cecilia Reclaimed: Feminist Perspectives on Gender and Music,* ed. S. C. Cook & J. S. Tsou. Chicago: University of Illinois Press, pp. 15–34.

Cusick, S. (1994), On a lesbian relationship to music: A serious effort not to think straight. In: *Queering the Pitch: The New Gay and Lesbian Musicology,* ed. P. Brett, E. Wood, & G. C. Thomas. New York: Routledge, pp. 67–83.

Dolan, J. (1993), *Presence and Desire.* Ann Arbor, MI: University of Michigan Press.

Esterberg, K. (1997), *Lesbian and Bisexual Identities.* Philadelphia, PA: Temple University Press.

Etheridge, M. (1988), Like the way I do. On: *Melissa Etheridge* [CD]. New York: Island Records.

——— (1989), Let me go. On: *Brave and Crazy* [CD]. New York: Island Records.

——— (1992), Ain't it heavy. On: *Never Enough* [CD]. New York: Island Records.

——— (1995), An unusual kiss. On: *Your Little Secret* [CD]. New York: Island Records.

Lang, k.d. (1989), Big, big love. On: *Torch and Twang* [CD]. New York: Sire Records.

——— (1992a), Wash me clean. On: *Ingenue* [CD]. New York: Sire Records.

——— (1992b), So it shall be. On: *Ingenue* [CD]. New York: Sire Records.

Leppert, R. (1993), *The Sight of Sound.* Berkeley, CA: University of California Press.

McClary, S. (1991), *Feminine Endings.* Minneapolis, MN: University of Minnesota Press.

Mockus, M. (1994), Queer thoughts on country music and k.d. lang. In: *Queering the Pitch: The New Gay and Lesbian Musicology,* ed. P. Brett, E. Wood & G. C. Thomas. New York: Routledge, pp. 257–271.

Post, J. C. (1994), Erasing the boundaries between public and private in women's performance traditions. In: *Cecilia Reclaimed: Feminist Perspectives on Gender and Music,* ed. S. C. Cook & J. S. Tsou. Chicago: University of Illinois Press, pp. 35–51.

Weston, K. (1996), *Render Me, Gender Me.* New York: Columbia University Press.

15

Lesbian Mothers: A Foot in Two Worlds

Deborah F. Glazer

While lesbians have been raising children for decades, if not centuries, lesbian mothers have typically conceived their children in heterosexual unions. It was frequently after the birth of their children that women came out to themselves and others. Increased access to reproductive technologies and single-parent adoption, coupled with advances in gay and lesbian rights, have allowed more women to conceive and give birth while already in committed lesbian relationships. As a result we are currently in the midst of what is referred to as a lesbian gayby boom. The experiences of motherhood and procreation are insufficiently discussed in psychoanalytic theory, as are issues of lesbian development and experience. As a result, explorations into the inner experience of lesbian mothers have been absent in psychoanalytic discourse. This chapter will provide an overview of some of the salient themes and issues confronting lesbians as they contemplate and undertake motherhood.

Gender, Object Choice, and Motherhood

Traditional psychoanalytic theory (Freud, 1920, 1925) has melded gender identity, object choice, and the wish for a child into one line of development. Deutsch (1945), however, believed that the instinct to mother is a primary drive resulting from a "bio-chemical source [that] lies beyond the psychologic sphere" (p. 19). Whether biological or psychological, Deutsch believed that the sexual urge and the desire to mother actually occur along different developmental lines, and that the maternal instinct, itself, was comprised of numerous developmental outcomes. She suggested that the confluence of the sexual and the reproductive motives was societally proscribed in the service of Christian ethics, aimed at warding off the recognition of pure, unbridled sexuality.

Current postmodernists (Goldner, 1991; D'Ercole, chapter 11) dispute the fixed, binary view of gender and sexuality taken by most psychoanalytic theorists. They concur with the idea that development of gender and sexual orientation is the outgrowth of more than one developmental sequence, and that those developmental pathways are powerfully influenced by societal configurations and expectations. Gender identification and sexual object choice grow out of a vast, complex mosaic of socially constructed, multiple, and shifting identities rather than binary and fixed traits.

Clinically, however, many lesbians exhibit difficulty reconciling their homosexuality, their gender identity, and their wish to mother. Many lesbian patients describe feeling a sense of gender inadequacy. This feeling of inadequacy may lead some women to feel that they do not have sufficient womanliness to conceive, carry, and raise children. This may be expressed in fears of not being able to conceive or fantasies that the babies will not form properly or be properly nourished/nurtured in the womb. Notman and Lester (1988) state that for a woman "awareness of her reproductive potential is part of her self-esteem" (p. 139). Until recently, societal and medical standards meant that growing up lesbian resulted in a relinquishing of reproductive potential. Recognition of one's lesbianism involved a recognition of one's barrenness, and by extension one's fraudulence and inadequacy as a true woman. Janice, a lesbian in her early thirties, described her grief and feelings of inadequacy at her childlessness by comparing herself to the female protagonist in television's The X-Files. This fictional federal agent had been kidnapped by the government and had her eggs surgically removed. Greenson (1964) wrote that individuals first develop a sense of their own gender, and subsequently become focused on their sexual desires. For homosexuals, "the awareness of homosexuality poses a threat to their gender identity" (p. 192). More recently, Butler (1995) theorized that gender develops out of a socially constructed, heterosexual matrix, which is an outgrowth of the renunciation of homosexual desire. Thus, "the fear of homosexual desire in a woman may induce a panic that she is not a woman; that she is no longer a proper woman; that, if she is not quite a man she is like one and hence monstrous in some way" (p. 168).

It seems that Janice fully recognizes that she is a woman, but feels damaged in her femaleness as a result of her lesbianism. In addition, Janice's homoerotic desires may serve to exacerbate the female genital anxieties initially addressed by Bernstein (1993). Fear of castration need not be a specifically male, or even penis related, experience. Girls, and later women, can experience female genital anxieties related to feared damage to inner and outer genital and reproductive organs. For some women, anxieties related to damage or disease of the genitals and reproductive organs may be seen as a fear of punishment for her same-sex desires. Others may erroneously believe that the same-sex desire is rooted in a body-based abnormality of the reproductive system.

For the lesbian who experiences this gender anxiety, the recognition that she can conceive, give birth to, and nurture a child can help heal the subjective experience of damage caused by the recognition of her lesbianism. Claire expressed strong feelings of self-reproach that she had never had intercourse with a man. She believed that her lesbianism and traditional virginity meant that she was flawed and inadequate as a woman. She feared that a healthy baby could not form inside her and that her breasts were too small to allow her to nurse. As her pregnancy progressed, Claire began to take pride in the womanly developments that were blossoming. After delivery, she brought her newborn son into her treatment and nursed during the session. For the first time she felt proud and adequate as a woman, and she was excited to exhibit her newfound female power.

It seems essential to consider that the experience of one's gender, one's sexual impulses, and the drive to mother result from varied and multiple identifications and internalizations. One's ability to identify as a woman is not incongruous with the ability to love a woman, as identificatory love and erotic love need not be mutually exclusive (O'Connor and Ryan, 1993). Similarly, the desire to act on the procreative instinct need not be contingent on the extent or adequacy of one's femaleness, or the gender of one's love object. Clinical questions address the fine internal balance of how each identification and line of development affects one's self experience and sense of adequacy and functionality in other developmental areas.

The Problem of Conception

The first dilemma faced by the lesbian couple who decide to procreate or coparent is how they'll have a child. In the case of biological parenting, they must decide which one of them will have the baby and who will be the donor/father. These questions are full of intrapsychic and interpersonal pitfalls.

Lesbians often grieve their ability to procreate through traditional means. Crespi (1995) discusses the mourning process that lesbians must experience in acknowledging the desire to make a family with someone with whom they cannot conceive a child. She likens this mourning to the grief experienced in heterosexual couples experiencing infertility. It is the resolution of this mourning that allows the lesbian to be free to conceive through alternative measures. Unresolved mourning leaves some women unable to have children in lesbian relationships, while others may feel a strong sense of inadequacy and fraudulence in their identity as mothers.

All developmental outcomes require a relinquishing or repression of the path not taken (Fast, 1979). The desire to bear a child can bring up long repressed feelings of longing for the relinquished heterosexual object. Some lesbians find an increase in heterosexual fantasies and wishes as they begin the process of reproduction or when they give birth. In addition, a sense of internalized homophobia can result in the sense that true motherhood can only be attained through a heterosexual union. Some lesbians choose to use a known donor to give the child a father and provide a heterosexual basis and validation for their parenting. Choosing a known donor may provide a rich, full family life. It may also result in a triangulation that can cause difficulty in the nuclear family if the nonbirth mother and biological father compete for their role with the child and birth mother.

The Stranger Within

Literary critics speculate that Frankenstein was a fictional account of Mary Shelley's fantasies about birth and motherhood. Moers (1996) notes that the work represents Shelley's "feelings as a woman" (p. 222), as well as her sense that "birth is a hideous thing" (p. 220). Johnson (1996) relates "the entire novel to Shelley's mixed feelings about motherhood" (p. 246). Both authors believe that the difficulties experienced in Shelley's multiple pregnancies, including early miscarriages, her young and unmarried state, and her familial rejection, exacerbated her fearful and conflictual feelings about motherhood and her unborn child.

Like Shelley, women of any sexual orientation may experience their unborn child as a frightening, destructive stranger within. Lesbians may experience guilt, shame, discomfort in their gender role, and familial rejection during pregnancy. For heterosexual women, societal support and rituals, coupled with knowledge of the genetic origin of the fetus, can allow enough structure to help neutralize the frightening fantasies of the unknown being growing inside. Lesbians considering parenthood often do not have the societal and familial support and ritual that heterosexual women experience to help them through this stressful time. In addition, the pregnant lesbian is often carrying a child who comes, at least in part, through the unknown origin of frozen sperm. Thus she cannot use the love for the father of the unknown fetus to further neutralize her fears and fantasies about the life growing in her womb. Finally, her self-esteem and adequacy as a woman may be more fragile due to her history of growing up lesbian. Thus, like Shelley, the conditions of her pregnancy may result in increased fear and anxiety related to the potential physical and emotional dangers that come from creating and loving the unknown stranger within.

Competitive Mothering

Traditional psychoanalytic theory has proposed that the lesbian outcome is a retreat from competition with the oedipal mother. In fact, same-sex intimate relationships are often fraught with competition. There is not the opportunity to use gender role stereotypes to rationalize the role division required in a successful partnership. Specifically, lesbian mothers do not escape from competition with the oedipal mother, as sharing mothering can evoke complicated feelings of competition.

Harris (1993) discusses the difficulties women have with competition. Intrapsychically, competition brings up strong fears of the powerful, dangerous, and retaliatory oedipal mother. External influences and expectations of gender roles teach women that competition is unfeminine. For lesbians who are coparenting, who may have unresolved oedipal issues, and who may not feel adequately female, issues regarding competition can be a likely source of distress. When both women have an intense desire to mother, conflict may arise over who conceives. In birth and adoption situations, one woman may be identified as the "true mother." The nonbiological/nonlegal mother may face unexpected feelings of anger and rejection related to breast-feeding, signing for medical treatment, etc.

The first competitive struggle may occur with the selection of who conceives, or who conceives first. Beth and Jean had always determined that Beth would carry the children, as Jean did not wish to be pregnant. However, Jean began to long for a biological child following a significant loss in her family of origin. As Jean was near the end of her childrearing years, and was six years older than Beth, the couple decided that Jean would conceive first. The months working toward conception, the pregnancy, and the neonatal period brought out unexpectedly powerful feelings of anger and competition in Beth, as she watched her lover attain what she had always craved. Sue and Tina had a simpler decision about who would bear the children, as Sue had unsuccessfully undergone years of fertility treatments in an earlier heterosexual marriage. Although she agreed to a family with Tina, Sue believed that if she could not conceive, neither would Tina. Tina conceived quickly and gave birth to a healthy child. This left Sue with a powerful sense of exclusion from the neonatal dyad. This was compounded by envy of her lover's joy in the biological motherhood which was unavailable to Sue due to her previously diagnosed infertility.

Once the baby arrives, lesbian couples often experience a sense of competition around the role of mother. With biological children, there is the distinction between the birth and nonbirth mother. The nonbirth mother may feel the same sense of exclusion from the neonatal dyad often experienced by the father, but she does not receive the societal support and camaraderie that allows males to work through that exclusion. It is not uncommon for the extended family of the nonbiological mother to express feelings that the baby is not truly one of their clan, leading to an increased sense of fraudulence and isolation. The biologically related family may treat her as an interloper who has less of a role than a true blood relative.

Nursing is another aspect of mothering the lesbian couple must navigate, as it signals the identity of the "true" mother to the world. One nonbiological lesbian mother would not allow her lover and child to come to her office Christmas party. She felt that her colleagues thought of her as a mother, and feared that her coworkers would join in her sense of fraudulence and inadequacy as a mother when her lover nursed the baby. At home that sense of inadequacy may be heightened if the nonbiological mother may not be able to soothe her baby as adequately as her nursing lover can.

The biological mother may envy the freedom the nonbirth mother has to go out and be free in the world. Dinnerstein (1976) points out that some of the most damaging aspects of traditional family life is that the father has freedom and power to go out in the world while the mother is homebound. She believes that this "sexual arrangement" leads to misogyny in male children, and a sense of inadequacy, self-denigration, and worthlessness in the female child. The new lesbian mother is often surprised when she finds herself in precisely the same situation that she believed her lesbianism had freed her from. She is homebound with a newborn while her lover is free to work, socialize, and interact in the powerful outer world. For four years, Camilla had been coparenting a son born to her lover. She was so frequently out of the home that her young son reported that he believed her home was in her office. When Camilla became pregnant, she began to experience anger at her lover for being out too late too many evenings while she was at home, pregnant, alone, and unable to sleep.

Dual Invisibility

Kiersky (chapter 2) speaks of lesbians growing up in the "shadowlands," unable to experience an authentic sense of self. Like the classic children's tale, *The Velveteen Rabbit* (Williams, 1958), a child begins to feel real because she is loved and validated by her family. When one's true nature is ignored or invalidated, there is a sense of unreality in one's being and experience. Furthermore, a child may learn to hide her true self to avoid rejection from her loved ones.

Lesbian mothers face increased demands in reconciling the multiple identities related to gender, object choice, and motherhood. They often wind up in the shadowlands of both heterosexual and homosexual worlds, feeling inauthentic everywhere. Motherhood enhances the presumption of heterosexuality, making one invisible or a curiosity in the gay community. There is no safe haven in the heterosexual community, where a lesbian family is often an anomaly and may face rejection and homophobia. This may evoke a painful reawakening of the sense of difference and unrelatedness experienced during the childhood and adolescence of many lesbians.

In addition, a small child may force self-disclosure in situations where the lesbian mother may feel unsafe and wish for invisibility. The striving for invisibility can be a self-protective stance used to ward off feared attacks and rejection in a traditionally heterosexist, if not homophobic, environment. Many couples discuss the discomfort and awkwardness of sitting on a bus or riding in an elevator with a small child who decides to introduce her two mothers to every stranger within earshot.

Children in the Lesbian Household

Lesbian mothers are navigating uncharted territory in child rearing. This new generation of children born to "out" lesbian mothers are not yet old enough to allow for full understanding of the intrapsychic and developmental influences of family configurations. Lesbian mothers must address questions their children face about the nature of their birth, and respond to the alternative oedipal configurations their children develop. They may also have to cope with discrimination against their children.

Emma is the 3-year-old daughter and only child of lesbian mothers. She knows she came out of her birth mother's belly, but believes that her imaginary friend came out of her other mother's belly. She has also asked if she can share her birth mommy's daddy if she lets mommy share her grandfather. Emma is clearly trying to make sense of why only one mother gave birth to her. She is trying to understand familial relations, and is working through her wish for a father. How the lesbian mother copes with her child's recognition that her family is different is often based upon the level of guilt and shame the mother feels about her own homosexuality. One lesbian mother expressed concern that her toddler son sometimes expressed a wish not to have a penis, noting that negative feelings about her own lesbianism have led her to fear she had harmed her son by raising him in an all-female, lesbian household.

As the child becomes increasingly involved in the world outside the home, the psychological stressors on the mother may increase. Having her child face bias or rejection may cause the lesbian mother to reexperience traumas dealing with her own childhood recognition of same-sex longings and the coming out experiences she faced in adolescence and young adulthood. A lesbian mother expressed the pain she felt when her young son came home from school and announced that he needs a father for his father's day project. Another girl could no longer play with her best friend from school when the classmate's mother prohibited her daughter from going to the lesbians' home.

Lesbian mothers and their children must also navigate alternate oedipal configurations. As in the traditional oedipal phase, there can be mother and "other." The nonbirth or nonprimary care mother may be the oedipal "other" used by the child to facilitate separation. However, she may feel guilt over the sensuality exhibited toward her by the oedipal phase child. Girl children may evoke distressing feelings when they exhibit an erotic attachment to the "other" mother, as some lesbian mothers may erroneously have guilt about passing homosexuality on to their children. Boy children may evoke discomfort as their eroticism may bring up repressed heterosexual feelings in a manner similar to the homosexual distress evoked in heterosexual mothers in response to their daughters' sensuality.

In addition, the biological mother may have to deal with periods of rejection at moments when the nonbiological mother is the preferred mother. In heterosexual situations, there may be more clearly defined expectations of what the father provides that the mother cannot. These gender-related expectations can help the mother deal with the losses as the child moves toward the father and separation. It can be more difficult and painful when the child moves toward another woman, as it does not have the same social meaning and expectation. In addition, the competition over mothering, even if it's with her child's comother, may evoke or reawaken earlier oedipal rivalries and feelings of failure.

Summary

Lesbian mothers and their children face bold new worlds both externally and intrapsychically. Increased societal acceptance is helping lesbians feel freer in their roles as women. Similarly, psychoanalysts are beginning to recognize lesbianism as a plausible and realistic outcome of female development. The lesbian is beginning to be seen as a "true" woman rather than a "fictitious" (McDougall, 1978)[1] emulation of a man. When lesbians are seen as real women, they will be seen, and see themselves, as wanting what women want; and for some, that includes children. Thus, the lesbian mother is becoming an increasingly common social phenomenon and must enter into the realm of psychoanalytic inquiry. The special problems faced in the development of lesbians in a primarily heterosexual environment affect the way lesbians cope with becoming mothers. The exploration of issues related to a sense of female adequacy, competition with her lover, fantasies about conception, and feelings about raising a child in a lesbian home are essential elements of the analytic work with lesbian mothers.

References

Bernstein, D. (1993), *Female Identity Conflict in Clinical Practice,* ed. N. Freedman & B. Distler. Northvale, NJ: Jason Aronson.

Butler, J. (1995), Melancholy gender—Refused identification. *Psychoanal. Dial.,* 5:165–180.

Crespi, L. (1995), Some thoughts on the role of mourning in the development of a positive lesbian identity. In: *Disorienting Sexuality: Psychoanalytic Reappraisals of Sexual Identities,* ed. T. Domenici & R. Lesser. New York: Routledge, pp. 19–32.

Deutsch, H. (1945), *Psychology of Women,* Vol. 2. New York: Grune & Stratton.

Dinnerstein, D. (1976), *The Mermaid and the Minotaur: Sexual Arrangements and Human Malaise.* New York: HarperPerennial.

Fast, I. (1979), Developments in gender identity: Gender differentiation in girls. *Internat. J. Psycho-Anal.,* 60:443–453.

Freud, S. (1920), The psychogenesis of a case of homosexuality in a woman. *Standard Edition,* 18:145–172. London: Hogarth Press, 1955.

---

[1]See chapter 1. McDougall's chapter included in this volume represents a critical shift in her thinking about lesbian identity.

———— (1925), Some psychical consequences of the anatomical distinction between the sexes. *Standard Edition*, 19:241–258. London: Hogarth Press, 1961.

Goldner, V. (1991), Toward a critical relational theory of gender. *Psychoanal. Dial.*, 1:249–272.

Greenson, R. (1964), On homosexuality and gender identity. *Internat. J. Psycho-Anal.*, 45:217–219.

Harris, A. (1993), Envy and excitement, masquerades and empowerment: The hidden dilemmas in women's ambition. Paper presented at the Ninth Annual Conference of the Los Angeles Child Development Center, "Women and Power: New Psychoanalytic Perspectives on the Development of Ambition." Santa Monica, CA. Sept. 18.

Johnson, B. (1996), My monster/My self. In: *Frankenstein: Mary Shelley,* ed. J. P. Hunter. New York: W. W. Norton.

McDougall, J. (1978), *A Plea for a Measure of Abnormality.* New York: International Universities Press.

Moers, E. (1996), Female gothic: The monster's mother. In: *Frankenstein: Mary Shelley,* ed. J. P. Hunter. New York: W. W. Norton.

Notman, M. T., & Lester, E. (1988), Pregnancy: Theoretical considerations. *Psychoanal. Inq.*, 8:139–169.

O'Connor, N., & Ryan, J. (1993), *Wild Desires and Mistaken Identities: Lesbianism and Psychoanalysis.* New York: Columbia University Press.

Williams, M. (1958), *The Velveteen Rabbit.* Garden City, NY: Doubleday.

Part IV

Twenty-Five Years of Psychoanalysis in the Lesbian Community

16

From Baby Boom to Gayby Boom: Twenty-Five Years of Psychoanalysis in the Lesbian Community

Lee Crespi

As we enter the twenty-first century, lesbian analysts have begun to achieve significant recognition and standing within the psychoanalytic profession. The debate and inquiry into the appropriate psychoanalytic understanding and treatment of lesbians have expanded to include voices from within the lesbian analytic community along with those of the larger analytic field. This volume and others like it represent a unique but growing body of literature that provides clinicians with long overdue theoretical, technical, and critical viewpoints to expand their thinking and clinical work.

It is only since the mid-1990s that psychoanalytic literature has offered a nonpathologizing approach to the treatment of lesbians. The seeds of this development, however, can be traced back to the early 1970s and

---

This chapter is dedicated to the memory of Jean Millar, C.S.W.

the influence of the lesbian and gay rights movement. During that time, many of today's theorists were studying, treating, and learning from their patients. At the same time, the patients themselves were in an evolving state due to the social and political transformations of the period. The following are some reflections on the past quarter-century of evolution both among lesbians who have sought treatment, and the lesbian analysts who have treated them.

The Seventies

In the 1970s, the sociopolitical movement for lesbian and gay rights was in its heyday. It was the perception of many gays and lesbians that the traditional psychoanalytic establishment could not be depended upon as a safe environment. The church, psychiatry, and psychoanalysis were felt to be the most conservative institutions regarding antihomosexual attitudes. Centers were established to provide counseling and psychother-apeutic services to the gay and lesbian community, primarily, although not exclusively, with gay and lesbian clinicians. In those heated political days there was much emphasis on peer counseling. The philosophy be-hind peer counseling was that many of the problems confronting lesbians who sought therapy were either caused or compounded by the isolation and stigmatization that they experienced in the world at large. The objec-tive was to provide exposure and contact with peers, that is, other lesbians who had shared many similar experiences and because of their own ther-apy and heightened political understanding could provide support, empa-thy, and role-modeling for their clients. Concurrent with this philosophy, there existed a strong mistrust of psychoanalysis for its history of misun-derstanding and mistreating homosexuals. For many, doing counseling and psychotherapy were logical extensions of political activism, a means to liberate others from the shackles of their psychological oppression.

As these peer counselors worked with their clients, they began to appreciate more of the complexity of the human psyche. The need and the desire for more training became increasingly compelling. Many sought advanced training through the various branches of the human potential movement. Approaches such as Gestalt therapy, psychodrama, cocounsel-ing, and other of the nonpsychoanalytic therapies were drawing much attention then, as an alternative to traditional psychoanalysis. Teachers and practitioners of these therapies were felt to be more progressive and open-minded, and less likely to impose antigay attitudes on their students. Also, these approaches themselves were not based on theories of pathology and cure but instead placed their emphasis on the experiential and on empowering individuals toward personal growth.

Some lesbians sought training in psychoanalysis despite its reputation, often because of their own positive experiences in analysis. By the late 1990s, most people in the profession were aware of the crimes committed against gays and lesbians in the name of psychoanalysis. Many accounts have been published or shared anecdotally. In the 1970s though, a new generation of analyst was emerging. Informed by the politics of liberation, they were baby boomers, the generation who questioned all authority and valued pluralism as its standard. Starting from the assumption of a lesbian affirmative psychology, they rejected the equation of lesbianism with pathology and believed in their patients' right to be healthy and happy and still be gay.

Not many psychoanalytic institutes accepted lesbians as candidates. "Being a homosexual analyst is like being a blind pilot" was one attitude expressed then. Some institutes accepted lesbians on a "don't ask, don't tell" basis (Drescher, 1995), a difficult position to maintain in a setting where one was expected to be fully open and self-examining. There were, however, a few institutes where lesbians were accepted for training and could be open about their sexual identities. Of course, this did not mean that antihomosexual bias was not in evidence in these programs and in the literature used for training. In classes and at lectures some students spoke up when they found course material questionable, while others kept their objections to themselves and focused on acquiring the knowledge and skill to equip them to challenge the theory. Many sensed that they were in a unique position in their clinical work. They could observe and analyze their lesbian patients from a new perspective and thereby add a unique understanding of lesbians and of all human sexuality and relatedness from this vantage point. For example, when one examines the dynamics of a lesbian relationship without imposing heterosexual assumptions of role-playing, one can observe how differences and similarities can be deceptive. All couples invariably resort to complimentarity of roles—not of gender roles necessarily but of character styles and degrees of intimacy. Also, studying the dynamics of same-sex couples can teach a lot about the differences between men and women in general. For lesbians who chose to train in psychoanalysis the hope was that in time they would be in a position to influence this bastion of antihomosexual theory. They would be the teachers, the supervisors, the analysts, and the writers. As I will discuss later, by the 1990s that hope was realized.

Identity, specifically Coming Out, was a primary issue in the 1970s (Vida, 1978). Many women who had been denying their sexuality or had never allowed themselves to even consider it as an option, were now feeling the courage and receiving the support to take the risk and explore their lesbianism. This was partly the result of the increased visibility of lesbians who did not fit traditional stereotypes, and the general atmosphere of sexual experimentation and freedom of the 1970s. Some of these women were young and had wrestled with their attraction to other women, but had been afraid to act on those feelings until now. Others, generally older, had married and even borne children in an effort to be "normal" and suppress their homosexuality. And still others, although in relationships with women, were unable to admit to themselves that they were lesbians. The idea called up disturbing images and threatened their sense of self.

Despite the supportive atmosphere of the 1970s, coming out, both to oneself or to others, could often be a confusing and overwhelming process. At gay and lesbian centers, drop-in groups were started to deal specifically with coming out. On the one hand, it was both relieving and exciting for many of these women to finally experience a level of passion and intimacy that was deeply satisfying after years of feeling unfulfilled and defective. Many said that they had always wondered what all the fuss was about. Heterosexual romance and sex had been flat and disappointing if not downright repugnant. Now they could understand. On the other hand, many still grappled with guilt, shame, and feelings of identity disorientation.

For lesbians who were in the closet and struggling with self-hate the possibility that they could feel good about themselves was also exhilarating. However, it was not an overnight process. Undoing internalized hatred and negative identifications brought many people to treatment as well. Then, too, were questions of whom to tell, how to tell, or even whether to tell, and subsequently dealing with the repercussions. For some people, this meant risking the loss of friendships and families.

Many lesbians during the seventies were experimenting with new models of relationships. The freedom of sexual liberation spawned diverse forms of sexual expression. All varieties of sexuality were being explored in both the gay and straight world—and sometimes combined.

S&M, fetishism, and group sex were all fair game, albeit not for everyone (*Heresies*, 1981). Establishing a long-term relationship was more of a challenge. Commitment in the face of all this opportunity could be difficult, as expectations were high and disappointment came easily. After the first blush of new love fades all relationships face conflict and require effort. For some, this was unexpected. Being lesbian was idealized. If the relationship did not fulfill every need, or the new partner was not everything one wanted in a mate, then something was terribly wrong. Whereas in the past, the lack of acceptance of homosexuality undermined the stability of many relationships, now the limitless possibilities created additional hurdles. As they experimented with varied forms of partnering, many couples rejected monogamy and explored open relationships. Threesomes and even foursomes became common, at times evolving into a kind of extended family. Sometimes the original dyad survived, but often threesomes reverted to twosomes with the original couple breaking up and one partner joining with the third member to start a new couple.

As part of the evolving exploration of relationships, butch and femme role-playing was largely rejected as a result of the influence of feminism. The intention was to move away from heterosexual paradigms and to create new ones. Equality in relationships was emphasized. At its extreme, the emphasis on equality took the form of sameness and blurring of genuine difference which could foster a tendency to merge with or idealize one's partner. The traditional psychoanalytic view of this was that it showed the essential preoedipal nature of female homosexuality. Lesbians were either fixated at the oral phase and seeking symbiosis with the early mother, or were narcissistic and only able to relate to an object who was perceived to be a reflection of the self. In retrospect, however, we can begin to appreciate the impact on psychic development of the tremendous isolation that lesbians experienced. This was the result of several factors: To begin with, their invisibility in society resulted in a lack of role-models and images necessary for adequate developmental mirroring (Buloff and Osterman, 1995). This was then intensified by the self-imposed invisibility necessary to maintain secrecy. As lesbians began to come out to their families and friends this isolation was further compounded by the resulting losses that they faced. There was great pressure to pull together against a hostile world. The lack of confirmation from parents and of recognition of their sexual desires led them to place excessive needs on their partners to be both lover *and* parent/sibling. In addition, we have come to understand through the work of feminist researchers such as Carol Gilligan (1982) that women have a naturally strong drive toward attachment. Whereas in heterosexual relationships this puts them in conflict with men who are more oriented toward autonomy, in lesbian relationships this drive puts them at risk for too much closeness and difficulty maintaining optimum distance (Boston Lesbian Psychologies Collective, 1987; Burch, 1987; Vargo, 1987).

Another consequence of the lack of parental and societal validation was the idealization of the lesbian community itself as the Good Mother. The need to be part of a community and the intense political mood of the seventies combined to create a somewhat authoritarian and rigid atmosphere. The new sense of freedom and experimentation had brought with it a great deal of anxiety, much as in adolescence, which caused many to create their own strict rules of rebellion.

Monogamy was becoming a dirty word, while jealousy, insecurity, self-recrimination, and a lot of broken relationships led more lesbians to question whether relationships could last. Self-doubt and anxiety increased when their feelings did not live up to the group's ideals. Of course, the heterosexual divorce rate was also skyrocketing. But the work for many lesbian patients was to develop a strong enough separate sense of self to respect what their emotions were telling them. This, then, would allow them to maintain psychic equilibrium when they had wants and needs that differed from the party line or the dictates of their partner.

I said earlier that the biggest issue of the seventies was coming out. As more people became visible and demanded their rights, one interesting effect of this was felt in the field of psychoanalysis itself. More lesbians were demanding to be treated by lesbian therapists. This was first seen in the private practice sector, and gay counseling centers had already been started for that express purpose. But by the end of the decade, lesbians had begun seeking psychoanalysis at centers associated with training institutes and were specifically requesting lesbian analysts. Many institutes still refused to train lesbians and those that did resisted the notion that a lesbian patient could request a lesbian analyst, arguing that the analyst's sexual orientation should be irrelevant. The patient's request was treated as a neurotic defense. Over time, however, the pressures of the clients' demands won out and these institutes began to seek out the lesbian analysts in their midst. As a result, it became easier for candidates to be ''out'' at these centers—they had become a valuable commodity.

Once these institutes accepted the possibility of a lesbian analyst treating a lesbian patient they began to observe that rather than *create* transference–countertransference resistance, these dyads often facilitated deeper explorations of the patient's emotional and sexual life. This was due to several factors. First, there could be a greater sense of trust that enabled the lesbian patient to examine her own conflictual or ambivalent feelings without fear, justified or projected, of manipulation and coercion by the analyst. Second, the analyst's greater personal familiarity with a lesbian lifestyle allowed the patient to feel that she did not have to instruct the analyst in order for the analyst to understand what she was describing, thus eliminating another potential source of resistance. Third, the lesbian analyst functioned as a positive role-model for the patient. The patient had the opportunity to internalize a parental introject that regarded her sexuality as valid and worthwhile and through identification could counteract the negative stereotype of the lesbian as sick and inadequate. The concern that lesbian analysts would be blind to their patients' pathology or that the patients would use the analyst defensively proved to be no more of an issue than any other resistance that might occur in any treatment; that is, it could be identified and analyzed.

The Eighties

In 1980 Ronald Reagan was elected President of the United States and the country entered its most conservative period since the 1950s. *Liberal* became the dirty word of the day and religious and social conservatives tried to roll back all political and social gains made by racial minorities, women, and gays. The outbreak of AIDS added to the already growing antigay backlash directed at lesbians and gay men. The optimism and hope that many lesbians felt in the seventies became eroded by fear, and the sense of unity and empowerment was gradually replaced by introspection and self-examination as more lesbians found themselves confronting depression, substance abuse, and other problems that political liberation had not resolved.

There were several clinical issues that emerged during the eighties. One of them was substance abuse. Many lesbians had used chemicals to suppress their self-hate about being gay or to help them cope in the straight world where they felt so terribly alienated. Bars had always been the social centers of lesbian life both before and after gay liberation, and by the eighties the dance club scene was in its heyday and with it came cocaine and other drugs. Although not exclusive to lesbians and hardly a new problem, by the eighties more patients recognized, in themselves and in their families, that alcohol and drugs had a crippling effect on their lives. For analysts working in the lesbian community, those not already acquainted with chemical dependency treatment were challenged to train and broaden their perspectives. Psychoanalytic training had been sorely neglectful of any serious recognition of substance issues as other than a symptom. Meanwhile, women who were in recovery through twelve-step programs, which emphasize a commitment to helping others, became interested in being therapists themselves and sought training in a variety of approaches, including psychoanalysis. More lesbians began entering the profession and thus having even more impact on training institutions.

Some lesbians, on becoming sober, discovered that they were using compulsive behavior to cope with histories of child abuse. In 1978, I saw my first patient who reported a history of incest. I can remember discussing her in my training and being met with disbelief at her description of the sexual abuse in her childhood. Today her story would not be considered unusual at all. Again, incest and child abuse were not unique to the lives of lesbians. The whole country was increasingly coming to grips with its reality in the lives of children. However, it has been proposed (Maltz and Holman, 1987) that incest may influence some women's sexual orientation resulting in a higher incidence of sexual abuse histories among lesbians. As a result, analysts working in the lesbian community were again challenged to learn and understand this new information and to expand their work and knowledge base.

Another picture comes to mind as well when reflecting on the 1980s. Increasing numbers of younger women were going into conservative, formerly male professions like law and business. The women's movement of the seventies had created these opportunities along with a new set of expectations. A distinctly novel breed with their progressive politics, openly gay lifestyles, and three-piece suits, some were lawyers working for legal aid or labor organizations. Others worked for large private law firms, while the bankers and corporate women were staking their claim on the "American Dream" previously denied them. In many ways, they were beneficiaries of the politics of the seventies. One young banker reported that for her best friend's birthday she was giving her a set of sterling silver shrimp forks. She explained that since lesbians couldn't get married they are unable to receive the kinds of gifts that heterosexuals do at their weddings. She felt it was important to provide these things for each other when the opportunity arose.

One of the most dramatic changes of the eighties was the emergence of the new lesbian family. There had always been lesbian mothers, women who had been married and had children from these heterosexual unions. Even so, the notion of a lesbian parent was an oxymoron. Everyone assumed that being a lesbian meant forgoing ever having children. So these parents were a challenge to everyone's assumptions and expectations. But in the eighties a new phenomenon began to take root. Lesbians began inseminating themselves with the sperm of gay male friends, relatives of their partners, or anonymous sperm donors. Lesbians were also quietly entering the adoption system as single mothers and having children placed with them. As the word spread and the idea caught fire, insemination and adoption became increasingly easier to come by. Adoption agencies began opening their doors to lesbians, and by the nineties we were in the midst of the gayby boom.

The 1990s

The 1990s were a decade in which the political climate of the country began to return to a more moderate one than that characterized by the 1980s. Despite attempts by social conservatives and the Christian right wing to make homosexuality a political scapegoat, the continued activism of gay political organizations, along with the increasing economic prosperity of the decade (and a general feeling that the far right had gone too far) led to advances for lesbians on several fronts. For one thing, there was a marked increase in visible images and public awareness of lesbians. In the media, increasing numbers of lesbian pop stars and television personalities began publicly announcing their sexuality. Articles began appearing in popular magazines concerning lesbians and their lifestyle. Gay issues appeared in everything from presidential campaigns to television sitcoms, not to mention sleazy talk shows. Even when the positions taken were antigay it seemed only to further the increased visibility and awareness that lesbians existed and were part of everyone's family and social network in one way or another.

Another interesting change that occurred in the 1990s was the dramatic rise in gay marriage and commitment ceremonies. While for some time there had been couples who had small commitment parties or exchanged rings and vows with close friends in attendance, by the nineties this phenomenon also became more of a norm than an exception. Mainstream churches and synagogues began discussing whether or not their denominations should sanction these unions, as more and more clergy were officiating at such ceremonies and defending the importance of them. First Hawaii, and then Vermont, debated in their state legislatures, bills that would grant some form of legal status to gay couples equivalent to that of straight marriage (as of this writing, the state of Vermont has passed such a bill). Even the United States Congress felt it necessary to pass a bill rejecting gay marriage, a sure sign that it was a phenomenon on the rise. In addition, large numbers of major corporations granted parity to domestic partners in health and other benefits in addition to including sexual orientation in their nondiscriminatory hiring policies.

And while all of this forward political movement provoked a wide range of reactions, positive as well as negative, such visibility became empowering for lesbians on a personal level. Young people coming of age, and parents as well, began having much greater awareness and understanding of gay issues which certainly enhanced the experience of many of those who were growing up gay and, as a result, a degree of psychological damage could be avoided. Younger lesbians were able to have a better sense of themselves and many more could be comfortably "out" to their families and their communities thus resulting in less self-hatred, shame, and conflict. At the very least, they could know that they were not alone and could seek out the support and the role models they needed to grow up with a healthy self-image. In addition, because lesbians no longer depended on a narrow community to provide sanction and support, it became easier for younger women to define themselves with great individuality, resulting in greater flexibility and confidence.

As previously mentioned, the nineties also found us in the midst of what has come to be known as the gayby boom. This change had a major impact on the lives of lesbians in a number of ways. One effect was that parenthood thrust many lesbians into greater visibility. Children put their lesbian parents in contact with the straight world to a much greater extent than they might ever have been without children. During pregnancy, one's personal life is suddenly open to the inquiries of strangers, and in adoption, one has to deal with the legal system, agencies, and birth parents. As their children began having play dates and attending school,

lesbian parents came in greater contact with heterosexual parents, teachers, and school administrators. For lesbians who were not used to being
open this required much adjustment. Even for those who were fully ''out''
in their lives, the experience of having to answer questions, discuss their
family structure, and negotiate people's reactions required a new set of
skills. In addition to dealing with outsiders, lesbian parents needed to be
fully prepared to be clear and deliberate in addressing their children's
inevitable questions and concerns about being part of an alternative family. By forcing greater confrontation and resolution of internalized homophobia in the lesbian parent, this process has resulted in a stronger sense
of identity and self-esteem. Many lesbians also found that having children
brought them closer to their families of origin: often the desire for grand-
children superseded any misgivings that straight parents may have had
about their gay daughters' lifestyle. This too could be very reparative.

On an intrapsychic level, the opportunity to become a mother enabled
some lesbians to have a stronger sense of their female identities, which
for some was less available either because of their homosexuality or other
factors that prevented them from identifying with their mothers' sexuality.
Raising a child can provide numerous opportunities to rework many
earlier issues within one's self and with one's parents (Benedek, 1959).
The opportunity to have children, whether or not that option is exercised,
has been a fortifying experience for individuals and for relationships.
Simply knowing that the option is available has served as an antidote to
some forms of internalized homophobia. For lesbians who chose not to
have children, the fact of having the possibility to make the choice, rather
than have it be beyond their control, has also been a meaningful emotional
opportunity (Glazer, chapter 15). The negative impact for these women
then was the pressure that was brought to bear by the reidealization of
motherhood in the culture both straight and gay (Lesser, 1991).

By the turn of the twenty-first century, much has changed in the lives
of lesbians and in the issues they bring to therapy. The gayby boom, for
example, brought a number of new issues to clinical practice. More lesbians have begun to seek treatment for the express purpose of examining
their feelings about having or not having children and to consider in what
form they wish to do so. Some couples have felt the need to examine
the differing roles they would have in relation to the child and to prepare
themselves, if this is ever entirely possible, for the dramatic changes that
their lives will undergo. Lesbian couples are in the unique situation of
having a choice about which partner will bear a child. This is sometimes

a mixed blessing as it can raise unexpected conflicts as well. As with heterosexuals, some lesbians have had to deal with the conflict of one partner wanting and the other not wanting to have children. The ongoing experience of raising a child and negotiating family relationships has also brought many new emotional issues to therapy with lesbians, as it does for any new parents.

Another change I have noted in many of the women that I see in my practice is that issues of merger and boundary confusion seem to arise less frequently than in the past. Couples seem better able to negotiate variations in the need for space and contact, for example, and are more able to value differences in each other rather than to be threatened by them. Even "butch and femme" role-playing has become an option again albeit with postfeminist modifications. This greater degree of independence in couples can be understood in several ways. First, the increased openness and mobility that lesbians now experience greatly decrease the sense of isolation that led to couples pulling tightly together against a hostile world. Second, an increase in self-esteem because of greater familial, societal, and self-acceptance has improved the quality of object relatedness and the capacity for autonomy that lesbians can experience. Third, because of increased visibility, a wide network of political, social, and professional groups, and a growing literature concerning lesbian issues, there is a more sophisticated awareness of some common pitfalls that lesbian couples have encountered, and a resulting desire to create stronger, more differentiated units. One thing I hear a lot less often is the belief that lesbian relationships don't last.

The 1990s brought many changes to the lesbian psychoanalytic community as well. Many more lesbians entered analytic training and began writing and publishing. In the same psychoanalytic institutes that once banned lesbians from training, candidates, faculty members, and supervisors can now be found who are openly gay, and courses in sexuality and gay issues are being offered from a gay affirmative position.

Throughout the 1990s the larger psychoanalytic community, too, began to take up the challenge as institutions and individuals entered the dialogue with greater openness to learning from their lesbian colleagues. In 1993, for example, the New York University postdoctoral program in psychoanalysis sponsored an all-day conference on Psychoanalysis and Homosexuality that included a panel of gay and lesbian analysts as well as leading analysts from each of its academic tracks. The first conference

of its kind for a mainstream psychoanalytic institute, it had been organized by the Gay and Lesbian Candidates Association in response to
complaints about antihomosexual bias in courses.

As psychoanalysis itself has evolved over these past twenty-five years,
by the 1990s there was a broader range of theory available for study.
Incorporating self psychology and the British school of object relations,
there was a greater emphasis on intersubjectivity and relational theories
that place their developmental emphasis on issues beyond the heterosexual resolution of the Oedipus complex and as a result have appealed to
many lesbian analysts. In addition, the increased interest in postmodern
thought opened the way for theorists to challenge even the basic constructions of sexuality and gender at all levels, creating opportunities to offer
innovative models of understanding sexual dynamics and preferences
(Butler, 1990).

Also, since the 1990s, there has been a proliferation of scholarly
books and papers written by lesbians on a variety of issues related to
psychoanalysis. Among these publications are: Noreen O'Connor and
Joanna Ryan (1993), *Wild Desires and Mistaken Identities;* Beverly
Burch (1993), *On Intimate Terms: The Psychology of Difference in Lesbian Relationships;* Ronnie Lesser (1995), *Disorienting Sexuality;* Judith
Glassgold and Suzanne Iasenza (1995), *Lesbians and Psychoanalysis;*
Schwartz, A. (1998), *Sexual Subjects: Lesbians, Gender, and Psychoanalysis,* to name a few. The Internet, too, has provided opportunities for
analysts from around the world to discuss and debate views on homosexuality along with other issues, through various on-line networks and fo-
rums. As it was anticipated in the 1970s, lesbian psychoanalysts *are* in
a unique position to hear and understand lesbian patients, not only to
serve them but to bring their truth to light to influence theory and practice
across the board.

I will close with an anecdote from my clinical practice. A few years
ago I began treating a young woman who was 25 years old and had been
raised in the South in a family of fundamentalist Christians: her mother
teaches Bible classes. That fall my patient informed me that she was
going home for a visit and planned to tell her parents that she was gay.
As I prepared to discuss this with her, I must admit I thought she would
be anticipating the worst: an ugly scene, denial, even outright rejection.
Surprisingly, she told me that she did not expect her parents to reject her
or to be unpleasant about it at all. Her concern was that they wouldn't
really talk openly about their feelings but would merely be "nice." I

confess that I was amazed. From the South? Bible toting Christians? And what about her? How could she be so sanguine about telling them? It seemed to me that though not entirely typical this young woman did in some ways represent a new generation, one that has truly benefited from the struggles of the past decades, is far more secure, and has a greater sense of entitlement regarding acceptance and rights. And, with the frequency of commitment ceremonies and the political fight for the right to marry well under way, the patient who in the 1980s had felt the need to buy her friend those silver shrimp forks will now have the opportunity to do so in the traditional way, perhaps even at a bridal shower.

References

Benedek, T. (1959), Parenthood as a developmental phase: A contribution to libido theory. *J. Amer. Psychoanal. Assn.*, 7:389–417.

Boston Lesbian Psychologies Collective, Eds. (1987), *Lesbian Psychologies: Explorations and Challenges.* Urbana: University of Illinois Press.

Buloff, B., & Osterman, M. (1996), Queer reflections: Mirroring and the lesbian experience of self. In: *Lesbians and Psychoanalysis: Revolutions in Theory and Practice,* ed. J. Glassgold & S. Iasenza. New York: Free Press.

Burch, B. (1987), Barriers to intimacy: Conflicts over power, dependency, and nurturing in lesbian relationships. In: *Lesbian Psychologies: Explorations and Challenges,* ed. Boston Lesbian Psychologies Collective. Urbana: University of Illinois Press, pp. 126–141.

———— (1993), *On Intimate Terms: The Psychology of Difference in Lesbian Relationships.* Urbana: University of Illinois Press.

Butler, J. (1990), Gender trouble, feminist theory, and psychoanalytic discourse. In: *Feminism/Postmodernism,* ed. L. J. Nicholson. New York: Routledge, pp. 324–340.

Drescher, J. (1995), Anti-homosexual bias in training. In: *Disorienting Sexuality,* ed. T. Domenici & R. Lesser. New York: Routledge, pp. 227–241.

Gilligan, C. (1982), *In a Different Voice.* Cambridge, MA: Harvard University Press.

Glassgold, J. M., & Iasenza, S., Eds. (1995), *Lesbians and Psychoanalysis: Revolutions in Theory and Practice.* New York: Free Press.

Heresies (1981), Sex Issue 3(12). New York: Heresies Collective.

Lesser, R. (1991), Deciding not to become a mother. In: *Lesbians at Midlife: The Creative Transition,* ed. B. Sang, J. Warshow, & A. J. Smith. San Francisco: Spinsters Book Co., pp. 84–90.

—————— Domenici, T. (1995), *Disorienting Sexuality: Psychoanalytic Reappraisals of Sexual Identities.* New York: Routledge.

Maltz, W., & Holman, B. (1987), *Incest and Sexuality: A Guide to Understanding and Healing.* Lexington, MA: Lexington Books.

McDougall, J. (1970), The homosexual dilemma: A study of female homosexuality. In: *Plea for a Measure of Abnormality.* New York: International Universities Press, 1980, pp. 87–149.

—————— (1995), *The Many Faces of Eros: A Psychoanalytic Exploration of Human Sexuality.* London: Free Association Books.

O'Connor, N., & Ryan, J. (1993), *Wild Desires and Mistaken Identities: Lesbianism and Psychoanalysis.* New York: Columbia University Press.

Schoenberg, E. (1995), Psychoanalytic theories of lesbian desire: A social constructionist critique. In: *Disorienting Sexuality: Psychoanalytic Reappraisals of Sexual Identities,* ed. T. Domenici & R. Lesser. New York: Routledge, pp. 203–223.

Schwartz, A. (1998), *Sexual Subjects: Lesbians, Gender, and Psychoanalysis.* New York: Routledge.

Vargo, S. (1987), The effects of women's socialization on lesbian couples. In: *Lesbian Psychologies: Explorations and Challenges,* ed. Boston Lesbian Psychologies Collective. Urbana: University of Illinois Press, pp. 161–173.

Vida, G. (1978), *Our Right to Love: A Lesbian Resource Book.* Englewood Cliffs, NJ: Prentice-Hall.

17

A Postmodern Comparative Study of Figure Drawings of Lesbian and Heterosexual Women: A Tribute to Ted Riess and Ralph Gundlach

Suzanne Iasenza and Sheldon Waxenberg

Introduction

In this paper we challenge from a research approach various categorizations of women with an avowed goal of clarifying certain conceptualizations of women, perceptions and formulations of them which in the past

Authors' Note: The authors wish to thank Heidi Gundlach-Smith for generously availing us of her father's archives; Dr. Patricia Sinatra for assistance with statistical methods, and Beverly Decker for her helpful reading of the manuscript.

have been confused, veiled, traditionalized, even demonizing. We do not, however, intend to strip away the substance or individuality of women. The census taker may ask, for example, "Is she married?"—so may the sociologist and the psychologist. Our focus is on psychoanalysts' labels of the past hundred years—a "failed" set of labels we think. Using postmodern and constructionist theorists' and therapists' insights about women, we shall emphasize some concepts useful for understanding women's multiple sexual and gender identities and will challenge traditional psychoanalytic theorists' tendency to conflate gender identity and sexual object choice.

Our exploratory mechanism is a projective technique of psychological science that was widely used in the 1950s and 1960s when the data of this research were collected. Specifically, our attention is directed to drawings depicting female and male human beings and animals, with whom individuals live and fantasize about throughout their lives. One motivation for our present endeavor is to apply ideas in a recently published book edited by Judith Glassgold and Suzanne Iasenza entitled *Lesbians and Psychoanalysis: Revolutions in Theory and Practice* (1995), which points in a distinctively new direction, eliminates many of the rigid sexist and devaluing modes of perceiving and classifying women by means of their sexual choices and their behaviors—as judged by male "experts" for the most part. The volume is representative of a movement within psychoanalysis to eliminate a view of homosexuality as pathological and to expand our concepts of sexuality and gender (O'Connor and Ryan, 1993; Domenici and Lesser, 1995; Magee and Miller, 1997; Kiersky, chapter 2).

Gundlach and Riess in 1968 published a groundbreaking paper on the sexual identity of women in which they highlighted the multivariate nature of female sexual identification. They pointed to the historical preponderance of research on men in studies of homosexuality. To even out that inbalance, they presented their data on the largest population of lesbian women studied anywhere in the world up to that time. Another motivation for our endeavor is to pay tribute to Riess and Gundlach's efforts by completing a segment of their work not completed at the time of their deaths in 1995 and 1979, respectively. We aim to complete their work in a way we believe they would approve, providing interpretations and understandings of human figure drawings that reflect the radical shifts in psychoanalytic thinking influenced by postmodern views of sexuality and gender, views that were anticipated with remarkable clarity by these two pioneers.

Background

Moving through the concepts current in the 1960s and 1970s leads to the realm of 1990s postmodern theory, but first it is appropriate to review Gundlach and Riess's findings and formulations of the preceding decades. Gundlach was a member of the team of researchers who worked with Bieber et al. (1962) on the study of gay men who were in psychoanalytic treatment. These data were originated by and filtered through the theoretical models of the analysts who treated these patients. None of the information was obtained directly from the subjects themselves. The direct approach was the preferred methodology of Gundlach and Riess, a further example of their advanced thinking when they fully entered this field.

Initially, Gundlach and Riess compared four major groups of subjects: gay and heterosexual adult males, utilizing data from the Bieber study (1962), and lesbian and heterosexual females. All of the men and some of the women were patients currently in therapy. Gundlach and Riess construed one's identity as a man or as a woman as part of a sexual–social role played and developed in a matrix of culturally determined values. They carefully traced out personality development as presented in the psychological literature of the 1950s and 1960s by Sears, Maccoby, and Lewin (1957), Lynn (1959), Spitz (1959), Maslow (1962), Loevinger (1964), Szasz (1961), Chess, Thomas, and Birch (1965), and others.

Gundlach and Riess deplored the earlier proclivities in sexual research to extrapolate from lower animals to mankind and to recklessly apply theories about men to women simply because there was an abysmal paucity of data on women. Alternatively, women were relegated to almost subhuman status, demeaning them as unimportant elements in the process of understanding human sexuality. Gundlach and Riess perceptively and presciently addressed another crucial issue: Does the choice of a sexual partner determine the kind of sexual–social role played by the person making the choice? Does a homosexual orientation imply that a gay man cannot be masculine or that a lesbian woman cannot feel and act socially in an expected feminine way? Lynn (1959) distinguished between sex-role identification, sex-role preference, and sex-role adoption. The first, identification, was defined as "the actual incorporation of the role of a given sex and the unconscious reactions characteristic of that role" (p. 127) and was deemed the most important feature as these concepts were delineated by others in the 1960s and quoted by Gundlach and Riess (1968).

Encouraged and assisted by some of the officers of the Daughters of Bilitis, a national organization for lesbian women, Gundlach in the early 1960s collected direct questionnaires and drawings from a sample of over two-hundred lesbian women. The organization members bonded together for social activities and for mutual protection as women who lived in lesbian relationships. In those days they were not "out" in public and were very protective of their partners and "sisters." They had felt themselves often misserved by the press and by social scientists, even seemingly friendly and empathic ones. They trusted Ralph Gundlach.

Gundlach and Riess were able, subsequently, with the cooperation of academic and therapist colleagues, to acquire life history questionnaires and drawings of a sample of heterosexual women matched for age, educational level, regional residence, and for whether or not the woman had been in psychotherapy. The questionnaire, containing four-hundred-fifty items, used the form and some of the questions from the Bieber study of gay men, but this material derived from the respondents themselves, not from therapists; and many of the respondents had never had psychotherapy of any sort. The self-administered personal developmental histories were appraised for comparison of the life experiences of the lesbian and heterosexual women.

Gundlach and Riess (1968, p. 208) studied "the multiplex factors involved in the choice of a love partner" and sought thereby to "illuminate some of the parameters of self-identification." They hypothesized that sexual identification is a response to tremendous and not-so-subtle environmental biases; that the choice of a love partner may therefore represent the result of many vectors playing on a woman rather than be a mirror image of the assumptions about male identity. Gundlach and Riess demonstrated (p. 215) that the daughter in a family does live in a differently perceived world from her brother, that the family and its interrelations are different for different family members. They felt that changes in the social system helped to confuse the mixture of new and old formulations regarding sex roles for both boys and girls. It seemed to them clear that the lesbian population had not had any universally strong prohibitions toward heterosexuality. Over three-quarters had inter-course with a male. Nearly 30 percent had been married, some for ten years or more; and one-fifth had children. These data need to be under-stood within the historical context of the 1950s and 1960s when there were fewer options for lesbian women to live without including men as partners. Sexual choices for women seemed to be unrelated to the establishment of feminine identity. More frequently, all women utilized sexuality to ward off loneliness or to supply a feeling of being wanted and needed, or of being "verified" (p. 228).

The lack of clear-cut patterns distinguishing the total lesbian and nonlesbian groups suggested that perhaps there are more pathways to homosexuality among women than among men. The unique crucial events in the history of each lesbian woman which led to homosexuality were far more scattered than in the lives of the men in the Bieber study. It also seemed that these events were not as strongly related to "sex role identity" in women as in men (p. 224). Among this wide sample of lesbian women few considered themselves masculine, a challenge to the traditional psychoanalytic theorist's tendency to correlate gender identity and sexual object choice. Gundlach and Riess state (p. 226) that "homo-sexuality among women in our society seems unrelated to the establish-ment of feminine identity." They quote from Simone de Beauvoir's *The Second Sex* (1957) to buttress this view (Gundlach and Riess, 1968, p. 226), parts of which we share here.

> One can say that all women are naturally homosexual . . . the female body is for her, as for the male, an object of desires. . . . with her sisters or her mother she has often known an intimacy in which affection was subtly imbued with sensual feelings. . . . " Between women love is contemplative; caresses are intended less to gain pos-session of the other than gradually to recreate the self through her; separateness is abolished; there is no struggle, no victory, no defeat; in reciprocity each is at once subject and object, sovereign and slave, duality becomes mutuality.

How remarkable that two male researchers at that time in history, when the feminist movement was just beginning, relied on a major femi-nist work to support their findings, a work that raised complex questions about sex roles, sexuality, and gender. Some of the parts of de Beauvoir's work that they selected foretold future feminist postmodern themes, such as the woman as both subject and object of sexual desire, themes that were beginning to emerge in their work.

Sources of the Research Data
Presented Here

The first set of data in the present study was collected from about a hundred women who identified themselves as involved in sexual relationships with women and who filled out a voluminous personal questionnaire and rendered three drawings: a drawing "of a person" and then a drawing of "a person of the other sex," and then a drawing of "an animal." Sixty-two usable sets of figure drawings resulted. Subsequently, when Gundlach and Riess were working together in New York City, at the Postgraduate Center for Mental Health, they jointly collected more than one hundred protocols from women in heterosexual relationships to be used as a matched comparison group, ninety-one of which included scorable drawings. These data provided the research base for an exploration of women's sexual identity and their sexual object choices as illuminated by their developmental histories and projective drawings. The personal developmental histories provided a valuable fund of information on these two groups of women and resulted in various publications (Gundlach and Riess, 1968, 1973; Riess, Safer, and Yotive, 1974; Riess, 1980).

Gundlach and Riess planned also to compare the drawings in accordance with projective technique methodologies of their era. They recruited as an assistant to their research group at the Postgraduate Center for Mental Health, Sheldon Waxenberg, who had completed a doctoral dissertation at Columbia University that depended on sophisticated use of projective data (Waxenberg, 1955) and who was completing certification programs in psychoanalysis and in group psychoanalysis. The protocol for quantitative and qualitative scoring of these sets of drawings was finalized between Gundlach and Waxenberg in 1977 in London, where Gundlach then lived and where he died in 1979. Two graduate students in psychology, Gregory Cole and Deborah Waxenberg, each scored the same subset of 57 drawings from the total pool of 153 in order to establish the reliability of the scoring. The reliability coefficient between them was 0.78, which was deemed satisfactory as a measure of standardized scoring. One of them then proceeded to score all of the drawings. Figures

17.1 and 17.2 are presented here as an example of one lesbian woman's human figure drawings. Data from the animal drawings are omitted; they do not seem cogent to the main point of this paper.

Riess, in Connecticut, and Waxenberg, in Manhattan, made efforts to complete the study, but Riess died at age 87 in 1995. Suzanne Iasenza of John Jay College of Criminal Justice agreed to join the effort to complete the task of bringing Gundlach and Riess's unique research data to publication.

The Draw-A-Person Test (DAP) in Historical Perspective

Figure drawings have been used to help assess psychopathology since Buck (1948) developed the clinical protocol for Florence Goodenough's DAP in 1948. As diagnostic sophistication developed, more and more signs of psychological distress were defined. The signs for homosexuality emerged in the 1950s, and one of the seemingly universal signs for both male and female homosexuals was the drawing of the opposite-sex person first, which was believed to indicate some confusion about sexual identification (Machover, 1951).

Empirical work using the DAP to examine homosexuality has included more males than females. A review of DAP studies on females revealed two major underlying hypotheses about female homosexuals when compared to female heterosexuals. The opposite sex being drawn first and poor sexual differentiation between male and female figures were surmised to mean that lesbian women show more confusion and conflict about sexual role, rejecting feminine identification. Poor quality in the rendering of the female figure and sexualized presentation of the female body image were taken to mean that lesbian women show more limitations in personal and social adjustment than heterosexual women.

Unlike DAP studies on gay men, those on women did not show lesbian women drawing opposite-sex figures first (Ferracuti and Rizzo, 1959; Armon, 1960; Gundlach and Riess, 1968; Roback, Langevin, and Zajac, 1974; Hassell and Smith, 1975). Additionally, data were not found to indicate that lesbian women revealed difficulty differentiating the sex of male and female figures (Armon, 1960). Mixed results were found regarding incompleteness and/or sexualized presentation of female figures (Armon, 1960; Gundlach and Riess, 1968, 1973; Hassell and Smith,

Figure 17.1 On this page, please draw a person (a whole person, not just a head). Please do this even if you feel you cannot draw. Please do *not* draw ''stick'' figures (⚥).

Figure 17.2. If you have just drawn a man on the previous page, please draw a woman here. If you have just drawn a woman on the previous page, please draw a man here.

1975; Janzen and Coe, 1976). Just as Evelyn Hooker's (1958) landmark Rorschach studies on gay and heterosexual men were not able to distinguish between them, these later DAP studies could not differentiate between lesbian and heterosexual women. In general, the results of DAP studies comparing lesbian and heterosexual women over the years have left us with three conclusions: (1) Female homosexuality is not a clinical entity; that is, no definitive pathology or etiology is found. (2) There are few personality features that distinguish lesbian women from heterosexual women. (3) There are differences in personality factors that distinguish lesbian women from gay men; indeed, personality differences seem to be more identifiable by biological sex than by sexual orientation.

Riess et al. (1974) stated that one of the underlying problems in understanding the projective literature on lesbian women is the inconsistency of methodology—different concepts, measurements, and samples—which make generalizations difficult. However, in a later paper, Riess (1980) asserted the accuracy of projective tests and further contended that the inability of projective tests to distinguish between people with same-sex orientations and those with opposite-sex orientations is consistent with results of larger survey studies.

Our interest here is not only to retest the original hypotheses of so many past researchers but to present alternative interpretations and clinical applications of DAP findings stemming from Gundlach, Riess, and Waxenberg's data which are informed by changes that have taken place in psychoanalytic theories of sexuality and gender over the past decade. We especially seek to understand differences and similarities in figure drawings while acknowledging separate continua for gender identity and sexual object choice.

Research Procedures

All subjects were divided into two groups, lesbian or heterosexual, on the basis of their self-declared object choice; that is, the choice of sexual partner—female or male—prevailing at the time of making the drawings. From a life-span perspective, some may be classifiable as bisexual, having had sexual relations with partners of both sexes; for example, a woman who had borne children within a conventional marriage, divorced in midlife, and then moved on to a committed partnership with another woman for the later years of her life. The stance of the researchers is that any "projections" in the drawings are relevant to the life of the drawer at the specific time the drawings are made.

Each of the two independent groups were compared with the other in terms of a large number of features of the drawings among which were: sex of figure drawn first; figures drawn full-face or left or right profile; figures vaguely or clearly delineated; drawings were "clean" or had line-overs, shadings, or erasures; figures integrated or fragmented; figures static or in motion, and the kind of motion.

We go back to our initial hypothesis, namely, that "projections" of sexual object choices in the drawings will not be expected to differentiate between women self-identified as lesbian and those self-identified as heterosexual. In other words, there will not be statistically significant differences in the performances, the productions, and the projections of the two groups.

Research Findings

Of initial interest was whether, as a possible reflection of her identification or interest or affiliation, a woman drew a female human figure or a male human figure first in sequence. Of all the women, 88 of 153 (58%) drew a female figure first. Fifty-nine of the ninety-one heterosexual women (65%) drew a female figure first, while twenty-nine of sixty-two lesbian women (47%) drew a female figure first. Chi Square as a statistical measure of the significance of the difference was 4.92, with one degree of freedom, rendering a probability of only 0.03 of such a finding being random.

A parallel finding concerned the degree of clarity of sexual differentiation of the female figure. Contradictory or ambiguous features of physical sexuality were more often found in the female figures drawn by lesbian women (6 out of 62; 10%) than those drawn by heterosexual women (0 out of 91; 0%). This finding was significant at the 0.01 level (Chi Square = 9.17, 2df).

One additional significant finding (Chi Square = 4.40, p = 0.04, 1df) related to the female drawings was in the continuity-discontinuity of body parts. Twelve out of ninety-one heterosexual women (13%) and two out of sixty-two lesbian women (3%) drew disconnected body parts in the female figure.

Most particular features or qualities of the female drawings did not differentiate significantly between lesbian and heterosexual women, among others: (1) the overall quality of the female drawing; (2) erasures in the female drawing; (3) shading; (4) activity indicated in the female figure; (5) head perspective in the female figure; (6) presence of protuberant breasts; (7) other female organs revealed; (8) female figure partial nudity; (9) female figure total nudity.

The drawings of male figures, as was the case with the female figures, reveal few particular features or qualities which significantly differentiate the lesbian and heterosexual drawers. The only exception is the number of erasures on the male figures. Thirteen out of ninety-one heterosexual women (14%) and three out of sixty-two lesbian women (5%) had many erasures. Seventy-eight out of ninety-one heterosexual women (86%) and fifty-nine out of sixty-two lesbian women (95%) had few or no erasures. The differences were significant at the 0.06 level (Chi Square = 5.55, $2df$).

Postmodern Interpretations of the Findings

Our hypothesis that projections of object choice would not differentiate between lesbian and heterosexual women was largely supported. The few differentiating results that were significant in this study were consistent with past findings, but instead of offering interpretations of pathology or providing evidence of one's fixed membership in some essential sexual category, we offer here feminist postmodern interpretations which give greatest importance to the role of social context and the intertwining of sexual and gender identities.

In this volume, D'Ercole (chapter 11) provocatively inquires: Is a lesbian a woman, or is she but a man in drag; not a real woman and only a copy of a man? Through D'Ercole's new postmodern lens, "the fluid constructs of gender and sexuality are expanded into a variable wardrobe of postures and poses worn and discarded as the fashion and context change." For D'Ercole, "Thinking of gender and sexuality as aspects of social relationships, rather than as traits derived from fixed developmental stages, moves them into the interpersonal interactive arena where relational acts are performed in contexts, and connected to subjective experience more than objective reality" (p. 181).

Our use of D'Ercole's novel imagery brings the act of drawing the figure of a person into the postmodern constructivist universe—available for interpretation in this realm of discourse—when she relates the idea of identities to "*performance*, the act of doing, of putting these identities into play" (p. 186), as when a woman takes pencil to paper. She urges that we do better to understand "both sexuality and gender as performative acts rather than as fixed, stable categories resulting from some normative developmental sequence" (p. 192).

The more frequent drawing of the male figure first in order by lesbian women may be interpreted as evidence of rejection of feminine identification in accordance with orthodox psychoanalytic theory. In our present context, another interpretation may be that lesbian women exercise more flexibility and diversity in the experiencing and expression of their sexual and gender identities and roles. In the same vein, the contradictory and ambiguous features of physical sexuality found in the female figures drawn by lesbian women may be interpreted as evidence of interest shown in recent generations in androgyny rather than traditional psychoanalysts' assertions of confusion and conflict about feminine sexual role. There is greater freedom today and many lesbian women accord themselves choices within a broad area of style of dress, gender roles, sexual roles, and behavior (Iasenza, 1995).

The finding that more heterosexual women drew disconnected body parts in the female figure might be interpreted by orthodox psychoanalysts as evidence of disturbed ego development in the heterosexual women. An alternative interpretation is that all women, heterosexual, bisexual, or lesbian, may understandably experience discontinuities in body image due to oppressive cultural pressures about women's weight, body shape, and stylishness. Perhaps lesbian women escape some of this stress or heal more rapidly from its damaging effects through the intimacy and contact with other women's bodies.

Heterosexual women produced more erasures on the male drawings than did lesbian women. Orthodox psychoanalysts would interpret this as evidence of heterosexual women's disturbed anxiety in relation to men. Our interpretation is that heterosexual women are taught throughout their lives to submit to men's control whereas lesbian women by making a departure from compulsory heterosexuality may experience a greater degree of social plasticity in relation to men. Since heterosexual women are doubly subjected to gender inequality, on the career as well as home fronts, more conflict and anxiety in relation to men may exist.

Object choices as made in the drawings do not define a "sexual identity" or a "gender identity" differentiation in these women, who actually are making choices every moment of their lives. Some of the decisions along the way are important, better regarded as momentous, such as a choice of a sexual partner for years or even decades of a lifetime. However, these choices do not differ because lesbian and heterosexual women are to be considered different "species" of human kind. These differentiations by means of choices are highly varied and are not categorical. The choice of a sexual partner, a same-sex choice or an opposite-sex choice, does not establish for an observer the nature of the choice maker, but only the nature of the choice itself. One such object choice does not render the chooser normal, nor the opposite object choice label her deviant. A person's sexual object choice may best be construed in the context of ordinary choice making of all sorts. The sexual object itself cannot be used to define totally the person herself, as has been done so often in discussions of human sexuality in the past.

Sexual self-identification, heterosexual or homosexual, here provides the research base for an exploration of women's biological, psychological, and sexual identities, and their object choices as illustrated by their projective drawings. What do these research results mean as we are now beginning to view female sexuality through postmodern and feminist lenses, views which put in doubt the connection between biological sex and gender, and gender and sexual identity, views which question that one particular sexual identity is more or less healthy than another? What this research explored is the assumed belief that sexual identity determines object choice. If this belief is valid, we should have more comprehensively been able to discern differences between heterosexual and lesbian women's object choices from their drawings. What was found is that sexual identity, although inclusive of sexual object choice (same sex or opposite sex), includes sex role (masculinity-femininity) and sexual self-image (how the person relates to her sexuality), a complexity that defies categorization.

By completing this research with these postmodern dynamic interpretations we honor the memories of Ted Riess and Ralph Gundlach who were moving toward such conceptualizations during the last half-century. We are grateful for their many contributions, radical for their time, namely, (1) insisting that statements about women be based on research with women rather than extrapolating on data from men; (2) being more interested in women's own subjective experiences rather than depending on "expert" (mostly male) opinions; (3) challenging orthodox psychoanalytic notions about the pathology of homosexuality; and (4) questioning the tendency to impose sexual categories on people. After all these years, Riess and Gundlach's work continues to inspire trends of thought that nourish us as we "perform" our professional lives.

References

Armon, V. (1960), Some personality variables in overt female homosexuality. *J. Projective Techniques,* 24:292–309.

Bieber, I., Dain, H., Dince, P., Drellich, M., Grand, H., Gundlach, R., Kramer, M., Rifkin, A., Wilbur, C., & Bieber, T. (1962), *Homosexuality: A Psychoanalytic Study.* New York: Basic Books.

de Beauvoir, S. (1957), *The Second Sex.* New York: Alfred A. Knopf.

Buck, J. N. (1948), *The H-T-P Technique: A Qualitative and Quantitative Scoring Manual.* Brandon, VT: Journal of Clinical Psychology Monograph.

Chess, S., Thomas, A., & Birch, H. (1965), *Your Child Is a Person: A Psychological Approach to Parenthood without Guilt.* New York: Viking Press.

Domenici, T., & Lesser, R., Eds. (1995), *Disorienting Sexuality: Psychoanalytic Reappraisals of Sexual Identities.* New York: Routledge.

Ferracuti, F., & Rizzo, G. (1959), Homosexual signs found through projective techniques in a female penal population. *Archivo di psicologia neurologia e psichiatria,* 20:193–203.

Glassgold, J. M., & Iasenza, S., Eds. (1995), *Lesbians and Psychoanalysis: Revolutions in Theory and Practice.* New York: Free Press.

Gundlach, R., & Riess, B. F. (1968), Self and sexual identity in women. In: *New Directions in Mental Health,* Vol. I., ed. B. F. Riess. New York: Grune & Stratton, pp. 205–231.

——— ——— (1973), The range of problems in the treatment of lesbians. In: *The Neurosis of Our Time: Acting Out,* ed. D. Milman & G. Goldman. Springfield, IL: Charles C Thomas, pp. 149–169.

Hassell, J., & Smith, E. W. L. (1975), Female homosexuals' concepts of self, men and women. *J. Personal. Assess.,* 39(2):154–159.

Hooker, E. (1958), Male homosexuality in the Rorschach. *J. Projective Techniques,* 22:33–54.

Iasenza, S. (1995), Platonic pleasures and dangerous desires: Psychoanalytic theory, sex research and lesbian sexuality. In: *Lesbians and Psychoanalysis: Revolutions in Theory and Practice,* ed. J. M. Glassgold & S. Iasenza. New York: Free Press, pp. 345–373.

Janzen, W. B., & Coe, W. C. (1976), Clinical and sign prediction: The Draw-A-Person and female homosexuality. *J. Clin. Psychology,* 31(4):757–776.

Loevinger, J. (1964), *The Meaning and Measurement of Ego Development.* St. Louis: Washington University Press.

Lynn, D. B. (1959), A note on sex differences in the development of masculine and feminine identification. *Psycholog. Rev.,* 66(2):126–135.

Machover, K. (1951), Drawings of the human figure. In: *Projective Techniques,* ed. H. H. Anderson & G. L. Anderson. Englewood Cliffs, NJ: Prentice-Hall, pp. 394–400.

Magee, M., & Miller, D. C. (1997), *Lesbian Lives: Psychoanalytic Narratives Old and New.* Mahwah, NJ: Analytic Press.

Maslow, A. H. (1962), *Toward a Psychology of Being.* Princeton, NJ: Van Nostrand.

O'Connor, N., & Ryan, J. (1993), *Wild Desires and Mistaken Identities: Lesbianism and Psychoanalysis.* New York: Columbia University Press.

Riess, B. F. (1980), Psychological tests in homosexuality. In: *Homosexual Behavior: A Modern Reappraisal,* ed. J. Marmor. New York: Basic Books, pp. 296–311.

———— Safer, J., & Yotive, W. (1974), Psychological test data on female homosexuality: A review of the literature. *J. Homosexuality,* 1 (1):71–85.

Roback, H. B., Langevin, R., & Zajac, Y. (1974), Sex of five choice figure drawings by homosexual and heterosexual subjects. *J. Personal. Assess.,* 38(2):154–155.

Sears, R., Maccoby, E., & Levin, H. (1957), *Patterns of Child Rearing.* New York: Row, Peterson.

Spitz, R. (1959), *A Genetic Field Theory of Ego Formation: Its Implications for Pathology.* New York: International Universities Press.

Szasz, T. S. (1961), *The Myth of Mental Illness.* New York: Hoeber-Harper.

Waxenberg, S. E. (1955), Psychosomatic patients and other physically ill persons: A comparative study. *J. Consult. Psychology,* 19:163–169.

Author Index

293

Subject Index

Abandonment, sense of, 6–8
Adaptive identity, 191
Adolescence, crisis of, 29–30
Affects, organization of, 28
Agency, 242
Aggression, female, 199–200
AIDS epidemic, 267
All the Women Caught in Flaring Light
     (Pratt), 204–206
Alter ego transference, 170–171
Alterity, 150
Analysts. *See* Therapists
Analytic discourse, 30–38
Analytic dyad
     gender panic in, 91–107
     maternal erotic transference in, 49–55
Androgyny, 289
Anti-identity, 225
Anxiety, imagination in mitigating, 87
Aphanisis, 160
Appartitional lesbian, xiii
Archaic selfobject, 161
Artificial insemination, 72–73
     among lesbian couples, 269
Attachment, 58
     desire and, 118
     drive for in women, 265–266
Attunement, 28–29

Authenticity
     in analytic relationship, 39–40
     theory of, 27–28
Autobiographical novel, 13–14
Autonomy, 58
     evolution of, 85–86
     of lesbians, 272

Bad me, 101
Bar Girls, 224–225
Big Big Love (Stewart), 243–244
Binary view, 218
     object choice and, 226–227
     postmodernist critique of, 248
Biomythography, 215
Bisexual completeness, wish for, 215–217
Bisexual myths, 217
Bisexuality, 225, 226–227
Body-ego image, lack of, 142
Body image, 145
Body language, 43–49
     in psychoanalysis, 49–55
Body self, 43–44
Body(ies)
     as assemblage, 148
     innately sexed, 152
     as natural and sociocultural, 146–147
     social values and, 147–148

297